From Point to Pixel

Interfaces ▪ Studies in Visual Culture

EDITORS Mark J. Williams and Adrian W. B. Randolph, Dartmouth College

This series, sponsored by Dartmouth College Press, develops and promotes the study of visual culture from a variety of critical and methodological perspectives. Its impetus derives from the increasing importance of visual signs in everyday life, and from the rapid expansion of what are termed "new media." The broad cultural and social dynamics attendant to these developments present new challenges and opportunities across and within the disciplines. These have resulted in a trans-disciplinary fascination with all things visual, from "high" to "low," and from esoteric to popular. This series brings together approaches to visual culture—broadly conceived—that assess these dynamics critically and that break new ground in understanding their effects and implications.

For a complete list of books that are available in the series, visit www.upne.com

Meredith Hoy, *From Point to Pixel: A Genealogy of Digital Aesthetics*
James Housefield, *Playing with Earth and Sky: Astronomy, Geography, and the Art of Marcel Duchamp*
William Kaizen, *Against Immediacy: Video Art and Media Populism*
Angela Rosenthal, ed., with David Bindman and Adrian W. B. Randolph, *No Laughing Matter: Visual Humor in Ideas of Race, Nationality, and Ethnicity*
Robin Veder, *The Living Line: Modern Art and the Economy of Energy*
Tanya Sheehan, ed., *Photography, History, Difference*
Ory Bartal, *Postmodern Advertising in Japan: Seduction, Visual Culture, and the Tokyo Art Directors Club*
Ruth E. Iskin, *The Poster: Art, Advertising, Design, and Collecting, 1860s–1900s*
Heather Warren-Crow, *Girlhood and the Plastic Image*
Heidi Rae Cooley, *Finding Augusta: Habits of Mobility and Governance in the Digital Era*
renée c. hoogland, *A Violent Embrace: Art and Aesthetics after Representation*
Alessandra Raengo, *On the Sleeve of the Visual: Race as Face Value*
Frazer Ward, *No Innocent Bystanders: Performance Art and Audience*
Timothy Scott Barker, *Time and the Digital: Connecting Technology, Aesthetics, and a Process Philosophy of Time*
Bernd Herzogenrath, ed., *Travels in Intermedia[lity]: ReBlurring the Boundaries*
Monica E. McTighe, *Framed Spaces: Photography and Memory in Contemporary Installation Art*
Alison Trope, *Stardust Monuments: The Saving and Selling of Hollywood*
Nancy Anderson and Michael R. Dietrich, eds., *The Educated Eye: Visual Culture and Pedagogy in the Life Sciences*
Shannon Clute and Richard L. Edwards, *The Maltese Touch of Evil: Film Noir and Potential Criticism*

FROM POINT TO PIXEL

Meredith Hoy

A Genealogy of Digital Aesthetics

DARTMOUTH COLLEGE PRESS
HANOVER, NEW HAMPSHIRE

DARTMOUTH COLLEGE PRESS
An imprint of University Press of New England
www.upne.com

Manufactured in the United States of America
Designed by Eric M. Brooks
Typeset in Quadraat by Passumpsic Publishing

Library of Congress Cataloging-in-Publication Data
available upon request

5 4 3 2 1

■ **To my parents,**
David & Jocelyn,
with love

Contents

Acknowledgments

The research culminating in this book began during my time in the Rhetoric and Film Department at the University of California at Berkeley. There, my interdisciplinary approach was encouraged and developed as I worked across departments including not only Rhetoric and Film, but also Art History, New Media, Performance Studies, and History. I am indebted to Greg Niemeyer for his contribution to my inquiry into new media theory and practice. In addition, Anne Wagner was instrumental in launching my sustained interest in the history of art—her investigative methods and her revelatory analyses proved indispensible in fashioning my outlook on art historical principles and practices.

This book would not have been written without the brilliant and generative intellectual support of Whitney Davis, whose insights first helped shape the conceptual foundations of the project. His breadth of knowledge and unique, incisive approach to theories of visual culture identify astounding connections across temporal, visual, and philosophical traditions. His mode of scholarship inspires and undergirds the methodological and philosophical structure upon which my own research is built.

My now years-long dialogue with Warren Sack has profoundly shaped my thinking about new media, as well as my professional career. His simultaneous roles as mentor and friend have been invaluable to me in my progression as a scholar, and his oversight of this project from nascent stages to fruition have demonstrated not only his dedication and attentiveness but also the complexity and depth of his thought. Our exchanges have left indelible marks on my knowledge of the philosophy and aesthetics of new media and added multiple elements to the framework of this text.

Abigail de Kosnik, Jeffrey Skoller, Martin Jay, Richard Doyle, and Kristen Whissel all aided in various stages of my research at Berkeley. Scott Bukatman, Frazer Ward, Mark Hansen, and Peter Brooks were also formative voices in early stages of my intellectual life.

In a very real way, this project was brought from the recesses of my computer into the light of day through the incredible, longstanding support of Frazer Ward. His commitment not only to our friendship of nearly twenty years but also to my intellectual and professional development is unparalleled, and his generous introduction of my manuscript to the remarkable University Press of New England catalyzed the very possibility of writing these acknowledgments.

I have been more than fortunate in my longtime connections to confidants and interlocutors whose intellectual dexterity motivated my process and my thinking about a range of subjects, only some of which are covered here. My deepest thanks to friends and co-conspirators Jennifer Johung, Zabet Patterson, Kris Paulsen, John Costello, Marius Watz, Andrew Uroskie, Monika Gehlawat, Brooke Belisle, Justin Underhill, Todd Cronan, Namiko Kunimoto, John Costello, Javier Cardoza-Kon, Shanda Hunt, Therese Hickey, Lauren Brackett, Winnie King, Kayla Fogarty, Robert Yeagle, Joshua McBride, Christine Gould, and Alexis Hersh.

To Adriene Jenik, who has believed in me and supported me in a myriad of ways, thank you for your exceptional dedication.

To the artists with whom I have discussed this book personally—Camille Utterback, Casey Reas, Jason Salavon, Jim Campbell, jodi, and Marius Watz—your generosity is beyond appreciated. The feedback given on my writing about your practice, your willingness to share images with me, and your interest in the topic of the current work has motivated me to strive harder to capture the excellence and rigor of your work. Many thanks to the Esther Schipper Gallery, as well as to Angela Bulloch herself, who graciously afforded me access to *Horizontal Technicolour*, and to the Artists Rights Society, which granted me permissions for images by Andreas Gursky and Victor Vasarely.

Thanks also are more than due to readers of this text who have remained anonymous. Their feedback was vital in revisions of the manuscript and the refinement of my thinking about the topic.

And, of course, within the University Press of New England itself, which has proved to be an amazingly helpful and delightful partner on the road to publication, I am incredibly grateful to editor Richard Pult, whose unending forbearance, wealth of experience, and kindness saved the day on many an occasion. The same can be said of Lauren Seidman, Naomi Burns, and Thomas Haushalter, as well as the wonderful design team that produced the layout of the book.

My heart of course belongs to my immediate family: Brian Beliveau, whose loyalty, belief in my abilities, and determination to keep me afloat even in difficult times has been my committed partner and stood by me through thick and thin; my beloved four-legged canine child, Hoss, who brings me joy every hour of every day, is my steadfastly loving companion and my little gray sunshine; Judith Beck, my most tireless advocate; Bill and Linda Benson, who have modeled for me since a young age genuine love of art and the mind. Finally, and above all, with the utmost gratitude and love, I thank my parents, David and Jocelyn Hoy, to whom this book is dedicated. They inspire me in all my efforts, leading me from reports on *The Hobbit* to graduate papers on Habermas and Heidegger, to my first book. Not only have they provided me with endless scholarly feedback during the research and writing stages of this project, but have supported me with limitless patience, love, and absolute and unwavering confidence and encouragement. They are, without question, the guiding lights of my life.

Introduction

The Digital ▪ An Aesthetic Ontology

Picture a screen before you, roughly the size of a movie-house projection. Then picture this screen divided into a four-by-eight grid of perfectly regular squares, each pulsing with a pale monochromatic light. As you read the description of this work, you notice that it presents digital footage shot by the artist at Zabriskie Point, the site of Michelangelo Antonioni's film of the same name, as well as footage, also shot by the artist, referencing the star gate scenes of Stanley Kubrick's *2001: A Space Odyssey*. A track recalling the soundscapes of the aforementioned films accompanies the shifting coloration within the boxes. Although any representational content is metaphorically "encrypted" through computational processing, at this point, the installation begins to make sense, perhaps as cinema redux, or cinema remixed. As you gaze at the pared-down coloration of the grid structure before you, you may be reminded of the seriated photographs of Bernd and Hilla Becher or the houses on the Sunset Strip photographed by Ed Ruscha. Perhaps you even think of the rich tones of Jeff Wall's lightboxes. But if you continue to wait for something like cinema to reveal itself to you, you soon realize that no image is about to shimmer into pictorial legibility. Instead, each square changes color with infinitesimal slowness and clings resolutely to purified abstraction of light and color; any pictorial content remains latent, hidden far below the human perceptual threshold. This is Angela Bulloch's *Horizontal Technicolour* (2002), not quite cinema, not quite sculpture, and not quite sound installation, but possibly intelligible as something else altogether, as a playful union of high modernist abstraction and digital programming. Bulloch, a London- and Berlin-based sculptor, installation, and sound artist who has been counted among the Young British Artists, performs a digital reduction of remediated references to scenes from Kubrick's and Antonioni's films and displays the results in a grid of colored "Pixel Boxes." These

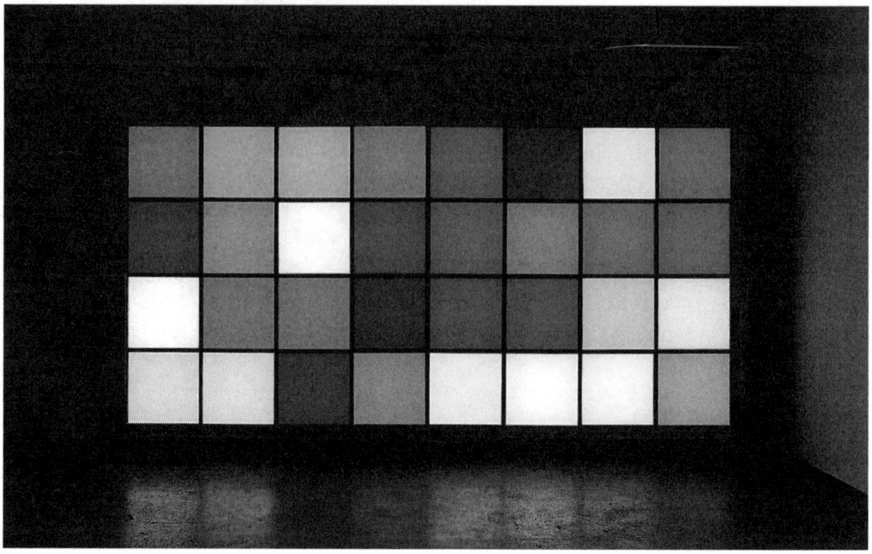

FIGURE I.1 ▪ Angela Bulloch, *Horizontal Technicolour*, 2002. 32 DMX module (waxed birchwood), aluminium plate, white glass, diffusion foil, cables, RGB-Lighting system, DMX controller. Sound system: amplifier, mixer, loudspeakers, cables. Wall: 4 x 8 boxes (Cinemascope Format). Programmed sequence 13:12 min (loop). Courtesy: The artist and Esther Schipper, Berlin. Photo credit: Carsten Eisfeld.

large "pixels" abrogate the possibility of image resolution and force the viewer to reconsider the structural composition of the photographic pictorialization that usually accompanies the cinematic experience. These Pixel Boxes appear as luminous, individuated tiles, as screens that produce their own strange glow rather than as image machines that reflect the familiar world back to the viewer. Here, the picture never supplants the technological apparatus, nor does it camouflage the grid of pixels, the very structure that engenders digital graphics at a cellular level.

Bulloch's work is best described as aesthetically digital, that is, it renders its visual data as a formal array of discrete elements that correlate to a definite informatic quantity. Because any kind of information, such as color, sound, words, or numbers, can be processed digitally once it is converted into machine-computable numeric data, the type of information conveyed may vary. But once the parameters of an element—its behavior within an overall system—are defined, it must reliably produce the same output with each iteration. Thus, if a pixel location is commanded to render a given numerical value corresponding to a particular shade of blue, the color will be the same each time it appears. Within a digital system, the range and complexity of the information that can be conveyed—the resolution, for example, or fineness of discrimination between color values—is dictated by systemic parameters. Binary systems process information through a series of commands that turn a simple switch to an "on" or "off" position, but increasing the number of possible switch positions dramatically increases the complexity of the tasks the computer is able to carry out.

More often than not, however, users/viewers attribute digital characteristics to digitally processed artifacts—video games, digital photographs, and cinematic special effects—not due to observable traces of digital processing on their surface (which are often registered instead as "glitches" in the system) but because their constitutive digitality is deduced associatively. If an image appears on a computer screen or monitor, one knows, logically, that it is a digitally processed image. One's awareness of technical parameters of digital computers tells one that the image that appears on it must be processed and rendered digitally, but one cannot necessarily discern evidence of digital processing embedded in the picture's formal configuration. When the computational ability of computers-as-machines meets or exceeds the maximum fineness of resolution registered by the human sensorium, this associative logic replaces direct observation in the determination of digital ontology. But some digital artworks use the medium reflexively, to consider how both objects and knowledge are reconfigured within a digital epistemological framework. In this instance, the appearance of discrete units on the image surface is not attributable to technological failure, insufficiency, primitivism, or a lack of technical dexterity on the part of the artist/programmer. An unfortunate peripheral effect of the expectation that technological development leads inexorably to seamless, transparent virtualization is the concomitant assumption that digital and analog modalities will converge and ultimately become indiscernible.[1] While this is certainly true in many cases, what should be guarded against is the blanket supposition that digital depiction always, or even in most cases, tends toward immersive pictorial virtualization. Rather, artworks, such as Bulloch's, that emphatically and obsessively explore the visible properties of digital discreteness are bound together in their profound investment in and investigation of the effects of the information revolution on patterns of seeing, thinking, and acting both individually and collectively. Bulloch formulates a visual (graphical) proposition in which the "digital" becomes a sensed and experiential, as well as a technological, category. She identifies the perceptual properties of digitality as a valid analytic problem within contemporary epistemology that necessitates both perceptual and intellectual negotiation.

Horizontal Technicolour is a work of art made with a computer, but it is not simply its computational ontology—the invisible processing of binary code

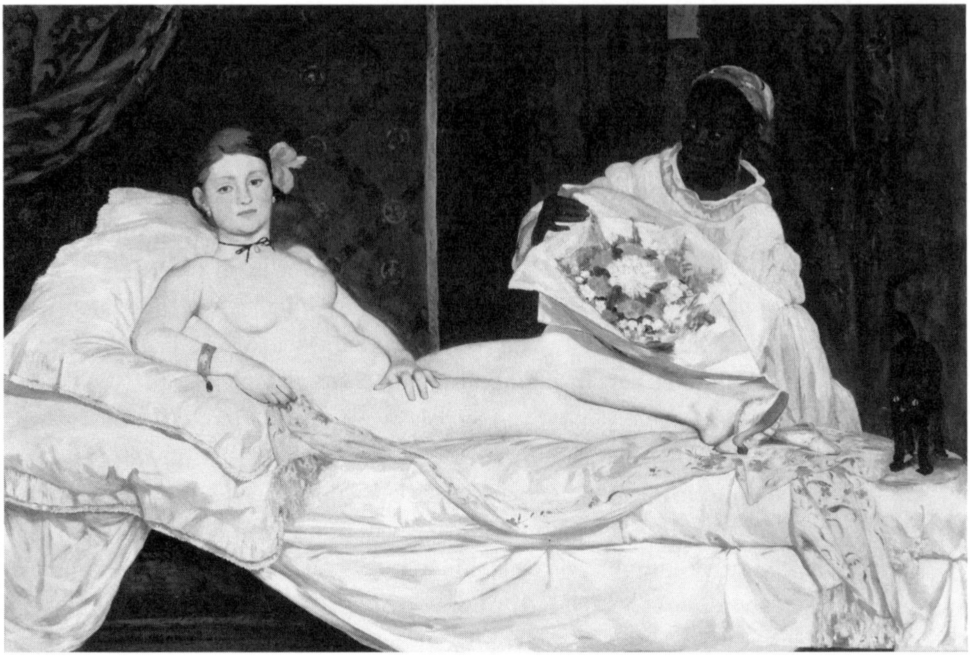

FIGURE I.2 ▪ Edouard Manet, *Olympia*, 1865. Oil on canvas, 130.5 cm x 190 cm (51.4 in x 74.8 in). Musée d'Orsay, Paris, France.

taking place prior to its graphical rendering—that lends it a digital aesthetic sensibility. In many examples of computationally generated works, such as the digitally manipulated photographs by Jeff Wall, their formal appearance is derived through the processing of binary digits, but they do not bear the stamp of digital processing on their pictorial surface. In other words, while these depictions are technically digital, they adopt the look and feel of analog imaging. Instead of foregrounding the piecemeal, additive processing of individuated pixels or even vector-based curves,[2] these depictions are computationally derived but bear the properties of analog pictures, such as continuity, density, repleteness, or irreducibility, ambiguity, and indeterminacy.[3] These terms come to light in chapter 1. However, to illustrate the distinction between digital and analog modalities more concretely, the following counterexample to *Horizontal Technicolour* exemplifies the ambiguity that lies at the center of analog aesthetics.

Edouard Manet's *Olympia* (1865) is a ubiquitous figure in university courses on the topic of modernity. As Timothy J. Clark has shown, this paradigmatic work not only exhibits a complex and potentially irreducible series of meanings at a level of narrative and iconography—the symbolism of the black cat, the model's pose, a direct reference to Titian's *Venus of Urbino* (1538), and the hovering presence of the African maidservant—but also reveals the way in which the appraisal, interpretation, and theorization of painting has thrived on, or even depended for sustained discourse upon, the indeterminacies, potential invisibilities, and discrepancies resulting from the application of colored pigment to canvas. The painting, first hung in the Paris Salon of 1865, immediately generated an aggressive critical response, in part due to what is taken to be latent aggression in the attitude of the painting, and its contents, toward the viewer. The overall mien of the reclining prostitute in the painting leads critics to read her posture, attitude, and hygiene as base, vulgar, and even dirty.[4] Overall, the instabilities of the painting, deriving at least in part from its painterly execution, define it in parallel to the poetry of Baudelaire, whose "meanings are so multiple and refractory, so unfixed, so unmanageable, in 1865."[5] But even more striking are the dramatic ramifications for the painting's formal, social, and narrative "meaning" effected by a single feature that hovers just outside the range of visibility, at least for its viewers at the Salon of 1865. Signifiers of Olympia's distasteful brashness and unclean nudity were present not only in the grey of her skin and the impudent refusal implied by the clenched hand covering her pubic area but also in her hair, which was to all appearances pulled back in a severe, "unfeminine" coif, made all the more ridiculous by the large flower pinned behind her ear. Caricatures of the painting conspicuously foregrounded this feature; in their satiric, performative reiteration of the painting, these drawings called attention to the sordid, off-kilter nature of the subject of the painting and of the visual encounter between viewer and object. However, as Clark reveals in the climactic moment of his essay, the subtlety of Manet's facture concealed for contemporary viewers, already unsure of how to classify the painting or its subject, a shock of loosened auburn hair that, once revealed, "changes the whole disposition of head and shoulders . . . the head is softened, given a more familiar kind of sexuality."[6] This significance of detail, and of course its social reception, or lack thereof, determines Olympia's placement as one of the great, discursively irreducible works of art of the nineteenth century. But this detail must be coaxed into view; precisely this coaxing supports the idea that the density of facture and a subtle handling of materials demarcate analog modalities in opposition to discretized digital ones.

Whether precisely linear or carefully blended, the pictorial landscape of a painting will never possess the numerical exactness of a digitally constructed picture, in which each pixel is programmed to behave in a determinate way —with an exact color value or degree of illumination. There is of course a scientistic mythology that develops from the fact that the digital-computational universe is, hypothetically, knowable in an absolute sense, where the "absolute" is coextensive with knowledge of a quantized color value, location, or other species of data. A supporter of a computationalist model would suggest that "meaning" is more accessible when an object or situation is filtered or mediated computationally. It might be supposed that meaning is more available to analysis because the object is numericized, transformed into searchable, comparable, quantifiable data. Computationalism is rife with its own problems, first and foremost its tendency to collapse semantic content into statistically verifiable data. But the opposite position is also problematic insofar as it would insist that relatively "more" or "richer" layers of meaning result from a representational model that constitutively resists or refuses exactitude.

Digital and analog modalities demonstrate their own particular semantic facilities; they tend to generate different types of meaning. But instead of valorizing one over the other, it is more useful to examine how the productive specificities and conditions of possibility, as well as the blind spots, in each model are clarified in their dialogic intersections and deviations.[7] Reconsidering *Olympia*, if the painting had been constructed digitally, the problem of the invisible hair would not have been obviated. Rather, it is precisely these types of debates, whether in the tradition of Morellian connoisseurship, with the identification of the telltale signatory mark (the *Grundform*) made by every painter, or in the social history of art, as in the present example, that identify the aesthetic and intellectual interest of a painting precisely in the ambiguities and indeterminacies supported, or even, in the strongest case, necessitated by the properties of the medium.

In contradistinction to *Horizontal Technicolour*, consider Andreas Gursky's 1993 *Paris, Montparnasse*. This work is a computationally assembled and retouched photograph that suppresses its constitutive digitality by rendering it imperceptible at the surface level of the picture. If there is a digital "look" to Gursky's photographs either before or after 1992, when he began to use computers to manipulate his pictures, it is not because surfaces are discretized and fractured, revealing an infrastructure of digital components, but because his photographs throw into sharp focus the dizzying partitions of human-inhabited city—and landscapes. *Paris, Montparnasse*, one of his earliest deployments of computationally aided montage, sutures two photographs of an apartment building in Paris and crops the ends of the building at the right and left edges of the picture. The building seems to continue panoramically beyond the limits of the frame, leaving an impression of a flattened, potentially infinitely extended grid of colorful windows sectioned by regular concrete bands. The photograph gestures referentially in two directions, oscillating between a tip of the hat to Piet Mondrian, the industrial/modernist grids of Gursky's teachers Bernd and Hilla Becher, and

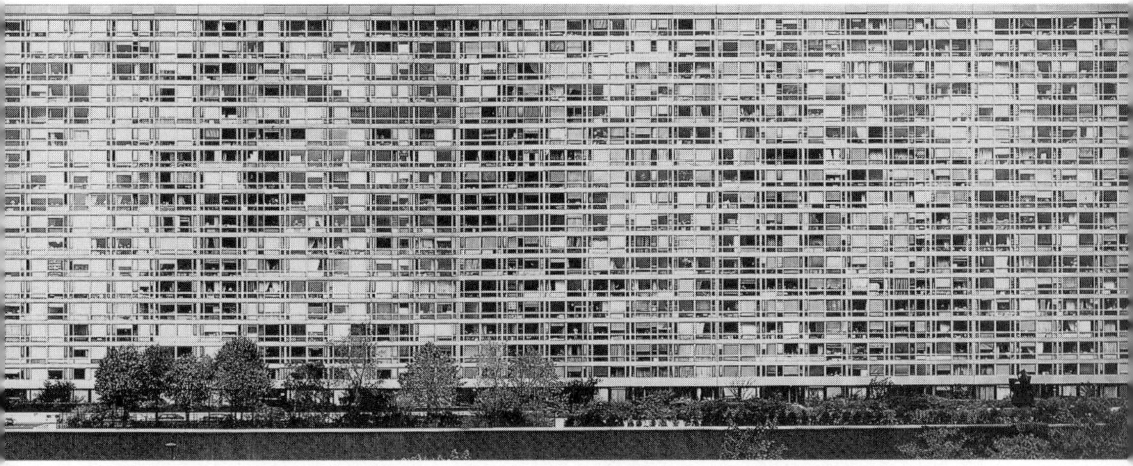

FIGURE I.3 ▪ Andreas Gursky, *Paris, Montparnasse*, 1993. C-print, 187 x 427.8 x 6.2 cm (73⅗ x 168⅖ x 2⅖ in). © 2016 Andreas Gursky / Artists Rights Society (ARS), New York / VG Bild-Kunst, Bonn.

the visibly bitmapped, pixelated landscapes of early computer graphics. Gursky makes nearly constant visual references in his photographic practice to his own historical situatedness within the technological horizon of digital computation. His pictures contain ubiquitous reminders of the new cultural fascinations and pictorial conventions in the digital age, most evident in his attention to the replicability and multiplicity of digitally recorded data. Within the hyperbolically partitioned pictorial field of *Paris, Montparnasse*, people—sitting, standing, and dancing—are visible through the windows, but they are subsumed by the overwhelming array of units, symbols of *both* the industrialized beehive of the modern lifeworld and the exponential replications of an informatic universe. Digital and modern worlds are thus seen in dialog, so that the digital presents an intensification and hypermediation, into the realm of "simulation," of modern mechanical capabilities. In Gursky's work, the figure of the digital, defined as the presence of discrete, interchangeable units, flickers in and out of perceptibility. The digital is an elusive target, simultaneously present and absent, and the work resists becoming an exemplary case of analogicity or digitality.

In a dramatic instance of suppression of the digital, Jeff Wall's *Flooded Grave* (1998–2000) also mobilizes computational montage. But it erases the sublime multiplicity visualized by Gursky by concealing the units or digits that are the building blocks of its smooth, apparently continuous surface. As such, it completes a recursive loop back to traditional analog techniques of image-making through the processing of binary code. Wall's photographs, and many of Gursky's, revel in undecidability. They preserve the intense coloration, the highly resolved crispness, and the emptied-out or sparsely populated visual landscapes of computationally generated environments. They also play the capacities of computational photographic technology in a complex counterpoint against the endlessly replicated, often deeply artificial realities of industrialized, digitized spaces of capital in which flows and feedback loops between money, technology, and architecture collude in the fabrication of a vertiginous, intensified version of Frederic Jameson's postmodern pastiche, embodied by Los Angeles' Bonaventure hotel.[8]

These initial references illustrate how the distinction between digitality and analogicity is easier to maintain in theory than in practical application. These categories have been debated most rigorously in the field of cybernetics and cognitive science, and perhaps most notably in Nelson Goodman's seminal text *Languages of Art*. However, they are infrequently addressed in relationship to specific works of art. While it might seem as if the digitized quality of digital art can be taken at face value, it becomes difficult to understand the term "digital" as an aesthetic category if artworks do not present themselves *as* digital, or if these works do not possess a set of characteristics that reference the digital processes that construct an image, bit by bit. Ultimately, "digitality" has no means to signify itself as such if the aesthetic properties of digitization remain untheorized. As a means of proposing a method for assessing these properties, *From Point to Pixel* considers when, how, and why digital artifacts appear to be "digitized," which is to say when they appear to be comprised of individuated units, pixels, or digits. The book employs various theoretical rubrics and examples to identify the surface qualities of digital works and evaluates whether these qualities can be distinguished in any absolute way from analog traditions of depiction.

The complexities of this endeavor and the potential pitfalls of a programmatic assessment of digital artifacts come to light when we notice that even a very brief survey of the varieties of digitally generated artifacts exposes a variety of trends in digital graphics.[9] Some of these tend toward a seamless remediation of older technologies, such as photography and film, and work to preserve a sense of indexical correlation between picture and referent. Others exploit the capacity of digital graphics programs to build three-dimensional worlds but use it for the fabrication of fantastical, fairy-tale universes, essentially fusing the imaginative conventions of Disney and Warner Bros. cell animation with the reality effect of naturalistic digital modeling. Still others veer away from naturalism toward information displays that, in translating complex data sets and sequences into a visually legible graphical form (i.e., a data "map"), blend qualitative (aesthetic) and quantitative characteristics. And finally, a subset of artists working with computational technology deploys the "glitch," or faults, in the system that register as a disruption or scrambling of the pictorial surface.

Not only is it in many cases increasingly difficult to recognize when an image is digital or analog, but it is also clear that being "digital" carries many potential meanings. The digitality of Pixar's animated feature films (e.g., *Toy Story* and *Ratatouille*) does not map onto the scrambling of digital signals performed by glitch artists, such as the Barcelona-based duo jodi. The theoretical parameters and evaluative methods applied to digital technology vary wildly, even amongst theorists who explicitly treat aesthetics as an analytic problem.[10] This book shows how particular media—in this case, computer technology, including both processors and other hardware and the hugely varied array of software programs—determine not only the structural conditions of the depiction but also how the assemblage of marks, the method and process of inscription, affects the way in which the image signifies. In other words, the affordances and constraints of a given representational technique (such as one-point perspective) or technology (digital computers) tend to produce artifacts that are better at communicating one facet or horizon of "meaning" than another. To wit, the greatest communicative facility of sculptures might lie in their ability to speak to the relationship between objects in space. Paintings might search for the best way to convey the essence of objects in the reduction from three to two dimensions. Computers, in contrast, are designed as engines of calculation—for the high-speed collection, collation, and manipulation of data. This means that even in the stage of graphical rendering, computers will be oriented toward the visual modeling of data patterns. The hypothesis presented here is that continuous, analog inscriptive modalities imbue depictions with a different set of signifying characteristics than do discrete, digital methods of composition, which index their own set of ideological, epistemological, and representational norms.[11]

Much of the best scholarship in media studies has offered cogent analyses of the political, social, and economic formations that emerge alongside digital technologies. These readings of "networked culture" focus on the systems of power/knowledge that arise from the Web 2.0 and a globalized world economy. Although this research proves invaluable to the understanding of a culture shaped by ubiquitous computing, a well-developed methodology for interpreting the role of digital technology in art practice must also situate digital artifacts in a specifically art-historical and theoretical context. This book considers how digital artifacts might overcome their dubious status as mere demonstrations of technical novelty and become artworks worthy of serious consideration. It looks at the importance of digital technology as an artistic medium and addresses how affordances, constraints, and technical parameters of digital processing influence the visible/sensorially appreciable configuration of computationally generated artifacts.

Despite its foundation in immaterial electronic pulses, digital technology produces material effects on culture and communication. The assessment of digital images is often based on their "reality quotient"—the degree to which they accurately reproduce the optical and haptic conditions of the external world. The fascination in digital cultural studies with virtual reality, second life, and other such practices supports this view and also leans dangerously toward the notion that progress in art is achieved by producing ever-more sophisticated techniques for rendering illusions of spatial depth. This concentration on the immersive capacities of digital graphics runs the risk of assuming a teleological progression in art toward "accurate" spatialization and virtualization. But an evaluation of art objects based on culturally determined signifiers of naturalism would exclude alternate visual models and historical traditions, such as abstraction. It is therefore imperative to consider depictions that exhibit visible evidence of digital construction—digital aesthetic characteristics—independently of the virtualizing capability of computational technology. The following chapters examine a subset of digital image-making practices that suppress virtualization in order to examine the structural principles undergirding digital graphics. In parsing these often-abstract, highly formalized pictorial strategies, it becomes apparent that they convey a different aesthetic and architectonic sensibility than analog depictions.

Concrete cultural artifacts and epistemological structures are discursively interdependent. As such, the omnipresence of digital images in both popular culture and high art would suggest a concomitant emergence of a digitally encoded representational modality and a generalized digital worldview, both of which would be directly traceable to the advent of computational technology. However, even a cursory glance at the art historical register discloses evidence of discretized models of symbolic communication (including but not limited to pictorial representation) that preexist computational technology by decades or even centuries. These artifacts, without the use of computers, point to the ways in which the fabric of meaning is often patched together out of small, disjoint, and highly articulated units. For example, instances drawn from nineteenth- and twentieth-century art offer an implicit critique of Romanticist or vitalist holism.[12] Without the use of computers, these works show that the physical world is not a totalized, closed system. They set up a world picture that paves the way for computationalism and provide a deep history of digital systems.

Theories of digitization and concrete instances of its appearance emerge from a wide array of disciplines, each of which constructs their theoretical models in support of distinct teleological and ontological narratives. The definitions of computation and digitality in this book operate independently of particular machines or technological formations. The digital is the fulcrum upon which its argument turns and is not technologically determined. Granting that "computation" may also refer to a number of mathematical and logical processes unbound to electronic digital computers, it is used in contradistinction to the discrete, schematic facture associated with digital aesthetics. Because a digital constructive method, and by extension a digital aesthetic, preexists, or is separable from, computational technology, the word "digital" signifies independently of its typical association with the technical specificities of computer hardware and software. While "digital" is for now a floating signifier that will acquire a broader semantic valence in the following chapters, the word "computation"—which of course possesses its own unique history and properties—is deployed as an abbreviation, or a metonymic stand-in, for electronic digital computing machines: contemporary computers.[13]

Over the course of four chapters and the conclusion, the text moves between theoretical analysis and case studies of artworks produced both with and without the aid of computers. Chapter 1 lays the theoretical ground for the cases examined in the rest of the text by identifying the constitutive characteristics of digitality and setting them aside from the aesthetic features of analog artifacts. This chapter investigates the possibility that there exists a set of formal qualities belonging to digital artifacts, which can be used to describe an object as aesthetically analog or digital. Understanding the particular language in which the object speaks facilitates a comprehension of the worldview or world picture evinced by that object. The premise of this chapter is that discretized, particulate digital artifacts are structured according to different principles than analog artifacts, which are relatively smooth and continuous with no perfectly regularized division between parts. This analysis of digital and analog sets the stage for the claim that a digital method of construction preexists electronic, binary computers and that a proto-digital way of seeing and representing the world can be observed in practices that precede the invention of contemporary computing devices. This analytic method provides for new explorations of artifacts that have not found a secure place in the artistic canon, and affords an interpretive schema with which to examine artists and artworks whose position in the art historical record demands renegotiation. The criteria for aesthetic success have been based on analog principles, which have not permitted digital artifacts to have a strong voice. Digital artifacts have appeared mechanical or even shallow by analog standards, but when framed in new terms, it becomes clear that their method of facture is performatively enacting a particular way of seeing the world, one in which the objects are configured from discrete units as opposed to a field of continuous lines. The theoretical model in this chapter proposes that the digital is a sensed and experiential, rather than a technological, category. The digital is placed in an expanded field, so that it is a mechanism, a process, and a constructive method that operates well beyond the boundaries of computational technology. Once digitality is disaggregated from contemporary electronic computers, it becomes a category that can be used to address works of art, techniques, and technologies that may speak in a different language and thus require a different interpretive framework than pictures and artifacts configured through analog processes.

Chapter 2 evaluates the extent to which modern painters Georges Seurat and Paul Klee exhibit constitutive features of digital systems. Conceptualizing these artists as experimenters with a digital method adds a new dimension to the theoretical, aesthetic, and historical significance of their work. Although it would be possible to delve further back into the art historical record for examples of digital aesthetic systems, even as far as Paleolithic cave markings, this chapter focuses on a comparison between modern, noncomputational proto-digital approaches and contemporary, electronically computed digital practices. Beginning with pointillism as its first test case, the chapter explores how proto-digital methods are established by Seurat in order to create a divisionist field of discrete units of color that resist fusion into analog continuity. The chapter engages the question of how the pointillist dot emerges rhetorically and descriptively as a digital, metric unit that allows Seurat's pictorial architecture and his digital aesthetic sensibility to emerge. Chapter 2 then addresses a second form of modern divisionism, that adopted by Paul Klee. Beginning with his so-called magic squares phase, developed around 1920, Klee gradually intensifies the digitality of his compositions until the 1930s, when he produced such iconic works as *Ad Parnassum*. As a painter, writer, and musician, Klee was deeply invested in notation, which contributed to his development of a proto-digital method for drawing and painting influenced by the notational systems of music. Characterized by precision and articulation, digital notations in Klee's practice become the underlying structure that makes possible the particular mode of expression he seeks to convey. The second half of the chapter addresses works of art produced after the advent of personal computing and with the aid of electronic computation. The grid of pixels, in these works, is a field of units syntactically and semantically distinct from one another. As such, the grid becomes a trope by which to identify digitality. The artists under consideration in this section tend to foreground the primary graphical elements of digital structure, most notably the pixel. In so doing, these artists dismantle the illusion of analogicity that many digital images seek to uphold. The computational examples in this chapter show how the principles of digital composition disclose the relationship between technology, structure, and composition as a philosophical, aesthetic, and material problem. Each of the examples, from Seurat to Jim Campbell, shows how the permutations of digital structures work to reshape the norms and limits of representation.

The next two chapters provide comparisons between artists who apply a digital method independently of electronic computation and artists whose digital aesthetic is computationally driven. Chapter 3 examines two artists of the twentieth century, one whose work largely precedes the invention of electronic personal computing devices, and the other whose artistic practice depends on computational processes to render colorful, abstract landscapes. The first artist, Victor Vasarely, is acknowledged as the progenitor of Op Art (Optical Art), a style recognizable by its vertiginous schemes that produce nearly hallucinatory visual effects. Despite enjoying some success contemporaneous to its production, Op Art has been broadly dismissed as shallow and gimmicky, able to produce phenomenological effects but lacking conceptual and aesthetic vigor and longevity. This chapter argues that Vasarely's approach to pictorial construction does not merely create novel optical-kinetic experiences but also prefigures a digital visual language that circulates within and expands a burgeoning digital epistemological horizon. Although Vasarely never used a computer, his works are often remarked as bearing a distinct resemblance to early computer art, capitalizing on austere, geometric configurations. This chapter contends that such a morphological resemblance to computer art can be accounted for by the fact that Vasarely explores and articulates a theory of plasticity that imagines matter, form, and structure in digital terms. He attempts to realize an endlessly recombinatory system of discrete parts, which, when set into motion, reveals a new way of seeing the architectonic configuration of world, universe, and even social organization. Vasarely's deployment of algorithmic processes, although not electronically computational, facilitates an understanding of digital composition as an aggregation of discrete, interchangeable units. Vasarely developed his ideas about a programmatic plastic language before personal computing was recognized as a viable artistic tool. In advance of bitmapping technology, he infused his works with a distinct digital aesthetic by conceptualizing the image as a field of discrete values arranged within and conditioned upon the structure of the grid. Moreover, his art practice evidences an epistemological shift in the mid-twentieth century toward a digital, computational, and informatic worldview that persists and evolves into the twenty-first century.

The second part of the chapter takes up Generative Artist Marius Watz's 2005 homage to Vasarely entitled *ElectroPlastique #1*. This work translates Vasarely's algorithmic visual language into computational generative code and ultimately into a screen-based, moving image in which a Vasarelian landscape develops, morphs, and eventually fragments. Watz's translation of Vasarely's visual language not only functions to recuperate Vasarely's artistic reputation but also presents a vigorous interrogation of the types of visual structure facilitated by computational technology. Both artists mobilize elemental modular structures, but what sets these structures apart from other modernist abstractions is their transformation based on the activating effects of algorithm and code. The dialog imaginatively enacted between Vasarely and Watz—the former employing analog tools to explore the still-gestating notion of digital systems, and the latter pushing digital visual language further into the domain of self-generating computational abstraction—reveals the conceptual and visual qualities of digital materiality. In contrast with digital images that cover over their constructive logic in a quest for ever-greater naturalism, the revelation of digital architectonics opened up in the space between Watz and Vasarely initiates in turn the question of what we might learn by bringing the underlying structural principles of digital images back to a visible surface.

Chapter 4 explores the differences between the digital aesthetic described in the preceding three chapters and the practice of making art using electronic computational devices, which does not necessarily yield a digital aesthetic. Artworks made with computers can obscure their digital origins, displaying instead many of the constitutive features of analog works, such as smoothness and density. Computation can be used, in short, to "analogize" the analog, or to create a hybrid, computational aesthetic. This chapter explores these ideas through an examination of the "programmed paintings" of Casey Reas, a contemporary artist who uses computers to produce images that are fluid and continuous, as opposed to being composed of a field of discrete units, as in the case of Vasarely. This chapter examines Reas's fraught and often contradictory response to the legacy of Conceptual Art in programming-based practices. Through a comparison between Reas and Sol LeWitt, Reas is shown to occupy an oscillatory position with respect to the values traditionally attached to analog aesthetics, such as immediacy and uniqueness/irreproducibility. By deploying algorithmically encoded instructions to automate artistic production, Reas reinforces the turn away from the cult of the artist initiated by conceptual artists in the 1960s. But at the same time, Reas's fascination with "handmadeness" and organicism preserves a link to analog aesthetic principles.

It is not accidental that Reas chooses the computer as his tool instead of a brush. His choice of medium can be construed as a manifestation of Reas's post-Conceptualist understanding of objects in terms of information architecture, in which a series of executions of discrete functions ultimately resolve into a complex landscape. Conceptual Artists, such as LeWitt, became deeply interested in the 1960s and 1970s in the notion that the world is comprised of information flows and that various forms of communication and exchange can be described quantitatively. This fascination on the part of many Conceptual Artists with information theory influenced the shape and thematic content of Conceptual Art and in turn inflects one strand of Reas's work, which takes up the algorithmic practices of LeWitt and transforms them into electronically processed computational schemes. This programmatic interpretation of LeWitt's wall drawings is deeply invested in the notion of algorithm, in the ceding of the artist's control to the dictates of the program. The results of these drawings, however, do not necessarily coincide with the model of digitality described to this point in the book. The presence of algorithm, in other words, does not automatically produce a digital aesthetic. The artist must choose to utilize algorithm in service of a sensorially apprehensible digitality. Thus, a computational aesthetic must be distinguished from a digital aesthetic, and the analytic category of the digital can be disaggregated from electronic-computational machines and from simple algorithmic processes. Artists can utilize computational technology in a multitude of ways—to highlight the properties of digital graphic composition through the foregrounding of pixels or other structural building blocks, or to occlude the picture's digital infrastructure, leaving only indirect clues, or none at all, to its digital ontology.

Finally, the conclusion examines the appropriation of the trope of "information" in computationally driven art practice, notably in that of Jason Salavon and Casey Reas. The conclusion articulates the relationship between art and information visualization. Shifting away from direct comparison between computationally and non-computationally digital art, the conclusion instead assays the discursive resonances available to artists in the widespread use of information visualization as a primary mode of mapping the vast amounts of data produced by the mechanisms of the "culture industry." The conclusion offers a final look at the mechanisms of digitality through the distinction between art and "nonart," identified specifically in the practice of information visualization, a valuable tool in science and industry that exhibits distinct aesthetic characteristics but is not typically accorded a place in the artistic canon. The artworks examined to this point in the text have all retained a certain degree of analogic ambiguity, thus operating in a liminal zone between a "purely" analog and a "purely" digital state. It is precisely this ambiguity that permits them to come to rest within the borders of art. By contrast, information visualization, which may or may not qualify as aesthetically digital, typically achieves success by eradicating ambiguity and communicating a particular set of values and relationships as accurately and efficiently as possible.[14] Information, according to Claude Shannon's theory, is inherently quantifiable. Because it is a graphical means for conveying quantitative measurements and relationships between measurements, information visualization is not generally included in an artistic canon that thrives on ambiguity and indeterminacy. In other words, while information visualization is a representational model, not all forms of representation will necessarily be considered "art." The conclusion takes up works by Salavon and Reas that engage the practice of information visualization but confound determinacy or the possibility of immediate legibility. Both Salavon and Reas adopt the figure of information as a new (im)material substrate for a particular model of representation.

Salavon and Reas, the emblematic figures of the conclusion, produce works that hover between the categories of art and nonart, and information visualization and information obfuscation. All of the their works addressed in the conclusion incorporate the trope of information into their compositional logic, but Salavon uses information against itself, to blend and blur quantities into indeterminate shapes that confound easy legibility. This use of information as a depictive entity is echoed in Reas's 2015 series, which utilizes computational processing in service of a much more clearly digital aesthetic than his earlier hybrid works (complicated by his continued use of digital "brushstrokes" in one video piece). Both Reas's and Salavon's work must be interpreted with the figures of digital and analog in mind, but ultimately each artist fulfills the parameters of both categories in different ways. Without a comparative analysis of analog and digital aesthetic qualities, their work loses theoretical vigor. But with the aid of these categories, their practice helps to reveal how an understanding of digital aesthetic principles expands the framework of what can be considered "art." Ultimately, digital depiction is part of a philosophical worldview that equates knowledge with quantification. Digital artificing is eminently concerned with the capacity of representation and symbolic forms to make the world measurable, to create schemas and algorithms that impose regularity and pattern on an otherwise analog universe. Accustomed now to computational formats, one can identify the digital as a structural principle and structuring force that shapes the architecture of depiction and disrupts analog aesthetic norms and expectations, both in the contemporary moment and extending deep into the past.

The broader stakes of an identification of systems and artifacts as analog or digital lie in discerning whether or not artifacts composed according to a digital method, logic, or aesthetic have been ignored, suppressed, misunderstood, or only partially understood because they fail to conform to the expectations, norms, and conventions for art objects that cohere within an analog-based framework of apprehension and interpretation. It matters whether an image is either digital or analog because digitally configured depictions have been cast into an interpretive limbo, where they can be interpreted neither as utilitarian objects nor as art objects, nor even, in many cases, latter-day examples of anti-aesthetic Conceptual Art. Examining a genealogy of digital systems sheds light on the patterns, norms, and internal disruptions that occur within the parameters of digital architectonics and paves the way for the account presented here.

To sum up, then, this book works toward a definition of a "digital method" that can be articulated without reference to the technicalities of contemporary hardware and software, allowing, however, the possibility that this digital method can acquire new characteristics when it is performed by computational technology. The artworks covered in the following chapters are treated as sensuous artifacts that are subject to change based on the constraints and affordances of the tools used in their making. But insofar as the word digital describes a series of technological operations, it often references the tool used to make the art but does not help a viewer/user relate to the art as a sensorially apprehensible artifact. Consequently, this book gathers together artworks that disclose visible evidence of their digital construction in order to identify the perceptible characteristics of digitally processed artifacts. It foregrounds not the hidden operations of computers—the intricacies of binary code and programming languages—but rather the surface qualities of digital graphics, or the disappearance of those surface qualities in a commingling of analog and digital modalities. While acknowledging that internal processes govern the aesthetic properties of these surfaces, it investigates the extent to which it is possible to encounter digitality at the level of the interface. Taking into account that the sensuous object will be informed by an underlying conceptual and technological framework or genotype, it sets out to discover whether certain phenotypic aspects of digitality will be inherently accessible at a phenomenological level. The chapters comprising the whole of *From Point to Pixel* coalesce around the question of whether the technical parameters of computation affect the way pictures are constructed, the kinds of subjects for which computers have the greatest representational facility, and by extension, the way digital pictures—the graphical index of digital technesis—will ultimately look.

The examples under consideration in the following chapters all formulate a claim that the "digital" is a sensed and experiential category. Think of the patterns visible in knitting, for example, how the stitching might analogize a pixel but in a "handmade" instead of a highly technologized sense. The definition of digitality laid out here has implications for the evaluative methods applied to both “new” and “old,” computational and noncomputational media. The series of examples that follow range from aesthetically digital artifacts made before the invention of electronic computational technology to “smoothed,” nondigital works made using computers, and to computational works that make visible the discrete, particulate, and schematic nature of the computational processes that generate the graphical output. Often, they reveal an unstable discursive exchange between the aesthetic perception of the digital and the technological specificities of electronic computation. The digital is placed in an expanded field, so that it is a mechanism, a process, and a constructive method that operates well beyond the boundaries of computational technology. Once digitality is disaggregated from contemporary electronic computers, it becomes a category that can be used to address works of art, techniques, and technologies that may speak in a different language and thus require a different interpretive framework than pictures and artifacts configured through analog processes. In my research, the contemporary figure of the digital becomes an analytic tool with which to examine both contemporary and historical artifacts for qualities other than those that would be recognized within the norms attached to analog picture-making. Once these qualities are recognized, they can then be put into dialogic exchange with existing theories and methodologies.

■ The digital, then, is a mode of visual understanding that has appeared at other times under other names. It speaks to the replicability of the pointillist dot and to the simulated matrix of perspective. Here, the digital ceases to be a highly technical term relevant only in contemporary discourse but becomes an art historical proposal about making connections. This is not to enforce congruence between all digital, proto-digital, and quasi-digital systems—perspective, pointillism, Op Art, and contemporary computational artworks are not reducible to historical, cultural, and formal equivalence. Instead, many of these works possess features that interface with this particular notion of the digital in complex and potentially idiosyncratic ways. This book opens digital representational technologies to renegotiation and renewed interpretation, and creates the possibility of a new conversation between contemporary art and that of both the recent and the deep past. The question of whether the “look and feel” of digital media is correlated to the appearance of individuated “digits” within pictorial structure is ultimately not merely a formal but also a social, philosophical, and an art historical problem. This book thus seeks to discover how an evaluation of digital composition might add a new narrative layer to the long art-historical discussion about how and why pictures “mean” and what they say about a given culture in a given historical moment.

1

From Analog Pictures to Digital Notations

In attempting to survey the rocky terrain around the fault lines of the digital divide, it is difficult to negotiate the formations that are beginning to sediment around disciplinary centers. Thinking about, and articulating, the nature of digitality seems to require polyglottal dexterity in negotiating the languages of philosophical thought experiments, mathematics-heavy engineering diagrams of complex circuitry, the procedural logic of programming languages, and the discourses of gaming and ubiquitous computing, to name a few. That is to say, the most crucial aspects of what it means to be digital might vary according to the features that one particular scholar or researcher needs to emphasize in describing what digital media can do. Depending on whether we are interested in the aesthetic dimension of digital artifacts (the way digital artifacts look), their principles of operation (binary switches and circuits, for example), or the symbolic effects of digital technology on culture, the enumeration of primary features will vary. In 1987, media artist Frank Dietrich argued that computers are most valuable as "tools for thought experiments" in order to "venture beyond the surface criteria that seem to dominate much of contemporary discussion of computer art. The 'look and feel' of computer-generated imagery is less interesting to me than extrapolating from known basic digital-symbolic functions into the future potential of this new medium."[1] That is, for Dietrich, computational aesthetics is less crucial than the sociocultural "effects" they elicit through the transformative capacities set into motion through their technological apparatus. I argue, on the contrary, that the aesthetic configurations of "digitally" structured images fundamentally transfigure the world picture we create through our visual, haptic, and auditory interventions into the normative expectations we hold for the significance of picture-making.

This chapter uncovers whether the "look and feel" of digital media is dependent on the appearance of individuated units or "digits" within the formal structure of the artifact or image. Specifically, it discusses the history of the distinction between digital and analog beginning in the mid-twentieth century with the Macy Conferences, leaving aside the colloquial definition of digital artifacts as those made by computers and analog artifacts as those made without computers. Thus, the distinction at hand is philosophical and theoretical and it is a distinction with a particular historical trajectory that is not technologically determined. Analyzing the distinction between analog and digital systems as it has been theorized in philosophy and information science makes it possible to discover whether digital characteristics are discernable in non-computer-generated artifacts, and conversely, whether computationally generated artifacts necessarily reveal their constitutive digitality.

Many of the categories of new media are easily explored in terms of their theoretical difference from analog media. Such considerations of new media often champion radical technological novelty or replace critical theory with descriptions or explanations of the technical specificities of computational processes and processors. But this approach tends to ignore the fact that theoretical, and often even technical, categories become complicated or even fractured when tested against sensory experience of concrete artifacts. A working comprehension of the operative principles of digital technology—the nitty-gritty of how the technology works—may deepen a viewer's conceptual grasp of an artwork or artifact. However, possible claims should be addressed about the kinds of perceptual experiences yielded by both digital and analog artifacts under the present technological conditions in which both types of artifacts are produced. Given the capacities of contemporary computational devices, it is conceivable that (a) the difference between analog and digital may have already become imperceptible and (b) if the work does not deliver any overt information about its status as analog or digital, the relevance of that distinction also disappears.[2] So the question arises whether one should continue to attend to this distinction in a "postdigital" age. Postdigitality entails that computation has become so advanced and so ubiquitous that images and artifacts may be saturated with technology but appear "naturalistic" in an analog sense, so that there remains no discernable difference between that which has been produced through analog and that which has been produced via digital means. The technologized, digital world has been effectively naturalized; nature is suffused with technology, but the digital resolution of the world picture is sufficiently naturalistic that its underlying structural principles become inconsequential and irrelevant. Zeuxis's grapes are more delectable than ever. The precise characteristics of the analogico-digital relationship will be discussed in further detail presently, but to return to the initial question of the value and relevance of the distinction, despite appearances it in fact becomes increasingly urgent to examine why certain makers choose to foreground analogicity and others digitality. Although these categories are becoming seemingly muddied, they appear at certain times and places to assert themselves perceptually and conceptually. And to what end? This chapter, and indeed the book as a whole, proposes that it is because our understanding of the structural properties of the world in which we live shift depending upon whether we assess it in analog or digital terms. Despite the apparent disindividuation of these categories in a postdigital era, which frequently celebrates their dedifferentiation, these categories persist beneath the surface layers of apprehension, waiting quietly for discursive articulation in service of a fuller understanding of how thinking about the world in terms of either category can drastically alter our expectations for how it is configured, how it will function, how it will appear, how we as humans will operate within it, and how we will form beliefs and knowledge about it. This chapter considers these larger questions through an aesthetic framework, using the phenomenon of pictorialization as a vehicle to reveal the ways in which digital and analog conceptual models alter fundamental ways of thinking, seeing, and knowing. The larger questions, then, are distilled into the query of whether, when we are faced with a pictorial schema that intuitively seems technological or artificial, the pictorial surface contains any particular elements that communicate its digital origins, and why this might be the case. In this way, the apparent confluence of digitality and analogicity in the postdigital age can be considered closely and potentially challenged in order to show their relevance to greater epistemological issues.

Media theorist Sean Cubitt has claimed that the *technical* distinction between digital and analog recording technologies becomes relatively minute when the rate at which data is digitally "sampled" and collated becomes ever more rapid and dense.[3] To illustrate this more concretely, take, for example, digital and analog recordings of a symphony. While an analog recording is literally analogous (bears a direct relationship to) its referent, insofar as a phonographic recording device responds to physical vibrations in the air, a digital recording takes discrete "samples" of sound, between which there is a smaller or larger gap in which sound will resonate uncaptured. In early digital recordings, a slower sampling rate would mean larger gaps and would thus result in an inferior, artificially sutured sound quality in the recording. However, in principle, as the technology advances and sampling rates increase, the density of analog and digital recordings will become fully commensurate.[4]

But to rely too heavily on the decreasing technical gap between digital and analog leads, potentially, to a misprision of the broader cultural and epistemological effects of technology, and specifically, the ways that the technological imagination contributes to the formation of a particular worldview, thought world, or lifeworld (depending on the preferred terminology), which necessarily tends to produce certain kinds of theoretical formations while passing over or suppressing others.[5] In other words, even if the technical specificities of digital technologies approach or surpass the fidelity of analog ones, and even if we live in an age of media convergence,[6] in which old and new media collide, presented through the same channels (over the Internet, for example), the distinction between analog and digital remains crucial for revealing the intricacies of pre-, post-, and proto-digital epistemology. The relationship between the two modalities may include both intersections and deviations; thus, I am not interested in claiming total continuity, nor complete rupture, but a theory of digitality and analogicity that attends to the dialogic, mutually informative relationship between them. And this relationship issues from their status as representational technologies, or at the very least architectonic strategies.

In ascertaining the extent to which a sensible quality of the digital is (or is not) coextensive with a quality particular to computational media, I trace a history of representation that not only permits historical specificity—the situatedness of a representational norm within an historical, cultural, and geographic nexus—but also constructs a view of the present, whose characteristics are notoriously difficult to qualify without the benefit of hindsight and the counterfactual ideal of critical distance. I do this both by finding past precedents and, more importantly, by evaluating which individual aspects of history become most prominent—most frequently cited, analyzed, and as such, become most visible as explanatory figures—in the contemporary imagination.

To restate, insofar as it is concerned with explaining the present with reference to the past, the present work is modeled after a genealogical instead of an archaeological method. It is not so much that the past *determines* a present view but rather that certain features of the past become visible, or become available to direct analysis in a unique way within the conditions of knowledge and perception that emerge within a given epistemic or paradigmatic configuration. Making an argument that a digital method for the construction of visual representations (whether in service of pictorialization or other forms of depiction and notation) appears prior to computational technology requires a concomitant account of how a new language for the description and interpretation of noncomputational digital aesthetics might change the "message" that these works deliver. And in addition, it necessitates a consideration of how computational digitization might communicate differently than proto-digitalizations, exemplified in the case of Seurat's pointillist "dot."

Within the humanities, which is to say outside of the technical fields of information theory and mathematics, the relationship between and identifying characteristics of analogicity and digitality have been most thoroughly covered in the analytic philosophical tradition. The *aporia* of these debates lies in their lack of application to specific test cases, such that analog and digital become conceptual game pieces greatly distanced from experience and sense perception. I aim to uncover how digitality reveals itself to sense perception—how objects offer up an experience of digitality and thus configure the digital as a perceptual phenomenon rather than conjuring it as a purely theoretical notion or one type of technological system. Thus, deploying the qualifying characteristics of analog and digital systems enables an exploration of how we *perceive* objects as analog or digital, and provokes the question of whether maintaining this distinction is necessary to understand how we observe, interact with, and find pleasure or displeasure in our observations of digital, or digitally analogical, art and artifacts.

Discursive Horizons of Digits, Digitality, and Digitization

In the context of this analysis, then, digital aesthetics refers not simply to the look and shape of computer hardware or the products of electronic digital computation, such as the Internet, but rather to a much broader, non-technologically specific method of image and artifact construction that was identified as "facture."[7] Although the following discussions in this chapter will challenge the possibility of an easy distinction between analogicity and digitality, at first glance the difference between analog and digital remains quite intuitively straightforward; analog technologies (which can be electronic) process "signals or information represented by a continuously variable quantity, such as voltage, spatial position, etc., which in the case of measuring instruments can be displayed on a dial or other fixed scale,"[8] while digital technologies operate "on data in the form of digits or similar discrete elements."[9]

As an illustration, take the example of "digitization," a term that refers to the translation of analog media into digital form. In its technical application, digitization is a process by which a continuously variable analog signal, or stream of information, is converted into a string of discrete units, or bits, that can be processed either individually or in multibit groups by a binary computer. When a scanner transfers a photograph of a painting from a book to a computer, for example, areas of the photograph are divided into units, such as pixels, and the information in that area is sampled and averaged. Low-resolution image files, such as JPEGs, render highly pixilated results under certain conditions. In a low-resolution image file, the color values of two adjacent pixels might differ dramatically, and the continuous, subtle gradations of hue and tone found in the analog photograph, or the painting of which an analog photograph is taken and subsequently digitized, give way to a jagged array of pixilated color. Moreover, blowing up the photograph to a larger size does not produce more pixels to fill the larger area. Instead, if the size of the image is increased by 300 percent, the pixels are scaled up proportionally, revealing a much larger pixel with the same amount and type of information (the color value of the pixel, in this case) as in the smaller, scaled-down version of the image. Thus, the same lines of code processed by two different computers render two images that have the same informational content—the same amount of bits and bytes—but might appear very different (and appear at different speeds) due to the differing technical specifications of the two machines and the two interfaces.

Even viewed simply through the lens of technical practice, digitization provokes a host of questions and problems relating to analog-digital conversion. In audio conversion, the amplitudes of an analog waveform are sampled at discrete points. The computer-readable "data" are the numerical values derived from the sampling process. But when the basic structure of the signal itself is altered so drastically, can we still claim that the digital translation is the same creature? Translation or conversion seems to transform the "essential" properties of the analog signal—the continuous waveform—into something more essentially digital: discrete numerical values. It might seem easy enough to argue, then, that the material disjuncture (where electronic materiality manifests as energized matter) between an analog and a digital signal nullifies any possibility of a successful, relatively lossless translation. Further, it would seem impossible that the material footprint (the index) of digitality or analogicity would not be left in the artifact itself.

But this is an argument that requires stubborn adherence to one polar extreme or the other of technological determinism; either digital technology will never become sophisticated enough to erase the perceptible differences between discrete, binary signal processing, or the distinction between analog and digital will become irrelevant when technology overtakes the human-sensory capacity to distinguish analog continuousness from—albeit very finely and highly resolved—digital discreteness. As Whitney Davis has argued, "There is often little practical difference between analog and digital modes of representation, despite the historical importance of the distinction. . . . If analog and digital cannot be perceptually or formally discriminated, they might have no informational or aesthetic status for observers."[10] Lev Manovich has also questioned the viability of separating analog and digital representation based on discreteness or continuity; for Manovich, the most compelling case for the uniqueness of digital media is made from the standpoint that computational media are *numerical* first and foremost.[11] Analog media can be notionally distinguished from digital media insofar as analog representations contain an indefinite amount of information in contrast with the definite number of pixels in a digital image. For example, as an analog photograph is enlarged, the outlines and tones of the figures within become increasingly grainy or fuzzy.[12] However, continual enlargement does not eventually reveal a grid of pixels that comprise the image, as is the case when a pixel-based digital photograph is subject to the same enlargement.[13] Depending on the number of pixels comprising the whole image, a digital photograph may maintain an appearance of analog consistency and continuity up to a certain level of magnification. However, a one thousand by one thousand pixel image cannot create more pixels to make the jagged edges of magnified pixels less harsh. In a poetic account of the light, texture, and mood of digital versus analog photography, Bernard Stiegler evokes the indeterminacy of the analog grain. "Even if the grain can be massively enlarged or diminished, one doesn't have differentiated access to the grains . . . which on the contrary is made possible by digitization and its 'surgical precision.'"[14] The grain in analog photography is sensed qualitatively, as a textured fabric of some more or less distant past. Graininess in an unfocussed or greatly enlarged photograph indexes the slow dissolution of memory as sharp images and sense perceptions "de-resolve" into a fog of indistinct shapes and continuous tones. Whereas the particular way in which indistinct patterns and texture overtake precise, legible figures is unpredictable in analog photographs, the fragmentation of digital images into a planar geometry of pixels never bursts the rigid framework of the grid. Analog figuration seems thus to decay, to return, like flesh, to dust and ashes, the molecules of which form into distinct but variable shapes.

Although the dissolution of a digital image may also evoke the fragmentation of memory, in a technical or metaphorical sense, the particular mechanism by which it becomes illegible as a pictorialization functions differently than analog granularization. If a digital photograph is created or stored as a low-resolution image, it may only require two or three successive and relatively small enlargements for the image to fracture into a blocky checkerboard. Despite the fact that, as Manovich points out, even by the turn of the twenty-first century, many digital tools, in this instance scanners, were capable of producing images at resolutions high enough to allow great degrees of enlargement without blurring into a field of pixilated noise, the finite array of pixels in the former creates a threshold of resolution that, once crossed, causes the image to dissolve into illegibility.[15] While it is the pixel that enables the image to form at the outset, it is precisely the limitations of these infrastructural components—the definite quantity of information contained in the digital graphic as opposed to the indefinite amount contained in the analog photograph—that result in the very undoing of the picture, its transformation from an organized pattern back into an incommunicative mass of distinct but seemingly random, nondepictive digital pixels.

Ultimately, Davis's claim that "analog and digital modes are now themselves wholly continuous"[16] is most applicable if we examine the digital as a *technological* category rather than an *aesthetic* category, one in which the digital is a particular configurative method that can be disaggregated from contemporary electronic computers. In this case, an artifact can have digital characteristics whether or not its underlying mechanisms are electronically computational, and an electronically computational picture might not bear any aesthetic index of its digital composition. Thus, the "look and feel" of digital images is, for my purposes, not a function of an electronic-computational ontology. The expectation for digital artifacts should move beyond the question of whether they are able to achieve a perfect mimetic resemblance to analog representation. Instead, I want to put pressure on what forms of both sensory and intellectual knowledge and experience digital facture *can*, in a more positive sense, produce. The historical development—the prehistory to the inception of computational technology—of digital artifacts requires consideration in terms of both history of art and the history of depictive technologies that circulate outside of the realm of art, such as maps, diagrams, charts, and other graphic modes of information visualization. Given that digital graphics often operate on the edge of art, it is essential to situate them in a broad context of visual culture, which considers the historical trajectory of imaging technologies whose dialog with high art is inextricable but does not always correlate with it in a direct or obvious way.[17]

To remix the words of Martin Heidegger, the essence of the digital is "nothing technological."[18] Digital facture is observable within and across a range of representational technologies, both pictorial and notational, and is therefore not merely an *effect* of computational technology; it is "nothing of the order of a machine."[19] Sensible digitality might appear to issue from the division of the picture plane into distinct units, such as dots, pixels, or other metric devices, including the points on a graph or tick marks on a clock face. But whereas division presupposes the primal existence of a unified whole that can be cut into smaller pieces, a truly digital universe relies on the principle that the world can be understood best as a quantized, metric system. This means that any section of the observable world can be computed and constructed from the ground up. Here, the whole is not merely subject to subtractive *division* into discrete parts; rather, the world is always already metric, always already composed of units that link together into an amalgamated individual object/form. If digitization were an epiphenomenon of a metricized conception of space, it would seem to be a theoretical more than a perceptual category. But what we want to begin to see, like the shape of a sieve as it pushes up through sand, is not just the sieve as a shaping device but rather the particular qualities and textures of the sand that are produced and made visible by the screen of the sieve.

■ Cybernetics and the Macy Conferences

Although heated debates pertaining to the definitional boundary lines of digital and analog arose in the Macy Conferences, held from 1946 to 1953, documentation of these discussions has focused more prominently on the signals, noise, and feedback loops of cybernetics than on the relationship between digital and analog information processing. Participants in these meetings congregated from a range of disciplines, including electronics, psychology, and anthropology, with the common goal of outlining the primary principles of a new, almost universally applicable epistemological model called cybernetics. This term has of course become emblematic of the age of information systems and personal computing, and has circulated widely in the history and theory of digital media. Notably, Katherine Hayles's book *How We Became Posthuman* was one of the first attempts by a humanities scholar to situate these debates in a detailed map of a cultural landscape and a set of epistemological conditions that give rise to a computationalist theory of mind, behavior, interaction, and representation.[20] Hayles's text quickly achieved recognition as the authoritative project on the legacy of cybernetics in the age of personal computing. However, for all the documentation and critique of cybernetics, in Hayles's book and elsewhere, very little writing has been devoted to the vehement disputes that circulated around the problem of analog and digital. Not only did disagreements about the nature of digital and analog systems dominate conversations among such central players as John von Neumann, Warren McCulloch, Norbert Weiner, and Claude Shannon, the implications of defining the parameters of these systems were significant and potentially threatening to the integrity of the very notion of cybernetics.

At the first conference, held in New York City in 1946, John von Neumann delivered the first talk concerning the problem of analog and digital.[21] In it, he argued that all "computing automata," defined simply as an automatically and independently functioning machine used for the purpose of fast computing, are divisible into two classes—that of analogy and that of digital machines—and that these classes of machines can also be transposed onto living organisms. These classifications thus function as powerful and consequential analytic tools, which, in conjunction with technological experimentation, aid in the scientific exploration of living systems.[22] But von Neumann's emphasis on the *efficiency* of digital machines in computing, in expanding the range of computable numbers, and in problem solving betrays a stronger interest in building computers for warfare and military strategy than in the intellectual development of cybernetics per se.[23] According to von Neumann, analog and digital machines are differentiated chiefly by signal-to-noise ratios. Because analogy machines are based on the numerical representation of *physical* quantities, such as an electrical current, they are necessarily subject to incursions of random noise into the "signal" that expresses the operation of the machine in a nonrandom, significant pattern. Random noise results unavoidably from the "uncontrollable fluctuations" that are part of any physical system. Whereas a digital system works *solely* by "representing numbers as aggregates of digits," where digits are all-or-none switches that are either on or off, without any intermediate state between them, "no analogy machine exists which will really form the product of two numbers. What it will form is this product, plus a small but unknown quantity which represents the random noise of the mechanism and the physical processes involved."[24] The advantage of digital systems, then, is that each computed result carries a maximum accuracy with a minimum amount of noise.[25]

However, what quickly became evident in the discussions of analog and digital in the first Macy Conference was that under close inspection the two systems tend to overlap, so that an absolute distinction between them becomes untenable. Norbert Weiner's claim that "every digital device is really an analogical device" would seem to contradict von Neumann's portioning of digital and analog systems based on signal-to-noise ratios.[26] However, a further look at von Neumann's "Theory of Automata" indicates that von Neumann himself accepted a certain degree of ambiguity and crossover between the two systemic types. Specifically, for von Neumann the nervous system cannot be considered either digital or analogical—both systems are present in physiological function. "The nerve impulse seems in the main to be an all-or-none affair, comparable to a binary digit. Thus a digital element is evidently present, but it is equally evident that this is not the entire story."[27] Functions dependent on chemical composition, such as the blood stream, von Neumann calls "humoral." Humoral processes are analogical. But generally, "feedback chains" in the body are mixed. If living organisms are part digital and part analogical, and these parts are often interdependent and thus neither fully one nor the other, the same can be said of many computers. Similarly, Weiner also argues that systems may have digital or analog aspects that overlap or even transform from one type to the other. In a contemporary instance of this analog-digital symbiosis, Timothy Binkley has pointed out that through the end of the 1980s most digitally computational interface design relied on analog (CRT and then, later, semidigital LCD) monitors to deliver information to the user graphically.[28] The development of newer, sleeker graphic user interfaces with higher-resolution capabilities has changed human-computer interaction at the perceptual level, but nevertheless, this analogico-digital oscillation shows that even in what we take to be digital systems, the incursion of the analog disrupts the apparently closed digital circuit.

It mattered to cyberneticians to define analog and digital because their theory was supposed to be all encompassing—to apply to all organic and physical structures and phenomena. But for their theory to work, the world needed to undergo a radical reconceptualization, to be reenvisioned in terms of digitality and computational systems. Claus Pias has categorized this new shift as one similar to the historical ruptures tracked by Michel Foucault; similar to the break in the eighteenth century, in which an "anthropological illusion" supplanted the preceding "metaphysical illusion," in the mid-twentieth century we begin to see the emergence of a new "cybernetic illusion."[29] As the birth of Enlightenment replaced metaphysics with the human sciences, epistemology converged around the figure of "Man," who instead of being defined as a reflection of God's will, becomes simultaneously the object and producer of knowledge.[30] A new epistemological rift begins to yawn in the twentieth century, when the participants in the Macy Conferences saw in the new interdisciplinary study of cybernetics an overarching epistemological umbrella, under which all knowledge could be reformulated, not, this time, in terms of Man or humanism but rather in terms of systems, feedback loops, signals, and noise, of which the human is only one instantiation in a total systemic ecology. However, running up against the indeterminacy latent in the analog/digital dyad threatened the stability of this new formation insofar as it undercut the possibility of an absolute differentiation between a world constructed according to calculable (statistically and probabilistically knowable) digital processes versus an infinitely fine-grained, aggravatingly flexible analog world.[31]

However, Pias also suggests that the very kind of thinking that proposes this typological distinction is dependent on the preexistence of a digital epistemology—a digital logic and terminology that activates a desire to see a system "as" digital or analog. Moreover, since many cyberneticians saw in digital machines the greatest potential for information processing, and since cybernetics as a discourse is heavily invested in the trope of information, they stand to gain the greatest benefit from attaining a thoroughgoing knowledge of the types of information transmission and feedback loops generated by digital machines or living organisms interpreted through a digital lens. Nevertheless, in Pias's selection of quotations from notable participants in the meeting, we begin to notice the persistent, shadowy presence of "continuity" well in advance of Nelson Goodman's typological study of analog and digital systems in the 1970s, which figures continuity against digital discreteness. Pias channels the anxious mood in the 1946 conference surrounding the persistence of analogy in the following synthesis of participants' commentary: "Not only for building effective computers, but also for building an effective discourse of experimental epistemology one has to be 'ignorant' (as Walter Pitts called it)—ignorant 'of the actual continuity' in all things that virtually might be digital."[32] "'Treat them as if these transition states did not exist. It is quite a good way of treating them,' said John Stroud."[33] An inconvenient preponderance of analogical continuity subsists even in ostensibly digital systems; John Stroud, Walter Pitts, and McCulloch himself all acknowledge the possibility that digitality will always be haunted by shades of the forbidden ground of analogy: intermediate states, in-betweenness, and continuousness. Analogy in all its messy physicality is forbidden because it allows randomness and noise to muck up the hygienic, arithmetical precision of numerically driven digital systems. Permitting the analog to extend its reach into the digital threatens to destabilize digital epistemology, the very thing that cyberneticians suspect will be their most effective tool for finding points of comparison between, or even rendering equivalent, machines and living organisms.

Theories of analog and digital have been imported from the cybernetic theories of the 1950s into cognitive science and the philosophy of mind in the twenty-first century. Here, digital systems are conjured not merely as *models* of consciousness, in which the model is a secondary representation, serving as a descriptive shorthand or approximation of its referent; rather, consciousness is itself a digital system. According to a strong, pancomputationalist view, then, digital systems do not *simulate* consciousness; pancomputationalists believe that consciousness, as well as other physical, chemical, and biological systems, exhibit digital states and that, consequently, these systems function computationally and can be most accurately replicated using electronic digital computing technology. In philosophy of mind, debates surrounding the degree to which natural systems, and by extension human consciousness, can be interpreted as computers cohere around whether consciousness processes information through computational operations or by building representations. In his article on representation in digital systems, Vincent Müller takes on the legacy of von Neumann and the Macy Conferences to assess the importation of definitions of digital and analog given by Goodman and the cyberneticists into contemporary computationalist viewpoints in the philosophy of mind.[34] The mode of inquiry and description mobilized by cybernetics treats both organisms and machines as feedback mechanisms and thus provides a backdrop against which living and technological systems can be made equivalent.

Digital Analytics: Nelson Goodman's Language of Notation

Twenty years after the last of the Macy Conferences, which galvanized the interdisciplinary study of systems theory, cybernetics, and computationalism, was held in 1953, philosopher Nelson Goodman published a slim but dense volume entitled *Languages of Art*. In it, Goodman set out to identify the formal and logical structure of symbols and to advance a conventionalist theory of how and to what end symbolic communication occurs. The ability of verbal, pictorial, and musical representational systems to successfully convey a particular meaning depends upon the transparent operation of cultural conventions that are maintained not through voluntary consensus but rather through consistent, iterative application of a set of terms to particular types of objects. The analytic problem at hand is the distinction between analog and digital, and the relevance of this distinction to the evaluation and interpretation of artworks and nonart artifacts. Of primary importance is Goodman's aim to show how pictures are differentiated from other types of descriptions and from other types of symbolic communication such as diagrams and maps, which will be called "notations," a distinction that requires explanation before I proceed further.

Goodman introduces several typological categories for the analysis of the symbolic structures not only of art but also of other symbolic modes of communication that operate outside the purely linguistic register, including maps, diagrams, and measuring devices such as clocks. Several key terms in Goodman's system of dyadic relations prove useful in establishing the types of expression and figural communication facilitated by analog or digital expression. A significant proportion of *Languages of Art* is devoted to Goodman's theory of notation, developed to test the distinction between the symbol systems at work in the nominal category "art" and those at work in "notations." These symbol schemes, which contain an array of differentiated characters, such as inscriptions defined as notes or letters, are arranged to stand for one particular correlating thing: the sound of the note or the letter denoted by its graphic symbol. Whereas in dense and replete pictorial schemes a mark or set of marks might have an infinite or indeterminable range of correlates, in a notational scheme one mark stands for one correlate in all, repeatable instances.[35]

Representations utilized in information science are more often notational than depictive. If they do refer to analogical representational strategies, these analogical modulations would be, more often than not, ornamental rather than information bearing. Aesthetics, here, diverges from the Kantian principle that aesthetics is purposive without purpose, which is to say, in vastly simplified shorthand, that aesthetic experience is not teleological or utilitarian.[36] Unlike ethical forms of social organization, such as laws that are created with a specific outcome in the minds of lawmakers and thus exist as means to an end, the value of a work of art is ascertained independently of the viewers' desire for the content depicted in the picture plane to exist or their desire to possess the object itself or its symbolic content. For example, the aesthetic pleasure I feel when viewing Paul Cézanne's *Still Life with Compotier* (1879–1882) is independent of my desire to eat or possess the apples depicted therein. My pleasure in viewing Jacques-Louis David's *Oath of the Horatii* (1784) is independent of my political views. And my enjoyment of Johannes Vermeer's *View of Delft* (1659–1660) should be the same regardless of my desire, or lack thereof, to move to the Netherlands.

Immanuel Kant's schema has been criticized on the basis that aesthetic experience is always political, always tied to ethical principles and epistemological frameworks. Nevertheless, the tenacity of Kant's separation of art and everyday life is never more apparent than in the art-science wars. "Aesthetics" in science is oriented toward functionality. A "good" example of information visualization is one that communicates its data immediately and effortlessly. It uses what it calls "aesthetic principles"—although these undergo a major semiotic shift as they move from a Kantian to a systems-theory framework—such as color, line, and shape, to erase indicators of its own selective construction of meaning. In other words, a harmonious aesthetic appearance can be utilized to mask the fact that there might be other potentially perceptible facets of meaning that would not only introduce visual discord but also change the semiotic parameters (the content) of the delivered message. If the markers of a picture's status as representation, such as framing or perspective, disappear, the information contained within can seem to communicate transparently, without the distortions and filtrations that inevitably result from any process of mediation.[37]

While the conventionally valorized aesthetic features of depiction consist of ambiguity and indeterminacy, notational schemes support the fantasy of flawless, transparent information transmission. As the density and irreducibility of analogicity, in which, for example, a mark carries direct correlation to the pressure of the instrument or quantity of paint in a brush, obviates the possibility of perfectly regularized precision, notational schemas are built on the dream of it. In her critique of the implicitly neo-Kantian (antifunctionalist) tendency to dismiss the aesthetic value of notational, point-based representational practices, Maureen Turim offers a compelling description of what we would usually think of as "analogical" inscription. "We usually think of [the] artisanal process not as a setting of points, but as a continuum. I draw a line, descriptive, expressive, gestural, fluid. If I am drawing from nature, then the line may be somewhat analogous to the referent."[38] Turim both equates analog drawing with continuity and emphasizes the correlative association between analog mark-making and direct analogy between the material qualities of the object and those of its representation. In contrast, Nelson Goodman claims that "plainly, a digital system has nothing special to do with digits, or an analog system with analogy," and develops his terminology along different lines, on the basis of, for example, syntactic and semantic density versus disjunctness, and repleteness versus attenuation. Especially given Goodman's focus on disjunctness and differentiation as constitutive elements of digital systems and continuity and density as fundamental attributes of analog systems, it is not in fact obvious that digital systems have nothing to do with digits or analog systems with analogy. It is quite common for analog systems to be identified as such because they demonstrate a direct relationship to what is being measured, or because changes in a system can be attributed to physical forces, as in the case of analog computers that operate on resistors, which open or shut according to the amount of electricity coursing through them.

There are several categories within Goodman's text that relate to the analogico-digital distinction but circulate outside of the particular oppositions that define the binary pairing. For instance, the relationship between digitality and notation, which will become relevant in my discussion of Paul Klee in chapter 2, is only cursorily addressed in the section of Goodman's text devoted to analog and digital schemes and systems. However, the digital is ranked as a subcategory within Goodman's general theory of notation. As is the case for all notational schemes, digital systems are required to be discontinuous, as well as syntactically and semantically differentiated, disjoint, and unambiguous, such that each character complies with a distinct correlate, can be used interchangeably in all situations, and are always "true copies of each other."[39] Thus, digital symbols, such as pixels, are regular, interchangeable, and exact copies of one another. If all digital systems are notational, and must conform to a stringent set of rules to fulfill the categorical requirements of digitality, we must assume that every digital system, and probably also every product of a digital system, is incontrovertibly unambiguous in both its formal construction and its denotative range. But this claim underscores one of the primary complications in evaluating digital artifacts under the same criteria applied to pictorial schemes, namely, artistic/aesthetic value traditionally increases proportionally to interpretive ambiguity, to an irreducibility of meaning to one determinate thread. This ambiguity can be understood as a product of the formal properties of analog pictorial schemes, wherein slight modulations of continuous marks or lines or zones of color bear semiotic content. In addition to the formal density and repleteness of pictorialization, it has been generally assumed that meaning in a good artwork is not easily reducible to a set of clearly articulated propositions. Stated in terms of Kantian aesthetics, the pleasure we derive from the contemplation of aesthetic objects is in the free play of the imagination. Free play is nonpropositional, nonteleological, and antireductive. Disambiguity and precision, which occur both hermeneutically and at a formal, configurative level in terms of syntactic and semantic differentiation, appear from the outset to exclude digital systems from a canonized view of aesthetics that embraces ambiguity, indeterminacy, and open-endedness.

Goodman's division between notation and depiction and digital and analog allocates a set of terms illustrating how the symbolic mechanisms of digital systems produce aesthetic criteria that operate independently of those typically used to evaluate analog representation. For Goodman, what "counts as" representation has little to do with the internal content of an image but is rather a matter of facture, or the architectonics of the image. Representation is encoded conventionally, by reiteration and comparison between internal iconographic similarities, so that an image may be interpreted as a "picture" if it is built using one symbolic system or a "description" if constructed with another.[40] Descriptive devices convey specific, condensed information, whereas pictorializations are apprehended in a more open-ended way. Although Goodman's text contains analyses of notational features of dance, literary arts, music, and painting, digital systems are exemplified chiefly by scientific instruments of measure. For Goodman, the differences between digital and analog are primarily operational—he treats digital systems as functional but not as incorporated into codes of artistic representation. Although he takes great pains to define the parameters of disjointness and differentiation at both a syntactic and a semantic level, he includes little discussion of how digital images and artifacts would manifest their constitutive difference at the level of the interface or image surface. While his conventionalist viewpoint explicitly provides for the expansion of artistic codes, in the context of *Languages of Art* he regards digital systems as notational and thus resistant to pictorial codes of depiction and representation that have traditionally relied on the presence of density and ambiguity in the mode of inscription. The central point I want to make here is that digital pictures—those that are fabricated according to a digital method—hover in between Goodman's categories and as such become an unstable, oscillatory representational type *because* they enfold what are for Goodman two different symbol schemes—dense, replete pictorialization versus disjoint, articulate (digital) notations—

into a single instance. Because for Goodman digital notations are not pictures or images per se, once a digital method is conjoined with pictorial strategies, the purity of the digital system is compromised through the process of blending distinct structural modalities.

Goodman's theory of pictures as independent from other descriptions depends on their correspondence to analog schemes, in which the inscription is both syntactically and semantically dense. Pictures are also dissociated from maps and diagrams because they are "replete," or in other words, are capable of communicating an indefinite amount of meaning given that every perceived modulation of the inscription potentially yields a new layer of signification.[41] In replete schemes, every observable property of the picture, whether formal or material—such as thickness of line, color, and texture—is relevant and conceivably multiply relevant. And, moreover, it is difficult to pinpoint, in a pictorial scheme as opposed to a digital or notational one, what *exactly* is being "represented" or denoted precisely because the informational content proliferates to an indefinite extent. Although certain elements, such as bodies, faces, and fauna, may be easily identified, it becomes more complex to determine exactly to what in the object-world the totality of the inscription correlates. There exists a potentially interminable number of overlapping relational possibilities —a horse, the horse rearing, the sun reflecting off the horse's flank as it rears, and so forth. Syntactic density obtains when the mark is unarticulated, or nondifferentiable into discrete constitutive elements whose boundaries can be precisely demarcated. According to Goodman, "a scheme is syntactically dense if it provides for infinitely many characters so ordered that between each two there is a third."[42] For example, a continuous line made by ink on paper cannot be broken into grammatical parts or discrete units, as a sentence can be parsed into words and then into letters. Until one arrives at the subatomic composition of ink and paper, there is no limit to the fineness of modulation within the line. Syntactic density, then, is the "fundamental technical-logical feature of analog representation."[43]

Semantic density occurs when there is overlapping or ambiguity with respect to the correlation between symbol and referent; for example, if we are presented with a collection of objects and asked to assign fractional values to describe the weight of each, there is an unlimited degree of fineness with which each weight could be discriminated, because no lower limit has been set to determine "significant difference." As such, the fractional assignation of weights, while numerical, is not digital (nor notational) and is semantically dense. Additionally, a system can be neither notational nor, as a notational subset, digital, if a referent can be named by multiple characters, or if a single character can apply to multiple referents.[44] For example, in a case of fractional weights, multiple fractional values can represent the same physical weight of a particular object. Thus, while digital machines are often identified as numerical processors, within Goodman's formulation a numerical system is not inherently digital.

Philosopher David Lewis offers the following summation of Goodman's differentiation between analog and digital inscription (and by extension, representation): "Digital representation is differentiated. Given a number-representing 'mark'—an inscription, vocal utterance, pointer position, electrical impulse, or whatever—it is theoretically possible, despite our inability to make infinitely precise measurements, to determine exactly which other marks are copies of the given mark and to determine exactly which number (or numbers) the given mark and its copies represent. Analog representation, on the other hand, fails to be differentiated because it is dense."[45]

As opposed to the density and repleteness that have become the standards by which analog depictions are evaluated, notational and digital schemes can only be classified as such if there is no ambiguity at the level of either inscription or reference. That is, only one distinct mark can correlate to a particular referent; consequently, one mark cannot stand for two referents, nor can there be two different marks referring to a single referent. For instance, the letter B refers to only one letter—there are not two letters that mean the same thing, nor can one letter refer to two different referents.

Given that the features associated with pictorial depiction have been more prominently allied with the fine arts, it is curious that Goodman marshals notation, and by extension digitality, in a book that attempts to systematize and catalog the symbolic structures that make meaning in art. Overall, the technical specificities of these terms are ultimately less important than the initial claim, that *pictures are distinguished from other symbolic kinds by virtue of their analogicity*—their density, repleteness, and so forth. Maps and diagrams are quasi-pictorial but do not fulfill the parameters for pictures insofar as they are notational, bearing specific informational quantities, rather than pictorial, or indeterminately replete. The problem that arises here, then, is what to do when an artifact that we would normally classify as a picture conforms more strongly to a digital schema, either perceptually, where digital characters are visible on its surface, or technically, as in the case of a digital photograph that appears to be analog but is constructed by digitally computational means. According to Goodman's typology, and his argument for the incommensurability between pictorial (analog) and other (notational) symbol systems, a digital picture would contain essential ontological contradictions that would frustrate any attempt to interpret them using the evaluative criteria assigned to (fundamentally analog) pictures.

This line of argumentation provides the foundational principle explored and expanded upon in this book. First, it clarifies why artifacts exhibiting a digital visual schema have not been easily incorporated into a canon of fine art, which demands semantic repleteness and density in order to achieve highest accolades. And second, it sheds new light on artifacts displaying the signs of digital facture, affording a new vocabulary and methodology with which to assign such artifacts the potential to signify on their own terms.

In appropriating Goodman's text toward a reading of digital art and artifacts, it is important to assess not only what analog and digital mean for Goodman but also how each category can generate a particular set of aesthetic criteria, which will become concomitantly perceptible in the structure of artifacts. In a helpful contextualization and exposition of Goodman's project, Whitney Davis argues that while many scholars of information theory and computation have encountered obstacles in the attempt to define the supposedly "primal categories" of analog and digital systems, Goodman's terminology allows an "independent and precise characterization of analog and digital modes of representation."[46] Even these primal and purportedly oppositional terms are subject to etiolation. Despite Goodman's claim that "the difference between analog and digital machines or systems is easier to illustrate than to define," both digital and analog artifacts often reveal elements of both categories deeply embedded within their basic structure, making a flawless illustration problematic if not counterfactual.[47] It is finally quite tempting to conclude that the categories slip all too often from their oppositional seats into "analogical" indiscernability. Indeed, Davis claims that "one of Goodman's most radical conclusions about analog and digital was simple: 'many [symbol] systems are of neither type,' including natural language. But this insight has been almost entirely forgotten in current discussions of media."[48] Popular terms such as *convergence*, *hybridity*, and *transvergence* are, in fact, attempts to account for media artifacts that demonstrate characteristics of both analog and digital or "neither" analog nor digital systems, though what this last category would look like remains to be seen. The subsequent chapters of this book are devoted to testing Goodman's terms against a selection of media artifacts, in order to determine whether his classificatory approach accounts sufficiently for traits found within these objects themselves, or where nuances within the objects problematize, or require an expansion of, Goodman's appraisal of the ontological and aesthetic character of digital and analog schemas.

One issue in particular that arises in in an analysis of pure structure (which is theoretically independent of representation per se) achieved through analogicity, digitality, and notation is the idea, raised as an objection to Goodman's enigmatic claim that "almost any picture may represent almost anything,"[49] that pictures, even if not overtly representational, are "object-presenting experiences."[50] One way of interpreting this is that all pictures present a set of associations leading toward a phenomenological apprehension of resemblances and an overall sense of objecthood or gestalt. However, while Goodman avows the denotative or referential function of pictures he declares resemblance inconsequential. What is denoted in a picture is determined by a conventionally determined "system of representation" or "plan of correlation under which the picture represents the object."[51] Dominic Lopes has written that pictorialization, both within and outside of familiar systems of depiction (in which a viewer's adjustment to and operation within a conventional schema ensures communicative efficacy), generates the "object-presenting experiences" mentioned above.[52] Pictures provoke a consideration of the object-world by confronting us with their object-ness and encouraging us to think about both how and why they are configured in the way they are and how and why we reflect them (pictorially or cognitively) back to ourselves in a particular way. Thus, when pictures are configured digitally they provoke a consideration of a digitally structured object-world. They present an alternative possibility for understanding and re-presenting the underlying structure of the things we see and feel in the world.

Looking forward to subsequent chapters, it is simple enough to say what is being represented, due to resemblance, in the case of many of the proto-digital examples, such as Georges Seurat's pointillist and Paul Klee's divisionist paintings. It is less clear what is being represented in terms of the "why" and "how" of the specific strategies of facture employed by each artist. It is the work of this book to uncover exactly how the structural or architectonic choices mobilized by these artists changes the semantic implications of the works. However, when we move further into the realm of digital-computational works, the way in which the structural principles of the works alter their signifying potential shifts again, because the class of objects to which the depiction refers is radically expanded, requiring a new correlative system for a viewer to recognize and sort the depiction into a range of objects potentially (re)presented by the visual schema at hand. For instance, the abstract permutations driven by Victor Vasarely's experiments with a visual, plastic alphabet activate a field of individuated elements (circles and ellipses) arranged in a multiple, combinatory array of possible patterns of color and shape, performatively enacting a predetermined system. His work moves beyond a simple formal proposition about the morphogenetic properties of a single shape-element and makes a broader claim about the way in which the creation of a proto-digital system can modify our apprehension and conception of a contemporary world picture. In keeping with their status as pictorializations using an imagined visual grammar, Vasarely's paintings bear a greater morphological similarity to typographic charts, such as that of Adobe's master font, in which visual permutations of each letter, such as elongation (stretching) and line thickness, are arranged in gridded rows and columns.[53] Vasarely explores the combinatory logic of a computable visual language, operating to a certain extent within the parameters of twentieth-century abstraction, in order to propose what can be called a digital (but nonelectronically computational) system and a digital ontology of the material world, phenomenological experience, and conceptual processing.

Complicating this setup is the fact that there exist instances of analog systems that use digits; they are discretized and differentiated, but similarly to the case in which fractional numbers are assigned to describe the weight of a set of objects, they employ analog representation. Electrical analog computers, for instance, receive input through resistors. The input is numerical, but the "representation of numbers by electrical resistances is analog representation."[54] Another example is spring-loaded valves that mete fluid. Analog computation is possible using this method based on amounts of fluid passing between valves proportional to an amount of time. The fluid could also be comprised of pellets, which adds a degree of syntactic differentiation, but the device still operates analogically. The relationship among the physical magnitudes in analog systems is more direct than that of digital ones, as in the case of resistors (analog) versus scanning/sampling (digital). Ultimately, while the complex disjunctures and affinities between digital and analog systems reveal sites of tension in digital, analog, and hybrid artifacts, it is also crucial to regard these artifacts through a macroscopic lens, to see how these distinctions manifest not only mathematically (Lewis) or within hidden computational operations (the hermetically sealed "black box" accessible only to a technocratic literati) but also in the level of interface, which is the "aesthetic surface" of computational processes.[55]

▪ Indeterminacy, Hybridity, and Incompossibility

One of the most compelling aspects of the philosophical debates surrounding the possibility or impossibility of maintaining a distinction between analog and digital is that these debates uncover the unstable ontology of digital states. Critical responses in analytic philosophy to the claim that digital states are constitutively discrete have pointed to the various indiscernabilities that arise between digital and analog mechanisms. For example, even if the hand of an analog clock moves in discrete steps, its calculations are governed by an underlying analog system. One response has been that analog devices may exhibit discreteness but that they lack true differentiation because they proceed serially.[56] Similarly, David Lewis has attested to the many cases of "representation that is as differentiated and non-dense as any digital representation and yet is analog rather than digital representation."[57] In the preponderance of circumstances, attempts to narrow the demarcation of digital and analog states is that they tend to gravitate back toward one another, so that just as one distinction is posed, it is problematized by a further instance of the constitutive hybridity of digital and analog systems. Clarifying an absolute distinction between digital and analog states becomes an ongoing process of iteration, feedback, and reformulation, such that there is a temptation to declare that digital states are relative and fully description dependent: that the boundary between digital and analog is vulnerable to permutation given the apparent flexibility and range of parameters that can be applied to define a system as either analog or digital.[58]

The difficulty of assessing whether a system is truly analog or truly digital suspends this relationship in a perpetual state of open-endedness; even the conclusions drawn within the strict constraints of philosophical logic maintain their viability only in a narrowly controlled range of circumstances. To return to the problem of time, or more precisely the digital or analog operations at work in instruments for measuring it, a number of possible tests for determining a clock's analog or digital status compete, ultimately leaving the solution indeterminate. In Müller's "first approximation, being digital means being in a discrete state."[59] But the situation becomes more complicated when we discover that analog movements and markings can also occur in steps. To state confidently that a system is analog, must it simply demonstrate continuousness? This cannot be sufficient, for "an analog watch does not cease to be analog even if its hands move in discrete steps," as a result of the fact that there is a directly analogous relationship between a physical force and its output.[60] This argument depends for its plausibility on the idea that analogicity is determined not by continuousness but by direct correlation between mechanism and representation. An equally viable claim, however, is that for a representation to be digital it need merely be discrete, which would imply the coexistence of analog and digital states in a singular mechanism, in this case the analog watch. As Müller explains, arguments for the mutual exclusivity of analog and digital representations dissolve when the notional analogy to the "flow of time" persists in both digital and analog timekeeping devices.[61] Although we can start by defining a digital state as necessarily and identifiably discrete, while analog states are continuous, many systems (which fulfill far larger functional roles than individual states) require conversion between signal types (analog to digital and vice versa), and thus contain analog and digital parts.

But why then insist, if this is so obvious, on reiterating the distinction between digital and analog media in the construction of art (or art-approximate) artifacts? If systems are bound to be so inconclusively both/and, what do we have to gain from identifying one from the other at the outset? While one possible response to these questions is that the persistent relativity and shifting lines of demarcation between digital and analog obviates the necessity to categorically separate them, I contend that alongside the technical definitions for these terms there exists a set of perceptual conditions (or a process of perceptual conditioning) that prompts us to recognize, if through purely imaginative exercise or direct observation, sensory and formal criteria that arbitrate, in a sometimes oscillatory rather than binding fashion, which side of a binary division (yes-no, digital-analog) the artifact will occupy. In other words, just as the first the cybernetic and now the pancomputationalist philosophical standpoint create a worldview in which all phenomena are interpreted in terms of computational processes (if all the world is a computer, then all its systems must also function computationally), we will have different expectations for the kinds of knowledge and experience upon which an artifact comments and/or reflects depending on whether we see it *as* analog or digital. If an artifact generates a perceptual effect of "being digital," not only are the truth-claims and indexicality of the picture called into question (if we are concerned with the matter of the waning of the index in digital photography, an issue that extends beyond the scope of the present discussion), but also that artifact falls into a different epistemological framework or "way of seeing" than does an analog instance. A viewer is, for example, expected to engage differently with a mosaic than with a painting by Nicolas Poussin, or with a heavily pixilated, digitized portrait of Abraham Lincoln than with the original photographic print that was the source of the digitization.

One important point to note is that "not all systems that have digital states are digital *systems*."[62] In colloquial speech, an implied equivalence exists between digital and computational machines. If computational machines exist to compute—that is, to generate an output (a result) from an input (a data set)—we must assume that their value is based on execution and thus issues from their functionality. In contrast with art, according to a Kantian aesthetic legacy, whose purpose may be to give pleasure, to revivify experience, or to provide a culturally sanctioned space for contemplation, the purpose of machines in general, and computers in particular, is to produce a controlled causal chain resulting in a specific, predictable and repeatable effect. But digital states may exist in nonmachinic systems that lack a prescribed chain of causality. The fact that computers compute, that they process information, defines them as tokens of a typology of functionalist systems. But their characteristic of being perceptually digital is separate from that typology. This means, then, that while it is easy to assume that digital states are notational indicators or symbolic representations of information-bearing values (i.e., the peaks and valleys on an EKG printout that "represent" numbers that in turn "represent" the range of systolic and diastolic pressures in the cardiac system), a system *need not* be computational, nor need it demonstrate a chain of cause and effect to fulfill the conditions of being digital. In other words, we can gather evidence of digital states in non-computational, non-mechanically generated works of art, such as the abstract painted mosaics by Paul Klee in the 1920s and 1930s that will be discussed in detail in chapter 2. These works have digital states but are not necessarily digital systems. Nonetheless, without distinguishing between digital mechanisms and observable digital properties of nondigital systems, it becomes all too easy to retreat into hard and fast functionalist distinctions between analog and digital and thus to become blind to the subtle network of relationships between and within each category.

At the same time, however, we can notionally uphold the separation between state and system in order to understand how computational digital systems produce different types of output than artifacts that display digital states without necessarily being a part of a digital system. Klee produces digital effects in his painting without creating a self-contained digital system. Pointillism contains enough digital elements from the beginning to the end of production to warrant consideration as a digital system, but it is not computational. And then there are examples of digital systems that, without attempting to conceal their underlying digital functionality, also digitally simulate analog processes, such as brushstrokes or drips of paint, in order to give an impression of contingency, spontaneity, or imprecision.

Camille Utterback's artworks, for instance, are generated within the technical, programmatic constraints of a digital, computational system but also incorporate analog elements to preserve a sense of "messiness" and handmadeness. This allows her work both to be technological—screen based, software driven, and interactive—and at the same time to appeal to an analog aesthetic sensibility, in which density and repleteness, manifested in the formal construction of the work, actively produce the indeterminacy, ambiguity, and open-endedness that occur at the level of signification. Specifically, her *External Measures* series, comprised of six individual, interactive "paintings," explores the aesthetic and experiential possibilities that emerge at the intersection of computational systems, bodily movement, pixelated formal construction, and abstract, painterly composition. Utterback's software responds to viewers' movements by creat-

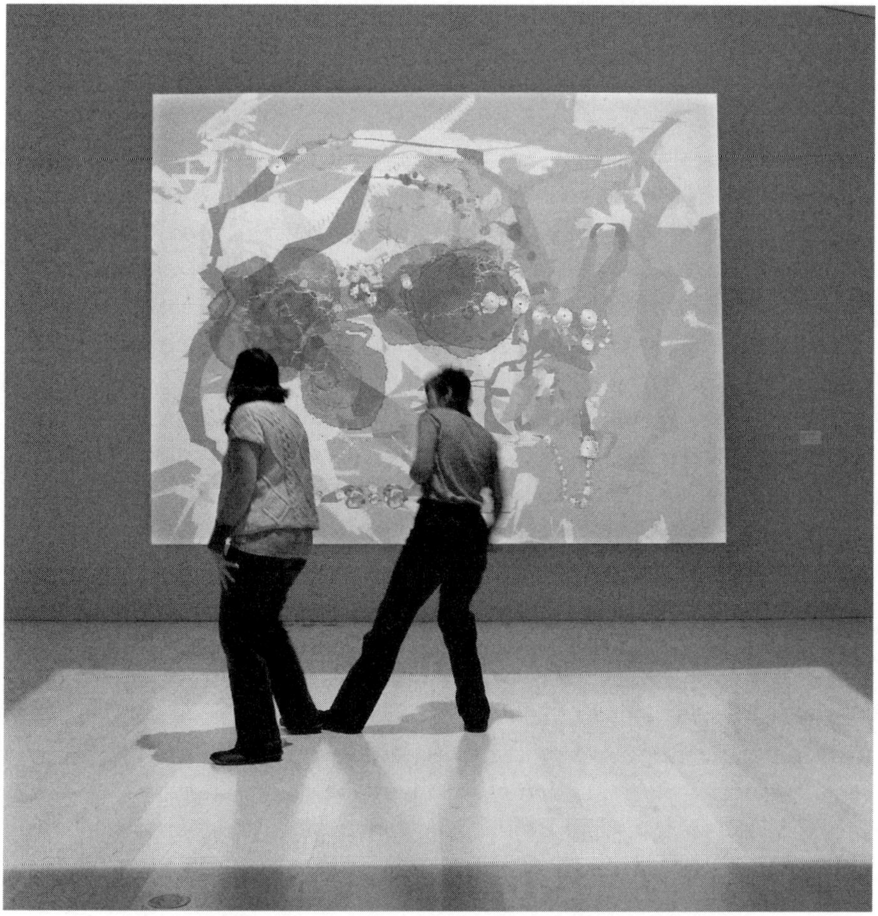

FIGURE 1.1 ▪ Camille Utterback, *Untitled 6*. From the series *External Measures*. 2005. Interactive Installation. Installation View. Photo Credit: Tom Bamberger, 2008

ing animated swaths of color and texture that bloom at the origin of a gesture, and decay and eventually fade over time. In *Untitled 6*, honeycombs of fine lines gather around the silhouette of the viewers'/users' bodies, and their path of travel is marked by black and white forms, indexing their movement while they cease to move and coagulate in colored blots when they collide with the bodily presence of another viewer/user.

In this work, the digital is visible in its functionality—the movements tracked and converted by the software into visible, textural patterns are evidently digital; they frequently reveal the pixel as their underlying structural component as the "analog" line loses resolution. In a more subtle sense, the work reveals its digitality in that the unfolding of the visual narrative in the work seems to be an effect of individual components acting on their neighbors, so that discrete elements create effects and disturbances in the overall system. In digital-computational systems, individual binary digital states are discrete, but their combined function is to work in tandem to support the entire system.[63] Thus, because individual elements effect changes within the system, and their underlying mechanism is computational, Utterback's interactive "paintings" would seem to exhibit all the necessary characteristics to conform to true perceptual digitality. Slyly, however, Utterback fluctuates between digital and analog aesthetic sensibilities. Recall that in a true digital system, each element in the system must be of the same type, such that each binary state will prompt an effect in another binary-switching mechanism. But some of her elements, stretching into linear, branching forms and blots of color, appear to be analog, mimicking brushstrokes and gestural swaths instead of representing the programmed system with regularized, interchangeable units. Digital systems combine these interchangeable units into an overall operational construction. Lev Manovich describes this relationship of part to whole in terms of "modularity."[64] Utterback's visualizations perform chain reactions that playfully engage the liminal space between pixilation and continuity. This variability, paradoxically, suppresses an overall mapping of the system's internal modularity, but also visually indexes the digital systematicity of the work at the level of the interface. In addition, the slightly juddering movement of the visual configurations (lines, shapes, and overall patterns) conveys a flavor of articulated digitality, so that computation is used toward a painterly end, on the one hand, to smooth out discreteness and disjunctness, but also toward a meditation on the phenomenological effects of digitality versus analogicity in the context of human-computer interaction.

Where she does invoke analogicity, it is not in service of a fully spatialized virtualization (as in "naturalistic," perspectival computer-generated imagery [CGI]), but rather to create a sense of continuity with analog mark-making systems. Utterback's choice to activate the analog in her creation of "interactive painting" links her work historically to analog practices including abstract expressionist painting, in which gesture and movement are mapped or "frozen" onto the canvas by skeins and drips of paint, and kinetic sculpture, in which moving parts and light effects create a dynamic and often immersive experience of plane, volume, light, and motion. In addition, her work generates a new instance of a (clearly purposeful) hybridity, in which the affordances and constraints of analog properties and the aesthetics of digital systems react to and interact with one another discursively and aesthetically.

However, as we have seen, the parameters demarcating computation and digitality become muddled due to the prevalence of description-dependent characterization of digital states. That is, if we have an interest in discovering digital features of an artifact, for example, a lamp that exhibits binary characteristics in its ability to be turned on or off, but is not productively defined as digital in any other sense, we will have a tendency to identify digital and computational characteristics coextensively. Müller attempts to circumvent the problems that arise in the description of digital and analog systems by relying on the distinction between type and token. "Every digital state is also on a continuum: the digital speedometer might change quickly from one number to another, but it does have intermediate states—just that these are not states of numbers, not states of these types, of these descriptions. What is crucial here, therefore, is that a digital state is *of a type*."[65] Defining types narrows the range of description, so for example, computation is of a certain type while digitality is of another, and accordingly constricts the range of tokens that will fall into that type by setting up the terms in advance by which the digitality or analogicity will be assessed. As we will see in chapter 4, there are instances, as in Casey Reas's software-based work, in which digital and analog states blur, introducing the possibility of a hybrid system. In the case of Utterback's work, the marks that operate as elements in an overall system indicate oscillation between analogicity and digitality. Her work approaches hybridity but demonstrates a greater degree of "switching" between analog and digital aesthetic modalities than will Reas's, which are almost indiscernibly digital. The *overall* typology in which Reas's hybrid works or Utterback's "interactive paintings" can be classified is restricted because the tokens, or the individual marks, must maintain consistency within their categorical distinction if they are to maintain their descriptive accuracy.

If Goodman's conclusions about digital and analog systems circulate around notions of discreteness, continuity, density, and disjointness, Manovich's analysis focuses on programmability and numerical manipulation. Contrary to Goodman, who treats the relationship between analog and digital systems as a subset of the larger issue of notation and depiction, Manovich emphasizes technological operations by embedding his discussion of "digits" in "numerical representation," one of what he considers the five principles of new media.[66] My own schematization of the primary characteristics of digital media deviates from that of Manovich; perhaps the most crucial deviation is in my disaggregation of digital from both numericization and computation. The separability of these two categories can be illustrated by examples of what Manovich calls "modern" media such as photography and film. These media forms emerge in the mechanical age and use analog technology to produce results that are partially discretized but not technologically (computationally) digital. Celluloid, moving-picture film generates the illusion of movement by stringing together individual frames of still photographs. The rapid shutter speed exposes seriated frames that, when projected at twenty-four frames per second, appears as a span of continuous movement. In a chart of digital and analog technologies, photographs fall on the analog side—they are continuous, not comprised of discrete units, or to use Goodman's language, nondisjoint and nonarticulate. Film falls toward the midline—it is syntactically, but not semantically, differentiated.

So while on the one hand Goodman's schema seems to provide a precise formula for ascertaining the digitality or analogicity of various objects, on the other hand it also permits indefinite and inconclusive analysis of many if not most representational technologies or systems. Manovich simplifies the distinction between analog and digital by placing greater emphasis on quantization than on discreteness. Thus, "while modern media contain levels of discrete representation, the samples are never quantified."[67] His initial explanation for the prevalence of discrete-but-not-quantified recording techniques of modern media tests the semiotic hypothesis that "communication requires discrete units."[68] If we refine this statement to engage more actively with Goodman, we would say that communication relies on symbolic systems, and symbol systems are built of discrete units, such as linguistic theory's phonemes and morphemes. However, Manovich quite deftly deflects a push into infinite regress when he calls attention to the fact that most "media" can be broken into discrete parts: drawings into lines, film into frames, and paint into brushstrokes. He also points out that a semiotics relying strictly upon discreteness proves untenable because "the discrete units of modern media are not usually units of meaning in the way morphemes are."[69] Thus, Manovich discards pure discreteness as a signifying system but ultimately marshals the phenomenon of nineteenth-century industrialization and the "separation of the production process into a set of simply, repetitive, and sequential activities that could be executed by workers who did not have to master the entire process and could be easily replaced."[70] If we are to conjoin Manovich's estimations with my own, industrialization, mechanization, and assembly lines seem somewhat "digital" on the basis of an interchangeability of parts and actions. Mechanical reproduction, mass production, and standardization and repetition in factories and on assembly lines characterize the ethos of modernity.[71] Rather than positing an absolute break between modern and contemporary epistemologies, my proposals find aspects of continuity between them, while acknowledging the rise of alternate social formations heralded in part by changing technological frameworks.

Digital Gestures

This chapter penulitmately concludes with a brief introduction of another constellation of thought about the digital, one that mobilizes etymological associations but also repositions the term, according it a strongly cardinal (bodily) orientation. The emphasis on the classical/etymological derivation of aesthetics from *aisthetikos/aisthesis*—sense perception—such that aesthetics is defined as knowledge produced from sense experience, rather than as an evaluative philosophical method, has implicitly signaled another manner of thinking about the digital that avers the connection between the body—specifically the "digits" or fingers of the hand—and calculating or counting functions. The digital becomes refamiliarized then, or reenvisioned in terms of intimate bodily practices that (seemingly paradoxically) yield abstract numericizing/counting techniques. Recent texts on new media practices have launched rejoinders against dystopic narratives presented in the 1990s about the disembodying and alienating effects of computational technology.[72] Authors such as Mark Hansen and Anna Munster have strongly advocated for incorporating phenomenology into assessments of new media artworks and artifacts.[73]

But another applicable model, which has not yet received adequate attention in Anglo-American media studies, reveals new points of intersection between the body and digital technology. What is most important is the way in which this configuration allows digital, computational, numerical processes and epistemological formations to be integrated with aesthesis—sensing, perceiving, and feeling—and bodily practice. This theoretical account emerges not from the school of phenomenology but rather from paleoanthropologist André Leroi-Gourhan's writing on tool use and hominization. According to Leroi-Gourhan, technics are always-already enfolded into the process of hominization; whereas it might be supposed that the brain enables the development of tool use, Leroi-Gourhan argues in contradistinction that it is the tool itself that drives the evolutionary process.[74]

Leroi-Gourhan's hypotheses have extended into some critical theorizations of "technics," notably in Jacques Derrida's *Grammatology* and French philosopher Bernard Stiegler's three-volume work *Technics and Time*, which argues for the central role of technics in shaping the historical and temporal horizons of the "human."[75] For Stiegler, humans are not the acting subjects of history while technology is the inert object; instead, humanity (and the human) and technology reciprocally/mutually constitute each other. While Stiegler's proposals work transhistorically, insofar as his theories address processes and relations—among humans, technics, and time—rather than a particular technological/historical period, Leroi-Gourhan speaks only indirectly to modern and contemporary regimes, taking prehistoric depiction as his primary technical milieu, which has been preserved chiefly in the form of cave drawing.

Using this method, then, it is possible to see how both digitality and computation have threaded through the deep history of artifact production, generally, and depiction, specifically. Whitney Davis has devised a research program around the "replication" of the ancient arts in the modern world, but more importantly, around identifying research methods that, while as with any investigative project are always culturally and historically situated, may yield pertinent information about an extensive field of cross-cultural and transhistorical practices.[76] Consequently, according to this model Paleolithic notations warrant consideration as digital practices, as do the examples I address in the following chapter.

Conclusion: The Digital as a Nontechnological Category

In sum, the problem of analog versus digital has been largely posed in terms of systems and machines. In other words, figures such as von Neumann and, more recently, David Lewis have addressed the problem at a systemic level; both thinkers, the former an engineer, the latter a philosopher, are concerned with defining the parameters according to which a whole series of operations belonging to one organism or machine describe the computing function of that machine, where the computing function is the processing of a particular kind of signal to generate an output distinct from the original input quantities. But in these theories, digital systems are being separated from phenomenally accessible—sensorially apprehensible—evidence of digitization in artifacts. I contend that the digital can be examined for its perceptual (aesthetic) as well as notional/theoretical valence, which is an unusual way of approaching the problem of digital aesthetics. Typically, as I have suggested, the digital and the computational will be collapsed, because digitality is most obviously, especially for information scientists, a technological and functional rather than a perceptual category. Arguments concerning digital and analog systems usually assume that these systems are computing devices, so that even the term "representation" is imbued with a computational *telos*. Representation, here, has to do with the way the mind organizes and processes "information," which encompasses all the kinds of stimuli—signals, symbols, and images—that we absorb, collect, and manipulate to make sense of the world and our relation to it. As understood in the disciplinary contexts of art history, visual studies, film studies, and so forth, representation enacts a selective interpretation and an "enframing" of the world to communicate a particular kind of knowledge or experience.[77] However, information and computer science attend more to the invisible operations of the nervous system or computer than to the way in which these operations become inscribed on a surface and thus are made available to the sensorial register.

As we have seen, according to an etymological interpretation of the origin and scope of digital and analog, analog movement analogizes that which the instrument measures—the movement of the analog clock correlates to the passing of time, which as Henri Bergson has argued, does not unfold in a series of jumps between steady states, as in a digital clock, but consists rather of a continuous durational flow.[78] But this begs the following question: "Which of the two characteristics is crucial for an analog state, the analogy to the represented, or the continuous movement?"[79] The digital in these cases is a way of thinking about measurement, the representation of information that can be measured using physical quantities (analog) versus purely numerical representations, or mechanisms that process information by translating data into numerical values. This suggests that digitality is a mechanistic tool and that defining the digital is a matter of evaluating the operating principles of computing machines. If this is the case, it is easy to see why the focus in digital media has been either on human-computer interaction (or on intrapersonal human relationships vis-à-vis the computer—for example, the formation of online communities) or on the technology itself. In the latter scenario, evaluators of digitally generated artifacts would tend to focus on how the machine works—how it numericizes information and how its numericizing functions and information processing support the idea of a computable universe. How computing machines work, and the kinds of output facilitated by the specific way in which they process data, leads to a mystification of the machine, whereby it is assumed we cannot properly appreciate computer-generated artifacts unless we know exactly how they work. This implicit demand for computational literacy can be dangerous, however, because it suggests that less technologically savvy viewers/users simply lack the education to understand works that would otherwise impart wisdom or produce a genuine aesthetic experience. But this instantly forecloses arguments for the potential of distributed digital media to induce political activism and to increase democracy. It also contributes to a technological elitism that returns digital art to a state similar to preprint culture, in which only the educated intelligentsia (usually clergy) could read, circulate, and make illuminated manuscripts.

Analog and digital characteristics are more often ascribed to technologies, organisms (or living systems), numerical systems, and the philosophy of mind than to art itself. And while the title of Goodman's text would lead one to believe that his methodology was devised in order to assay the aesthetic properties of artworks, his test cases are not artworks at all but rather instruments—clocks, counters, and other measuring devices. The breadth (applicability) of Lewis's and von Neumann's definitions seem limited to the particular domains from which they gather their evidentiary examples, insofar as their discussions describe computing machines rather than digital and analog as categories of visuality. Goodman's introduction of density and differentiation as correlative but more theoretically generalized terms for analog and digital expand the scope of his argument beyond the instrumental tools he uses to demonstrate the distinction between analog and digital into the realm of artifacts produced for sensory apprehension alone, rather than for utilitarian ends.

Goodman's text reinvigorates analogicity and digitality as a set of evaluative terms that allows one both to determine the status of given system or schema with greater specificity *and* to apply the terms to a greater range of objects and artifacts. The conceptual architecture of Goodman's argument is useful to tease out the deviations in how different symbolic systems make meaning, or in how we imbue them with meaning (how we make them mean rather than what they mean inherently), and what kind of signification is facilitated by each system. But when we turn our attention to artifacts themselves, the successful parsing of these objects, or the successful application of these terms to objects, their utility as explanatory or exploratory devices becomes somewhat murky. Upon further examination of philosophical debates surrounding digital and analog systems, we discover that it may be digital and analog states themselves, not simply the terms in which they are theorized, that are susceptible to breakdown.[80] As von Neumann, Stroud, McCulloch, and the others suspected in the 1940s, hybridity is built into most systems, such that careful examination of their operations reveal a fundamental indeterminacy in their status as *either* digital *or* analog. If a sweeping secondhand on an analog clock seems to identify it as analog, the underlying system of marking time is already at least partly digital.[81] Questioning the nature of time in terms of analogicity and digitality is a philosophical abstraction of a problem that manifests itself much more locally and more concretely in the timekeeping instrument, a previously mentioned example that can now be refined. Clocks are in essence measuring tools that can perform their task according to either an analog or a digital logic. In either case, the primary function of the device is to measure an abstract quantity that is otherwise unavailable to direct perception; we cannot touch or see time and therefore cannot use our own observational faculties to measure time in itself; we can only measure its effects (the sun climbing higher on the horizon and the temperature of the air growing warmer and colder as the day waxes and wanes). Although we may experience the passage of time phenomenally as a perpetual flow, the symbolic representation of time divides it into discrete elements. The digital representation of time is functionally oriented—hours and minutes transform time from an a priori condition of being into a quantitative informatic tool, so that to experience oneself as a temporal being is now equated with one's ability to process the information-bearing symbols that stand in for time. Clocks can be understood as transcoding devices that partially "digitize" time in the technical sense by translating an analog "signal" into digital information-bearing quantities.[82]

Returning in conclusion to the exemplary case in the previous section, while Paleolithic "art"—which seems to range in type between depiction and notation, or may hybridize or not distinguish between the two types of symbolization—might seem an odd point of reference for a theory of digital aesthetics, it is highly apposite to the overall goal of the current project. Namely, the digital is less about a particular and highly specific technical configuration—in this case, the electronic digital computer—than about a *method*. Indubitably, computationalism, cybernetics, and the technological reality of the hardware and software at work in computational machines supply the possibility condition to renegotiate objects that appear as early in the artifactual record as the Paleolithic. It should be stressed that it is the particular epistemic horizon of the current contemporary moment out of which the digital practices under consideration here become visible. Nevertheless, reevaluating the past through the lens of the present allows digital and computational practices to come to light across a broad span of historical periods and geographical locations. The greater significance of this comes from the fact that evaluating artifacts in terms of a digital method will allow them to signify in new ways, effectively opening the interpretive field within which artifacts both produce and reflect cultural knowledge systems.

2

Points, Divisions, and Pixels ▪ From Modern to Contemporary Digitality

A quick look into the literature on digitality and analogicity illustrates the degree to which the distinction between these two categories is more theoretical than actual. Recall that both Norbert Weiner and John von Neumann acknowledged that analog and digital systems tend to overlap, so that most systems are neither wholly analog nor wholly digital but contain elements of both. The difficulty of applying these categories not just notionally but also in the object-world bears out in the fact that many analog measuring instruments, such as analog clocks, have digital elements—namely, the tick marks on the face of the clock—and that digital instruments often approach the analog by representing numbers in physical magnitudes.[1] Most treatments of analog and digital emerge in a context of information theory or philosophy and as such deploy only notional examples as demonstrations of theoretical models. They thus do not examine whether the theoretical distinction obtains across a range of object-models. David Lewis, von Neumann, and the other cyberneticians discussed in chapter 1, for example, do not discuss "art" at all. When we turn to an examination of artifacts (art or nonart), formal evaluation of a work's perceptible digitality will often most easily identify moments of blending, partiality, or indeterminacy between the two modes. And additionally, when addressing works of art, and pictures specifically, the disentanglement of digital and analog becomes more complex. This is especially the case when the works in question are constructed by traditionally analog means—particularly when created by hand—and when, because they were produced in a context in which analog and digital pictoriality had not yet been conceptualized as such, their digital communication must be evaluated retrodictively.

This chapter ascertains whether there exists a formally digital quality, visible on the surface rather than hidden from sensory perception in the black box of computational processes, that is unique to digital media. It searches the art historical record for the emergence of digital or proto-digital artifacts prior to the inception of electronic digital computers. As a corollary, I determine whether the computational digit and the noncomputational digit display different perceptual effects dependent on their computational or noncomputational origin. Identifying the visible (or otherwise sensorially apprehensible) characteristics of digitality, which preexist or exist independently of computational technology, helps to construe more accurately whether or not the digital is in fact a unique and constitutive aspect of the phenomenological (aesthetic and sensory) *experience* of contemporary computer graphics or "new media." Where chapter 1 addresses the history in the twentieth century of the philosophical distinction between analog and digital, chapter 2 considers how this distinction imports itself into the domain of art, establishing the phenomenological parameters for a digital aesthetics.

The series of artworks in this chapter fall into two categories: those that precede the invention of electronic computers but still evince a digital aesthetic, and those that use computers to emphatically and obsessively explore the properties of digital discreteness. The paintings of Georges Seurat and Paul Klee exemplify the former case; despite the lack of electronic computational processing used in their construction, the presence of the digit is resolutely surfacial, available for all to see. Instead of thinking of the digital as a term that describes the technology used in its making, wherein an object is "digital" if it is a product of electronic computational processing, this chapter marshals both works that use computers and those that do not to define the digital as an aesthetic category. "Aesthetic" is deployed etymologically, to refer to the apprehension of features of an artifact that are available to sense perception. The digital then becomes a configurative and aesthetic modality.

Consequently, although a picture is created using an electronic computer, whose underlying processes are computed digitally, it might not necessarily exhibit perceptibly digital features. In contrast, an artifact that is made without computational processing might have digital features. Surface-level digitality does not automatically indicate that beneath outward appearances binary computational processes are hard at work. After examining neo-Impressionist divisionism, Klee's transcriptions of musical notation into a pictorial language, and his own divisionist period, it might be assumed that digitization emerges out of industrialization or that the digital is the visual-cultural offspring of the advent of mass production. But numerous classes of artifacts, such as mosaics and even Paleolithic cave drawings, trump this claim. Mosaics, in particular, resist the smoothing effect of line drawing (analog continuousness), the gestural index of the negative handprint, the line drawing, or the painted brushstroke (digital "fingery," explained below), and the messiness of paint splattered, splotched, or brushed-onto canvas (analog ambiguity, irreducibility). Of course, this is not to say that the technology used in making an artifact becomes irrelevant when discussing digital and analog aesthetics. But disentangling the digital as an aesthetic quality from the constraints of electronic computational processing allows an assessment of the specific ways in which it appears over a broad span of historical and technological milieus. The digital, then, is a quality that either is or is not sensorially apprehensible via direct observation, irrespective of the technical particularities used to achieve it.

Embedded in the term "digital" is its etymological connection to the hand, to the fingers or "digits" that become discrete units for tallying and counting. Fingers not only are tools for gestural communication but can also function as calculating devices, or at least placeholders to aid in calculation. They are articulated at the joints and seem to facilitate the development of schematic, iterable inscription, as well as patterned, informatic notation. Digital symbol systems may appear in the form of pixels but may also manifest in a variety of other mark-making practices, such as points on a graph, in which a unit of measure has been assigned and outside of which no indeterminate state can be registered. Information is, of course, processed digitally in today's electronic computers, but the digital as an analytic and perceptual category can be disaggregated from the technical specificities of today's hardware and software. The digital refers to a particular configurative schema—to a state in which materials or signals operate and are operated upon as discrete states, as distinct from the continuous variation of the analog.

As discussed at the end of chapter 1, Bernard Stiegler's theory of technics, influenced by the paleoanthropology of André Leroi-Gourhan, links the development and definition of "the human," as distinct from the animal, and all else that is not human, with innovations in tools. But more particularly, Leroi-Gourhan posits that the making of marks is a materialization of the coordination of hand and eye. The process of inscription actualizes bodily rhythms, externalizes them, for example, on stone or other surfaces, and becomes an imprint—or what Jacques Derrida would call a trace—of the human organization of its own sensorimotor apparatus. Mark-making, or inscription, is thus intrinsically "digital," an externalization of the handedness of human communication. Derrida, Stiegler, and Georges Bataille, for example, refer frequently to the digital quality of writing, or in the latter case, of "grammaticalization of the visible."[2] Grammaticalization relates both to the institution of individuated rules that are said to regulate and govern verbal communication and to the structuralist manner of parsing channels of signification (speech, music, art, etc.) into grammatical "units" in an effort to isolate and identify the most elemental unit of these systems out of which more elaborate formations can develop.

Moreover, according to Leroi-Gourhan, technologies of inscription emerging from the use of hand tools forward operate within the logic of "hand-operated machine"—which can also be conceptualized as the digital machine if we take into account the connection between the digits implied in handedness and the digits deployed in more traditionally understood digital systems. The relationship between the human body and its technological extensions is pushed further with the claim that "punched cards and electronic memory," the endpoint of Leroi-Gourhan's technological appraisal, as well as the computational binary systems of the twenty-first century, take over the comparative, memory-collecting function of the human brain.[3] Punched cards and computers radicalize the process of externalization, which started with the feet and the shift to uprightness and then moved through many stages of evolution, until ultimately the hand achieved sensorimotor coordination in the act of inscription. "Books in their raw state are comparable to hand tools: However sophisticated their presentation, the reader's full technical participation is still required."[4] Technical participation, in Leroi-Gourhan's estimation, is linked genetically to bodily operations. I contend that while there exists a process of distantiating technology from the body, traces of technology's fundamental connection to embodied action must be identified in order to prevent misguided proclamations of the body's eventual obsolescence. Later machines will, Leroi-Gourhan predicts, complete the total exteriorization of processes once originarily located in the body, thus guaranteeing its outmodedness. As numerous theorists have suggested, however, the early pronouncement by writers such as Hans Moravec of the desuetude of the body in the age of computers must be contravened by alternate considerations of the ways in which the body is engaged by technology rather than excluded by it.

Digitality removed from computation can nevertheless be thought in terms of technics, so that it is a technology of facture envisioning a universe constructed in elemental parts, which can be configured and reconfigured by a digital method of composition. The Jacquard loom is "digital" because it uses discretely punched cards to produce a replicable pattern. But as Walter Seitter has stated, weaving itself is digital, just like the grammatically, phonetically discretized practice of writing, insofar as fingers "which can be formed into a concentric fist, placed in parallel rows, spread out and hooked into each other, provide the proto-types for the tools and products of these activities."[5] Fingers, or digits, are perhaps our most direct and intimate examples of discontinuous, repeated units, which mimic the interchangeability of fully externalized digital technologies. "That which applies to the pianist and to the precision engineer is also true for the activities of drawing or writing, and equally so of plaiting or weaving. It is not only that all these activities require the dexterity of the fingers, but that fingers . . . provide the prototypes for the tools and products of these activities. . . . The fingers of one hand are the original pencils; the fingers of the other are the original graphs or letters."[6] Fingers as individuated units provide the mechanism by which activities such as drawing or weaving are performed. This evidences the underlying digitality of inscriptive and constructive modes and in part can be deployed to explain the emergence of a digital technics and digital aesthetics in modern strategies of depiction.

In the information age, digitality has come to signify something else than an application of mnemonics or metrics to bodily configurations. Despite the fact that electronic-computational systems bear metaphorical traces of these connections, as in our description of information storage as "memory," the production of pictures and other forms of depiction is more often than not assumed to be rendered through code rather than by hand. Thus, traditionally gestural, indexical, bodily modes of artificing, such as painting, must speak, when produced in the contemporary moment, about technology; they now must either adapt or reject computational technology, which increasingly enframes all forms of cultural production, so that, as Knut Ebeling has written, "in the age of digital media, painting is less about making references than about encoding."[7] With the inception of electronic computing devices comes a shift in modes of production and conception by which all processes of depiction must grapple with the fact of computation and encoding. The omnipresence of computational technology entails that images are always-already (self) aware of resultant epistemological changes.

When we begin to refer to the technological category of digitality, which finds its origins in the fingers but gradually supersedes the body and even the calculating capacity of the mind, the "digits" in digitality are recognizable as such because they are switching elements: they can only occupy an on or off state, without any intermediary states between them. In her article outlining possible theoretical intersections between "aniconic" Islamic and computer art, Laura Marks's discussion of Basrian Mu'tazili atomism offers an elegant and intuitively accessible explication of the theory of binary digitality over which our analytic philosophers have labored so heavily. "According to the Basrian Mu'tazili, atoms occupy space, form larger units additively, measure space by occupying it, and prevent other atoms from occupying the same space."[8] Marks captures several of the crucial elements of digital signals and systems: their fundamental role as measuring devices (although as we have seen, the same can be said, if contentiously, about analog signals); their singular, exclusionary occupation of one state or another; and their modular, fractallic structure in which the whole not only is an aggregate composite of smaller parts but also mirrors the structural form of the smaller parts.[9]

Thus far, the word "digital" has acquired several meanings—it can be used to refer to technological, bodily, or aesthetic milieus, all of which converge around the way discretization affords particular kinds of knowledge and experience. Digital tools can be seen to trace the process of externalization by which the tallying, counting, and ordering system afforded by the physiological structure of the hand is gradually dissociated from the body and refigured in symbolic and depictive inscription and memory storage devices from books to portraits and computers.[10] Given their inability to handle ambiguity—their determinate, causal execution along a precise chain of encoded commands, not to mention their processing speeds and capacity for memory storage alone—digital tools have become associated in various documents of the postcybernetic, Western cultural imagination, from Stanley Kubrick's *2001: A Space Odyssey* to James Cameron's *Terminator* series, with a profound sense of the inhuman, a concept that shall be explored further in chapter 3. But when considering Walter Seitter's disimbrication of digital meaning and digital structure, the seemingly nondigital, nontechnological, and decidedly human practice of painting is instructive of the way digitality incurs in numerous practical usages. "If two applications of red paint are placed next to each other, and if these two applications of red are mixed or smudged together to produce a uniform red mark, then the digital or discreet method of painting is trying to disguise its own *digitality* in order to create the effect of having come from, perhaps even, of having developed from the same source."[11] An application of paint to canvas in individual brushstrokes or marks is "digital" in the sense that it deploys a tool as an extension, and externalization, of the hand and the fingers.

But even if the marks are applied using the digits of the hand, or even if a computer generates a screen-based picture using binary code, this does not mean it will exhibit a digital aesthetic in the terms I am proposing. A painting whose digital structure is visible on the surface is not only composed digitally but also communicates *about* digitality; it speaks, in a visual language with its own distinct syntax, about the relationship between surface and infrastructure, and between representation and technology, and it speaks about the fact that all composition originates, to a greater or lesser extent, in a piecing together of disjoint units. In other words, a picture can be technologically digital, or constructed of syntactically disjoint units, but this does not necessarily imply that this structure will be sensorially apprehended because those units can be highly resolved, smoothed over, and occluded. A "whole" image—seamless, continuous, and dense—is the result of a careful process of suturing and smoothing. When a painting uses a digital syntax to communicate a digital meaning, this in turns shows that a totalized, coherent image surface is inherently illusory.

Pointillism: Modeling Digitality

In 1889, Seurat painted *Eiffel Tower*, a heavily discretized canvas whose insistent digitality—its enlarged, individuated touches of color and a preponderance of high-contrast and primary colors—destabilizes the opposition between figure, ground, void, and volume by allowing matter and ether to bleed together due to the juddering placement of the dots. Painted before the tower had reached completion, Seurat's canvas creates a digital screen through which the structure is filtered and architectonically reconfigured. His rejection of decisive linear strokes in favor of the application of unitary dots causes the top of the tower to dissolve progressively into the blue of the sky, rendering indiscernible the exact moment in which iron lattice gives way to its enveloping atmosphere. Especially because it is painted by Seurat, the most technical of painters, this work can be read as a convenient testament to the changes, whether viewed as advancements or abominations, in the Parisian landscape wrought by the spectacular forms of industrial technology. But the work also points to radical ruptures occurring in the theory and technique of pictorial representation. What is most compelling about this work—the punctum or perceptual fulcrum that then inflects this reading of the composition as a whole—is the zone of indiscernability at the juncture of tower and sky. Seurat chose to paint a construction zone rather than a ruin, a monument to the imagined future rather than a nostalgic view onto the classical architecture of a distant past. But it is, oddly, the modernity of his technique—its digital systematicity—that confers a sense of the pastoral onto this structure, interpreted variously as monstrous or elegant. In other words, it is precisely the ability of the highly articulated dots to construct a dispersed, low-resolution pictorial architecture that deemphasizes the incompletion of the structure itself, instead causing it to blend organically and harmoniously with its surroundings. The lack of distinction between figure and atmosphere lends this painting a sense of abstraction that is a specifically *digital* rather than geometric abstraction. It is an abstraction that feeds not simply on the flattening or simplifying of shapes but plays with the possibilities for perceptual surprise that emerges with the early consideration of a digital methodology for composing on a canvas.

Pointillism, the method of applying small dots of paint to canvas most no-

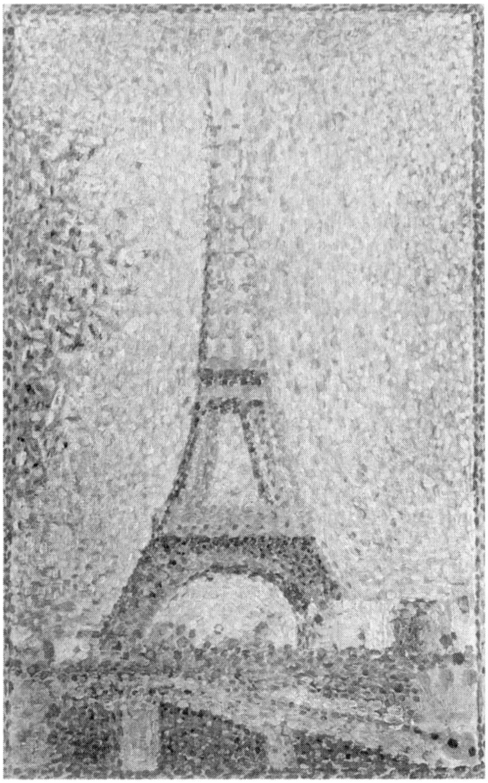

FIGURE 2.1 ▪ Georges Seurat, *The Eiffel Tower*, 1889. Oil on canvas, 24 x 15 cm (9.5 x 6 in). Fine Arts Museums of San Francisco.

tably embodied in the paintings of Seurat, appears almost too conveniently as a morphological precursor to the pixilated architecture of bitmapped computer graphics. But is there indeed any productive comparison to be made between pointillist dots and pixels beyond a quick observation of their perceptual similarity? To insist on a *causal* technological lineage from nineteenth-century pointillism to twentieth-century computer-generated imagery would be not only strained but also somewhat farfetched. There is not a perfect similitude between Seurat's dots and the pixel of the electronically computational graphical user interface, nor does pointillism *predict* the technological and cultural milieu associated with the emergence of electronic computers. However, pointillism (also known as divisionism or chromoluminarism) emerges as a technologized method that produces its particular effects, its pictorial architectonics, and its aesthetic sensibility by envisioning and deploying a systematic, digital configurative method: a *program* designed to produce a particular range of affect and sensation that made these paintings stand out from stylistic models that both preceded it and were contemporary to it.[12]

William Innes Homer's 1964 *Seurat and the Science of Painting* has been largely acknowledged, both by supporters and critics, as the most circulated and exhaustively detailed classic text concerning Seurat's application of scientific principles, specifically the physics of light and the psychology of perception, to painting.[13] Homer's account reads Seurat's technique as an attempt to perform the final transformation of Impressionist naturalism into a rigorous scientific method that has less to do with any specific pictorial aims (any theory of representation that would align his practice with, say, figuration or abstraction) and more to do with specifically perceptual ones. Subsequent attempts to reevaluate Seurat's work have taken issue with Homer's large-scale acceptance of Seurat's grasp of the scientific theories in question, by which the adjacent application of pointillist dots was supposed to produce heightened, shimmering luminosity and brighter color effects than those achieved by color-mixing techniques, because the color would be blended optically (by the eye itself) rather than on the palette. Alan Lee, for example, shows that already in 1886, Seurat's contemporaries (in this case, Émile Hennequin) simultaneously and contradictorily noted the failure of the technique in practice. Nevertheless, they adhered unquestioningly to the perceived scientific validity of Ogden Rood's arguments, presented in *Modern Chromatics*,[14] that greater luminosity is achieved by optical, rather than material, blending.[15] Directly subsequent to endorsing Rood, Hennequin avers of the *Grand Jatte* that "you cannot imagine anything more dusty or lustreless."[16] The debates, then, over Seurat's work, extending from supporter Félix Fénéon to Homer and to respondents such as Lee and Martin Kemp, have centered largely on Seurat's degree of success in applying late nineteenth-century theories of the science of optical color blending to his canvases.[17]

However, Seurat's understanding or misprision of color theory is less relevant here than another aspect of his technique, one that is largely taken for granted in these scholarly debates despite numerous and rich opportunities for evaluation. This is Seurat's technique of applying paint in adjacent "dots," the digital *method* that underlies the theories of color blending outlined in Rood's *Modern Chromatics*, the book that not only informed Seurat's goals toward optical blending but was also reported by Rood's son Roland to be the "bible" for the Impressionist painters. As Martin Kemp has argued, it was not only the neo-Impressionists who would have adopted theories of optical color blending but also the Impressionists, who participated in a less systematic divisionism by employing highly individuated, visibly unblended brushstrokes.[18] These brushstrokes were more gestural, aimed at the impression of instantaneity or spontaneity rather than a regular, mechanistic array of dots that becomes the trademark of pointillism. Recall Walter Seitter's claim that the side-by-side application of painted marks is "digital" whether or not it attempts to disguise its digitality through blending. For Seitter, blending functions as a disguise, the analog is no more genuine, no more natural (in the sense of lacking artifice), than the digital and in fact is always "simulated."[19] Seurat's technique reveals its discreteness and its function as a kind of "tally"; it is a record of each finitely countable touch of paint to the canvas through the digital extension that is the brush. Each dot is a single, unblended, and thus disjunct, point of color.

To be sure, if we move back into a technical (instead of etymological and physiological) definition of the digital, these points show themselves to be at least partially analog; they are *not* mechanically applied, nor are they truly regularized and thus interchangeable. As such, their limits are not quantitatively bounded, and thus each "point" contains ambiguity and indeterminacy. Pointillism thus cannot be fully or perfectly discrete, disjunct, and therefore purely digital. However, we find again that in practice, when we are looking at materials and products of material processes, it becomes difficult to adhere to notionally "pure" definitions of digital and analog, because pointillism tends nevertheless toward digitality in numerous ways; it is chromatically discrete, in its unblendedness, and also syntactically and semantically verges toward the disjunct. Moreover, the inexactitude of the size and spacing of the dots is an important, and intentional, analog aspect of this technique that is surprisingly deployed to enhance the perceptual digitality—the appearance of individuated units—of the paintings.

In pointillism, the dot as the unit of measure hovers on the surface of the picture, creating a directly perceptible digital aesthetic. Whereas in analog pictorialism, direct indices of metric armatures are usually suppressed, in pointillism, the "dot" asserts itself, mischievously and uncomfortably, by bringing the metric to the foreground. What we begin to see in Seurat's method is technique as program, a program for creating affect and sensation. This act of making visible the "unit of measure," even if it turns out to be one that is, in Seurat's case, imprecise relative to a bitmapped pixel, provokes a consideration of the long history of utilizing metric systems as the frameworks supporting pictorial depiction. Perspective paintings, for example, are constructed according to precise, metric rules; the matrix that structures the spatial arrangement and proportion of objects to one another on a picture plane is computed manually instead of automatically by an electronic machine, but perspective is nevertheless a computational system. What viewers are seeing when they gaze at a perspectival construction are the visually apprehensible results of a metric system at work. And while viewers see the *effects* of this system, direct indices of that system, the scaffolding of orthogonals and transversals supporting the structure, are by and large painted over. Thus, the pictorial illusion of space in perspective is governed by a notional, but not a directly apprehensible, matrix.

Perspective is not only a technique but also one aspect of a philosophical conception of matter, space, and world, in which quantitative values are increasingly viewed as the most accurate and viable means with which to describe, annotate, and depict our physical surroundings. But perspective is seen not only as a "symbolic form" but also as an ideological structure in part because the technical apparatus, including, for example, orthogonals and transversals, and the famously monocular viewpoint, are occluded.[20] The science of perspective has been critiqued for advancing an illusion of transparency, for announcing itself as the closest approximation to "natural" vision, while in truth it involves a high level of artifice to be carried out properly. The development of Albertian perspective shows how Western, analog pictoriality often configures its depictions metrically. The artistic decision to reveal or conceal any indices of the undergirding metric system is however highly significant and must be viewed as responding directly to the Western conventions of spatial representation and pictorial artifice.

In the existing literature on Seurat's pointillist technique, the presence of the "dot" is generally deemphasized because it is seen as the vessel, medium, or vehicle—the syntactical unit—that communicates Seurat's more *semantically* complex ideas about color theory. In other words, the dot is seen as less significant than the fact that it is employed in service of producing the sensation of luminosity in the viewer. However, if one reads this literature with attention to what *is* said about the dot, it becomes clear that there is an analytic subtext that warrants attention. To understand Seurat's digitality, it is necessary to read against the grain, to look at the structural foundations—the technical means—that become the conditions of possibility for color, brightness, luminosity, or the lack of all of these, to be delivered to the viewer. For, in fact, it is argued more often than not that Seurat *failed* when it came to color. What is celebrated more, or is more consistently remarked upon, whether with approbation, disdain, or even fear, is Seurat's delicacy, his strangely immobile, geometric shapes and volumes, the sense of insubstantiality that, oddly, accompanies the stillness of his compositions.

Both Meyer Schapiro and Turner scholar John Gage have turned their attention to the dots in Seurat's painting. Gage adopts the view that "Seurat was not so much interested in the optically-mixed tone as in the lively texture created by the separated dots themselves," while Schapiro remarks that the dots are "a refined device" and that "this artificial micro-pattern serves the painter as a means of ordering, proportioning and nuancing sensation beyond the familiar qualities of the objects that the colors evoke."[21] Thus, whether Seurat's method succeeded or failed to achieve his chromoluminarist ideals, or whether he understood or misunderstood the finer points of Chevreul, Zunnul-Zadé, or Helmholtz, Ruskin, and Maxwell as ventriloquized by Rood, the dot emerges rhetorically and descriptively as a digital, metric unit that allows Seurat's pictorial architecture and his digital aesthetic sensibility to develop.[22] Despite Seurat's, and many of his interlocutors', primary interest in color, rhetorical slips of the tongue and inconsistencies in the writings about his work hint that there was something else happening in pointillism—a concern for the dot itself, not as a mere vessel for vibrant sensations of color but as Seurat's approximation of a metric, digital unit. To attend to the semantic valence of the dot and the pointillist method of facture, which allows the digital, systematically applied touches of paint to remain visible as disjunct units, instead of "simulating" the analog by blending the marks, is not to claim the insignificance of color. Rather, it calls attention to other facets of Seurat's work that are less distinct when color is the central focus of analysis.

This transposition of the metric unit from the invisible background to a highly visible foreground demonstrates one aspect of the digitality of Seurat's pointillist technique. Digital signals and systems have a fundamental role as measuring devices. Digital units are also metric units, but they are metric units that are singular, interchangeable, and binary insofar as they occupy one state or another exclusively, without overlap or intermediate positions between states. Digital units are modular and composite, and digitally configured structures are aggregate, composed of many smaller parts. In a true digital system, the elements comprising the system are all interchangeable and perfectly regularized, even if this proves to be only a notional possibility.

Viewing Seurat's technique from the standpoint of color theory, the dot serves as one effective tool to apply points of color adjacent to one another, rather than blending them in the traditional manner. The hypothesis, the accuracy of which has been debated from Seurat's first painterly experiments with it, is that the adjacent, disjoint placement of colors stimulates the viewer's visual cortex in such a way as to produce a shimmering luminosity, hence the adoption of the alternate term "chromoluminarism" to this method of painting. But Gage asserts that not color but *texture* shimmers and shifts in our visual field as a result of pointillist technique.

The argument according primacy to the dot itself, instead of color, centers on the issue of fusion. If, as Meyer Schapiro has averred, the dot emerges at Seurat's "tangible and ever-present unit of measure,"[23] and if, as Seurat himself wrote to his friend Fénéon in 1894, technique is the "soul and body" of his art, the field of individuated dots brings the metric apparatus to the pictorial surface.[24] Proponents of the color theory model look for the degree to which Seurat was successful in producing optical mixing, which depends upon the fusion of the dots into a relatively smooth surface. In his discussion of viewing distance, Homer cites two passages, one by Fénéon, the other by Camille Pissarro, to support the claim that the paintings should be viewed at a distance at which optical fusion can be achieved. Fénéon notes that as a viewer retreats from the painting, "all the multicolored specks melt into undulant, luminous masses. *The technique, one might say, vanishes*: the eye is no longer attracted to anything but that which is essentially painting."[25] Here, Fénéon clearly ascribes to the conventional expectation that the paintings should be viewed at a distance at which the digital technique is no longer perceptible, and the painting can present itself as reassuringly continuous, smooth, ambiguous, and aesthetically analog. Likewise, Pissarro was reported to have instructed pointillist paintings to be seen "as Nature is seen, at a distance sufficient to allow its colors to blend; or generally speaking, at a distance as long as three times its diagonal."[26] Homer also dictates that the distance of three times the length of the diagonal (six feet in the case of the small canvas of *Les Poseuses*, 1888) prescribed by Pissarro is also the distance at which the eye will register the greatest degree of shimmering luminosity, or what Rood calls "luster." But luster is most evident when only partial fusion is achieved. Here, at this fixed distance, an oscillatory effect occurs, between fusion and separation, so that, "as hard as one tries, at a distance of six feet most of the colors can neither be made to fuse completely nor can they be seen individually. One's eye is simply caught between the horns of a visual dilemma."[27]

Gage, following but pressing further than Homer, has attested that the standpoint from which Seurat's, and fellow neo-Impressionist Paul Signac's, paintings would have been viewed was *not* at a distance at which the viewer could have achieved optical fusion. Instead, the dots would have remained visible as discrete points. As such, the makers of these paintings would not have used a digital technique to produce an analog aesthetic experience but would have used a digital technique toward digital aesthetic ends. The pointillist method did, finally, parade its digitality, and by extension, implicitly rejected the occlusion, as in perspective painting, of the technical, metric scaffolding underlying the pictorial structure.

Homer nudges toward this conclusion by asserting that the ideal viewing position of a pointillist painting is not the point at which the discrete dots fuse into a smooth contoured shape or plane of color, but rather the standpoint from which the eye cannot quite resolve the dots into an integrated whole. And

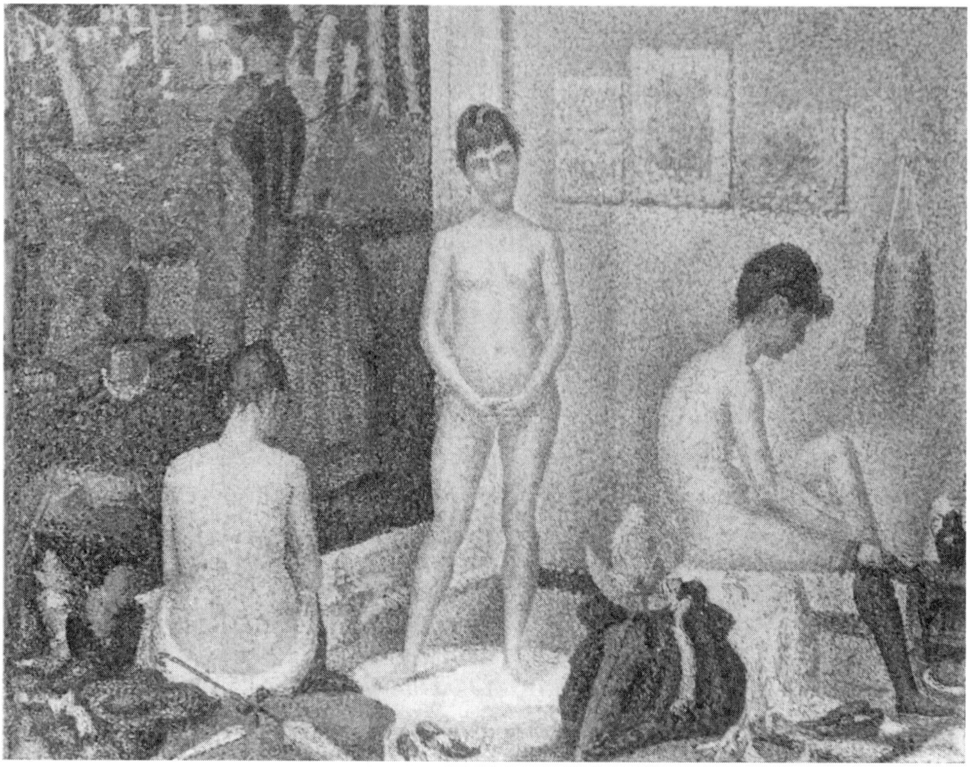

FIGURE 2.2 ▪ Georges Seurat, *Les Poseuses*, 1886–1888. Oil on canvas, 200 x 249.9 cm (78¾ x 98⅜ in). Barnes Foundation, Philadelphia.

despite evidence that both Signac, in his early pointillist works, and Pissarro, as indicated above, designed their canvases to be viewed from a distance at which the dotted brushstrokes would blend into an even mixture of color, Gage notes Seurat's variation in the size of the dots. He emphasizes in particular the areas in which Seurat reworks the canvas, increasing rather than decreasing the size of the dots, thus rendering perceptual fusion impossible unless the painting was to be situated at a great distance from the observer. Gage speculates that in *La Grande Jatte* and *Les Poseuses*, this variation in size and shape of the dots may be due to the fact that the two paintings "were painted in a studio too confined to allow the artist to stand back very far, with the result that he found the dots too small for the size of the canvas."[28] It is also striking that despite Signac's recommendation in a journal entry from 22 November 1894 that the observer situate himself in a favorable condition for fusion of the dots, after this date Signac himself enlarged the dots "so that by the end of the 1890's fusion can no longer be in question."[29]

According to Schapiro, already in 1958 too much had been made of the scientific basis of Seurat's artistic methodology. Unlike Homer and later respondents, such as Alan Lee, Schapiro distantiates Seurat's scientific interest and intention from the paintings themselves, placing his focus on technique, in particular. In this way, Schapiro shows the perceptual and aesthetic affordances given by Seurat's (digital) technique, which combines precision and austerity with a sensitivity to variation, a richness and complexity that counters accusations that Seurat's painting were so riddled by his programmatic, technical theorizations that they balanced on the edge of failure.[30] Roger Fry reports that as Seurat's practice developed until his untimely end, brought by diphtheria in 1891, his great passion for his method overtook the "sensibility"—the sensitivity to minute gradations and variations in tone and value (analog traits)—that was visible in his earlier paintings. This analog sensitivity can be observed in Seurat's *Bathers* of 1883–1884, made a year before his adoption of the pointillist method, which was unveiled to the world in the form of the *Grand Jatte*. Fry, during the course of Seurat's life, attests that "demonstration would replace inspiration and theory passion."[31] Regardless of Seurat's scientific and theoretical influences, Schapiro counters (in 1958 to Fry's essay of 1924) that they matter little when faced with the paintings themselves, which exhibit a virtuosity that make them more than mere demonstrations of the validity of his method.

Numerous scholarly studies have emerged on pointillism and optics, pointillism and color theory, pointillism and industrial technology, and pointillism and the printing press, to name a few. These treatises attempt to identify the ways in which this rather short-lived moment in the history of art reflects the massive cultural and technological changes coinciding with and resulting from the industrialization and the rise of mass culture. Schapiro's critical response to these scientifically inflected readings of pointillism appears to be a way to recuperate the autographic uniqueness of Seurat's practice. It is a way of reframing Seurat, of viewing his painting not simply as a series of weak dabblings in popular science by a late nineteenth-century dilettante but rather as a complex, ambiguous, and artistically ambitious meditation on the effects of culture and technology on human perception.

Schapiro, unlike Homer and his later respondents, maintains that Seurat's interest in color theory, optics, and the science of perception doesn't significantly affect the aesthetic import of his paintings. In contrast, Lee sets about to contradict the view that Seurat was a great pioneer, in the manner of Leonardo da Vinci, in the conjoining of art and science. Lee claims instead that it was Seurat's blundering with and fundamental misunderstanding of optical principles that led to the development of chromoluminarism.[32] However, there are many "sciences" of painting, and many scientific and mathematical discoveries have exerted influence on norms and conventions of depiction for centuries. Whether Seurat's grasp of science was virtuostic or naïve, accurate or false, his method makes visible a particular *technology* of depiction and a correspondingly technological worldview.

Seurat's technologized application of paint to canvas in grains or dots introduces a form of handmade or gesturally implemented digitality. It is systematized and algorithmic, and in its systematization often evokes mechanical and industrial metaphors in the critical literature on his work.[33] But it is precisely the fact that it is handmade and not mechanically produced that preserves its palpably digital aesthetic, even if it is also this very handmadeness that prevents the dots from exhibiting a digitality in a strict sense, insofar as they are not definitively interchangeable; their limits are not quantitatively defined beyond their reference to metricality and thus not perfectly syntactically disjunct. However, as we have seen, not only is optical blending *not* necessarily Seurat's goal —a conclusion that can be reached by considering the conditions under which the work would have been viewed—but also it is the analog inconsistency of size and placement of the dots that prevent perfect fusion. Lee has conjectured that "the technique of pointillism *cannot* give perfectly uninflected areas of colour, even when the surface is viewed from a distance sufficient to ensure optical blending. This is so simply because it is not possible manually to apply spots of paint with perfect regularity. If, by some mechanical means this had been possible, then completely blended and uniformly flat colour surfaces could have been produced."[34]

But to suppose, as Lee seems to do, that Seurat *would* have increased the resolution to the point of perfect uninflected fusion seems to run contrary to the fact that the ideal viewing position is one at which fusion is impossible. Lee's presupposition that Seurat imagined a teleological progression toward analog smoothness opposes the argument presented here. Instead, Seurat can be ranged among artists who work *against* smoothness and resolution, choosing instead to foreground discrete, disjunct, digital or semidigital systems of depiction.

In concurrence with Schapiro's claim that pointillist technique contains a significant aesthetic and political import in calling attention to "its own mode of operation," Seurat's, and later, Signac's greatest contributions to modern aesthetics lie in their ability to render connotatively equivalent their painterly mode of operation with technology itself.[35] Operational modalities can be interpretively defined as encompassing the material and symbolic tools marshaled for the act of representation. Seurat and Signac both refuse to smooth over the mediating nature of media. But whereas the Impressionists employ self-reflexivity to capture the transience and subjective contingency of vision, Seurat and his compatriots use a quasi-regularized system to conjure an image of a highly mechanized, mass-produced modernity. As Stephen Eisenman has written, "Painted in discrete dots of color, applied according to a preconceived system, Neoimpressionist pictures are a kind of exaggeration or parody of the very type of industrial and alienated labor then expanding in France" with the rise of industrialization.[36] Consequently, while the origin of Seurat's technique in science and optics may have been overwritten,[37] the notion of technologically mediated vision embedded in the texture of their painting speaks volumes without having to embody conclusively any optical scientific theories of the day.

Although Schapiro minimizes the scientific aspect of Seurat's practice, the multiple references to mechanical production in the historiography of pointillism cannot escape notice. Mechanical image-making technologies are not of course automatically digital, so it is not this facet of chromoluminarist painting that lends it comparative value to computationally generated digitized images. In fact, while he contrasts the atmospheric haze of Pissarro's and Claude Monet's painting with Seurat's "sympathetic vision of the mechanical in the constructed environment," Schapiro emphatically refutes accusations that Seurat's painting tries so hard to be scientific that it ends up being overly mechanistic, devoid of the luster and vital liveliness that Seurat sought to achieve through this new technique.[38] Later, after the turn of the twentieth century, strains of modernist art such as Futurism elevated the incorporation of modern technology into pictorialization to new heights by integrating mechanistic elements into the form and content of painting. But Seurat's technical application of pointillism does not constitute a fetishization of industrial technology per se. He does indeed depict the Eiffel Tower, a grandiose symbol of modernity, but he is more interested in technical method than the representation of the objects signifying modern technological advances.

After the seeming ease with which Impressionists injected a sense of immediacy and dynamism into scenes of industrial and urban life, Seurat's apparently "rigid" systematicity seems to challenge the traditional aesthetic standard that art be allographic: that it must bear the unique mark of the artist's hand.[39] Of course, in the variation of the size of the dots and in their actual handmadeness, they do in fact assert the presence of the artist in the process of depiction. But the critique of pointillism often lies in the accusation that it is too technical to be aesthetically dense and replete, two of the points upon which the assessment of art objects often turns. Pointillism, according to this line of critical appraisal, is too scientific to achieve full aesthetic potential; to be sure, art is made possible by the invention and repetition of technique, but if that technique appears to impinge upon or even override the harmonious realization of form itself, then it detracts from instead of contributes to the aesthetic value of the artwork. Thus, the accusation that Seurat's painting is mechanical is implicitly pejorative. In order to valorize Seurat, Schapiro is careful to frame his "virtuosity" in opposition to his alleged mechanicity. And though Schapiro concedes that Seurat's method confers a quasi-metric order upon his paintings, he is also quick to rejoin: "I cannot believe that an observer who finds Seurat's touch mechanical has looked closely at the pictures."[40] For Schapiro, the variety in size and shape of the dots confirms the allographic nature of Seurat's painting and reasserts his conformation to a properly allographic/auratic aesthetic sensibility. But as I have maintained, it is precisely this choice to enlarge the dots that preserves the visibility of his digital pictorial architecture, which at least in part confounds the expectations of continuity, density, and repleteness attached to analog aesthetic criteria.

Pointillist technique undeniably imposes a deliberate, ordered structure to the paintings that stands in opposition to the looser, intuitively applied daubs of paint exemplary of Impressionism. Schapiro himself, despite his argument for Seurat's nonmechanical virtuosity, proclaims that "the world is not perceived as a mosaic of colored points, but this artificial micro-pattern serves the painter as a means of ordering, proportioning, and nuancing sensation."[41] Order and nuance coexist in this painterly dimension, which preserves the allographic quality of these paintings. But this is not just any type of order; in fact, Seurat's dots, according to Schapiro, "are his tangible and ever-present units of measure."[42] Here we are faced with another possible contradiction: is pointillism a technique of nuance, luster, and sensation? Or is it an ordered, metric system —the kind of system that compels interpreters to remark upon its calculated, quantified, and mechanistic style?

One way around this interpretive polarity is to propose that Seurat's method is digital rather than mechanistic. The antecedent form of the mosaic is almost universally marshaled in descriptions of pointillism. And as Walter Seitter has noted as a justification for his argument that painting has always been digital, the mosaic "has clearly stood up for and demonstrably displayed the inevitably digital quality of painting. . . . If the mosaic can be described as an archaic form of the picture that stubbornly insists on its constitutive digitality, then the ruin would be the late form of the picture, which . . . would finally admit that it was built from strokes, blotches and spots."[43] And further, "one of the directions adopted by the painting of the nineteenth century was the path to voluntary ruin, that is, the mosaic: first in Impressionism, which constructs the painting from a multitude of small dots of paint without smoothing out the resulting *coarse* structure; and then Cézanne, whose apples dabs of paint on top of previous dabs of paint."[44] Neither Impressionism nor the uncategorizable modernism of Paul Cézanne bear sufficient evidence that they fulfill the requirements for digitality. The perception of shared "points"—the atomic building blocks of pointillist figures—is manifested quite differently in pointillism than in Impressionism. Neither Impressionists nor Cézanne assert both syntactic and semantic disjointness in their inscriptive practices. However, pointillism marks a point of departure precisely because it is syntactically and semantically disjoint, and even leaves traces of this aggregate character when viewed at a distance from which fusion is possible.

Impressionism is a method of capturing fleeting impressions and sensory ephemera. In fact, it was exactly the Impressionists' desire to capture "fugitive appearances" that led to the rejection of this painterly model by the neo-Impressionists.[45] Contrastingly, as we have seen, Seurat has been accused of being "rigid and systematic in his method,"[46] which has led to comparisons between his figures and the Panathenaïc frieze of Phidias on the Parthenon.[47] The frieze-like character of neo-Impressionist painting has been attributed partially to the positioning of the figures and their appearance of frozen statuesque immobility but also to the dots themselves: to the particular organization of shape, volume, surface, and depth imposed by the constraints of pointillist technique.

Recall that modernism has often been characterized by the ubiquitous incorporation of technical or industrial model into art production. Seurat commented to Fénéon that writers and critics "see poetry in what I do. No. I apply my method and that is all."[48] The notion that Seurat proceeds according to a method invites comparison to programming. His "method" is, effectively, a program with specific configurative parameters that gives rise to depictions of a certain character. The aesthetic characteristics of his paintings are a direct result of the fact that his programmatic approach yields a sensory experience associated to a greater extent with technics than expression or intuition. Schapiro writes that Seurat appears as an "engineer of his paintings, analyzing the whole into standard elements . . . and exposing in the final form, without embellishment, the working structural members."[49] Fry surmises that Seurat "proceeded perpetually by analysis and classification" and that his synthetic analysis "appeared to him to be a mere logical deduction from the classified data of sensation—a deduction which could be stated by perfectly ascertained and preconceived methods."[50] By articulating his subjects as the outcome of a logical process of deducing and organizing raw data, Seurat demonstrates how to render pictorially the rigorous, programmatic logic that emerges with such force in the Enlightenment and progresses into the modernist era. He offers an instance in a lineage of pictorial digitality that is applied all the way to the computationally automated algorithms of the digital age.

Let us take another look at Seurat from a different angle: his relationship to the traditional aesthetic model of *disegno*. For Jean-Auguste-Dominique Ingres, drawing not only facilitated recognition of the object at hand. Skilled draughtsmanship was tantamount to poetic expression; without drawing, the artist could not manifest the complex relationship between inner feeling and the external world. However, in the latter years of the nineteenth century, the ascendance of a "light-dark continuum," charted by Linda Nochlin and others, ends the reign of *disegno*. Whereas lines individuate objects by designating their limit with a sharply contoured edge, a regularized application of dots both alters the appearance of volume and depth in the object and challenges the notion of the "edge" as the limit of the body, the point at which one object ends abruptly and another begins. Lines preclude the commingling of matter or the indiscernability of limits. The emphasis on line instituted by proponents of *disegno* discourages or even precludes an indeterminate "sharing" of particles between depicted objects. Under the regime of *disegno*, the edges of a body cannot remain indistinct, wherein a mass reveals itself slowly and coyly, without the sharp decisiveness of the draughtsman's pen.

The use of dots to produce shapes and contours paradoxically lends Seurat's paintings a sense of indistinctness, a slight haze and dispersion of figure into ground despite the precision of his method. His technique, notwithstanding its airs of mechanization and its vulnerability to criticism on the basis of the wooden frozenness of his figures, dismantles the notion that individual bodies are distinct, self-contained, and autonomous.[51] His paintings suggest instead that bodies, or objects, foreground and background bleed into one another and maybe are not so absolutely differentiated after all. While this blending is a perceptual effect of Seurat's paintings, it is unequivocally part of Seurat's artistic or philosophical program in its approach to the issue of boundaries and their pictorial delimitation. In one sense the digital methodology that amalgamates individuated dots suggests a worldview governed by principles of atomism, in which matter shares particles and is therefore indistinct.

However, claims for Seurat's atomism are somewhat confounded by the initially perplexing fact that there is also evidence in Seurat's paintings that he was concerned with contour, as well as object distinction. In order to stay within his self-imposed algorithmic program (applying paint in dots rather than lines), he dealt with this problem not just by deploying the contrast of light and dark regions but also by turning to the specifically digital issue of *resolution*. Seurat makes his dots smaller when he is defining a contour; as such, the variation in size of Seurat's dots correlates to the tradition of *disegno* but uses dense, highly resolved chains of dots to produce a linear effect. Where contours require solidification, the dots become smaller and therefore tend toward continuity. Decreasing the size of the dots effectively increases resolution; in shrinking the granulated dots and placing them more proximately to one another, Seurat mimics linear contours and dissimulates analogicity by creating the effect of "the large, smooth curves that respond to Ingres' norm of good drawing."[52] Thus, while Seurat concerns himself with the analog values of linearity, he approaches this through the avenue of resolution, demonstrating once again that a strict delineation of digital and analog aesthetics frequently proves to be a counterfactual ideal, and suggesting a model of hybridity in which digital and analog modalities inform one another. They instead exist in dialog and invoke an oscillatory worldview in which digital and analog epistemologies both collide and collude.

Whether or not this smoothing of the digitized surface and the creation of an illusion of continuity is necessary for Seurat's ostensibly naturalist program, it does suggest a certain anxiety in his practice, or even provokes anxiety in his viewers by setting up an apparent contradiction in terms. Seurat's greatest aesthetic innovation—his contribution to the expansion of received aesthetic parameters—is that his pointillist method manages to produce a strong aesthetic effect from its own refusal to smooth over the constitutive digitality of painting. In contrast with the sometimes grotesque immobility of his figures, his method redefines, potentially, the very definition of "the image." His strongly programmatic method, unexpectedly, creates painterly surfaces and objects whose shimmering insubstantiality reveal the images as fundamentally evanescent, always already on the edge of fragmentation and disaggregation. As Schapiro has shown, without Seurat's "peculiar means" we would not have "his surprising image-world where the continuous form is built up from the discrete, and the solid masses emerge from an endless scattering of fine points —a mystery of the coming-into-being for the eye."[53] Seurat's painting reveals to viewers a digital territory, a universe built up of an aggregation of points that refuse a smooth linearity and the illusion that analog continuity is more true or natural than digital disjunctness.

Paul Klee's Pictorial Notations

By 1931, Paul Klee had applied his own theory of divisionism to an even greater level of abstraction than that of Seurat, painting works such as *In Copula* (1931), *Fermata* (1932), and *Tendril* (1932), in which a delicate tiling effect produces an

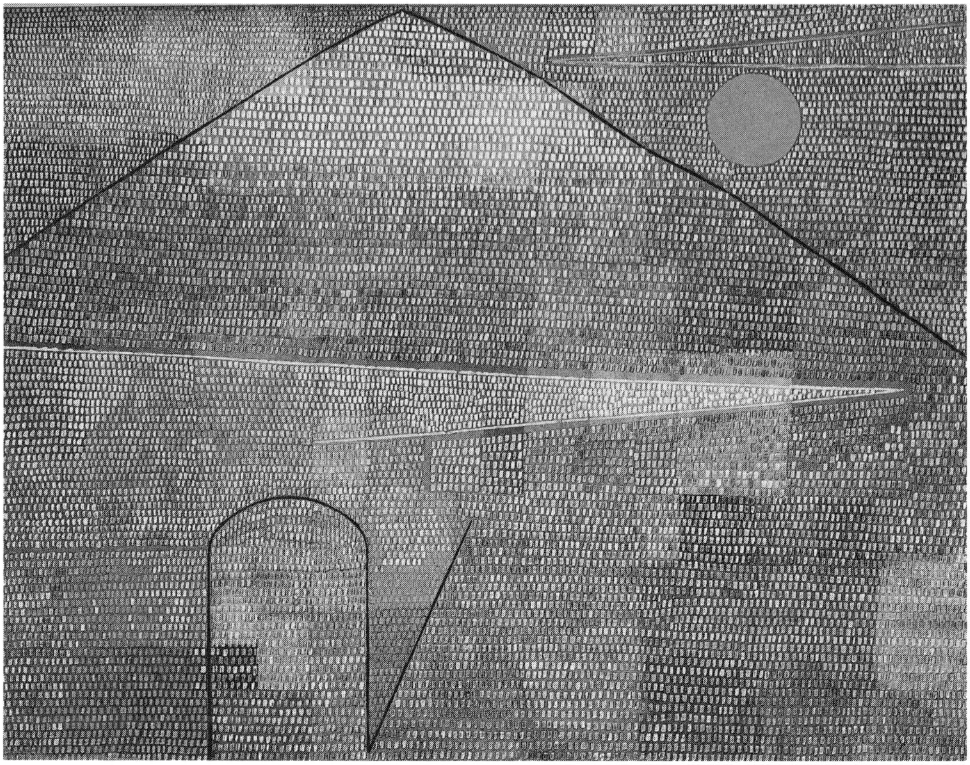

FIGURE 2.3 ▪ Paul Klee, *Ad Parnassum*, 1932. Oil on canvas, 100 x 126 cm (39 x 49 in). Kunstmuseum, Bern, Switzerland.

impression of an ethereal, light-and-fog-mottled atmosphere onto which curling or swirling lines, arrows, and circular suns are superimposed. These dark, continuous strokes punctuate the textural surface and function as a reminder of the canvas's flatness instead of implying the recession of objects into space. These paintings, a series that also includes his masterpiece *Ad Parnassum* of 1932, demonstrate Klee's strategy, developed around 1920, of arranging rectangles of color in grid patterns on the canvas. While his earlier "magic squares" experiment with visually conveying musical harmony and counterpoint through the juxtaposition of tones and colors in a rectangular grid, his divisionist phase intensifies the digitality of his compositions. By reducing the size of the individual unit, he turns the focus away from the geometric quality of the module, shifting attention instead to its aggregative function and emphasizing the notionally extended world created by this metric or quasi-metric configuration. Klee's deep concern for structure, for the building blocks of the material world, and the relationship between spatial and musical structure (where each rectangle is conceived dually as a physical block and a distinct musical note), is evident in paintings such as *Static-Dynamic Gradation* of 1923 and later paintings, such as *New Harmony* of 1936, which employ the earlier technique. Viewing the products of both of these artistic phases, in conjunction with a consideration of his interest in graphical notation, specifically the possibility of visually annotating rhythm, calls attention to the conceptual and visual digitality of his artistic practice.

Working between the first decade of the twentieth century and 1940, a year in which, before his death in June, he had already completed 366 works in various mediums, Klee during the course of his lifetime produced a massive and stylistically diverse oeuvre. Alongside his approximately ten thousand etchings, drawings, prints, and paintings, which to date fill a weighty nine-volume catalogue raisonné, he also meticulously documented his practice in a compendium of notebooks. In addition to painting and writing, Klee was a practicing musician. This multimedia approach to art—one that comprises writing, pictorialization, and music—resulted in a practice that brought each of these branches of the arts closer to a common source and was deeply invested in the notational systems that enable musical, verbal, and pictorial composition. Similarly to other early twentieth-century artists, such as Wassily Kandinsky, Klee was fascinated with the possibility of creating a visual language that could build a synesthetic bridge between music and painting. Ileana Marcoulesco, alongside other modernist historians, has put it succinctly: "In that period, the kinship of music and painting was in the air. Ravel had launched the notion that the laws of harmony were the same for music as for painting. Since Rimbaud and Baudelaire, artists had been on the lookout for correspondences between colors and vowels, and colors and moods. . . . Colors were first of all qualities; secondly, they had weights, thirdly, they could be measured, and so forth."[54]

In 1849, Richard Wagner envisioned grandiose stage productions that would incorporate a multitude of artistic media into a "total work of art" (*Gesamtkunstwerk*).[55] In his 1911 treatise *On the Spiritual in Art*, Wassily Kandinsky proposed an aesthetic theory heavily dependent on synesthesia, a condition in which neural pathways cross, producing sensory responses that do not necessarily correspond to the kind of stimulus applied. A synesthete, then, might taste colors, or hear musical tones when viewing certain shapes. As Kandinsky gleefully insisted, "Our hearing of colors is so definite that it would be hard to find anyone who would try to express bright yellow in the bass notes, or dark lake in the treble."[56] Whether actual or metaphorical, the implications for synesthetic perception were clear to Kandinsky. He believed that as painting approached the condition of musical composition through its unfettering from naturalistic representation, it would achieve an ever-greater level of purity.[57]

Klee's point of entry, the term that illustrates for him the most productive point of intersection between the visual arts and music, is *rhythm*. Rhythm, like writing or other digital modes of inscription, is articulated, metric, and algorithmic. And as Nelson Goodman shows at length in *Languages of Art*, scoring, the method of graphically notating musical compositions, is notational; as such, it is an inscriptive modality classified as a superset of digital systems.[58] Notational systems share different rules than those typically associated with pictorialization, which, as discussed at length in chapter 1, is most often conceptualized as a fundamentally analog system in its density, richness, and continuity. Klee's "creative credo" of 1920 reads like a formula for a notational painting practice, or more precisely a notational system, as in music, that can be used to "compose" a painting. Painting, as a system of depiction rather than notation, deviates from musical composition in that there exists no regularized set of notational marks. If a painter adopts a notational "system," as in the case of Seurat, it is likely to be unique to his or her own practice and thus not fully replicable in the manner of a true notational system. Although, as I will show in chapter 3, Victor Vasarely develops a "programming language" for painting that is replicable across platforms and painters, typically, the semantic content generated by a painter's syntactical system will not necessarily extend unambiguously into other artists' practice. Thus, we cannot "read" a painting by Barnet Newman according to the system advanced by Klee. True notational systems, such as musical notation, must contain what Lev Manovich calls "transcodability," or what can also be called transmedial legibility.[59]

Riddled with references to elementary units, dots, centers, points, elements, bits, and planes, Klee's early texts describe a quasi-notational schema. Klee narrates the movements he will take with his reader, namely, a "little trip into the land of deeper insight," and provides instructions to achieve graphic purity, which we will navigate "following a topographic plan." When we "stop to catch our breath," the topographical mark will be "the broken line, or the line *articulated* by several stops."[60] Distance traveled is a "sheaf of lines," a boat is a "wavy line," and a bridge is a "series of curves." When we "travel joyfully together" lines converge, but when we inevitably disagree, the lines are drawn "independently of each other." We cross an unplowed field that is a "plane traversed by lines." A cart becomes a wheel; a child with curly hair, "corkscrew movement." Lightning flashing on the horizon is a "zigzag line," and stars are "scattered dots." At some points, however, Klee's desire to convey the potential vivacious dynamism even in his "notational" or hieroglyphic system begins to break through his rhetoric. His description of static graphic elements is replaced by reference to dynamic, expressive movements, catalyzed, we can only assume, performatively by the marks themselves. The child's hair is not just a corkscrew but also a corkscrew movement; our excitement as we travel is manifested in vibratory qualities within the marks: "expression, dynamism, emotional quality of the line."

The notational aspects of Klee's work have been recognized frequently, usually with respect to his attempts to translate both quantitative and qualitative aspects of music into a pictorial form of graphic depiction. In other words, musical scores and alphabets, as notational systems, use inscriptive systems that communicate a field of "meaning" (a melody, a sentence) irrespective of certain aesthetic elements of the configuration.[61] Thus, it does not affect the content of a written sentence, or a bar of music, if it is printed in red or blue ink, or if it is typed in one font or another. As long as the system is truly notational —if each symbol is, for example, discrete and replicable—the message can be transmitted within a range of media. Klee's paintings and drawings acquired notational characteristics because he was interested in conveying meanings that are, arguably, more reliably communicated through precise notational systems rather than pictorial ones, which, we recall, are generally understood to thrive on ambiguity. Klee's paintings, then, can be read not simply as hybridizations of pictorial and notational systems but rather as experiments that test what kinds of meanings can be transmitted *both* notationally and pictorially, or how different facets or valences of meaning might be exposed depending on whether they are notated or pictorialized.

For example, while teaching at the Bauhaus in the 1920s, Klee worked directly with musical scores to develop graphic methods of annotating and depicting the wide range of media in which music can be said to exist—from the notational score to the sonorous event—and the many ways in which it is experienced—as a text, as a rhythmic composition, and as a continuously variant tapestry of pitch and timbre. In the pages of his notebooks, Klee attempted to annotate several layers of musical structure that escape the boundaries of the traditional score, with its measures, notes, and time signals. In one sketch, Klee places two bars from Bach's sonata no. IV in G major for violin and piano. Below the score he sets up a grid, on which, arrayed along the vertical axis, each row stands for one note. The grid covers all the notes in three octaves. Along the horizontal axis, Klee divides each row into columns and uses these rows and columns to notate the pitch of each note by drawing lines that increase or decrease in thickness as the pitch changes. The resulting graphic impression is of a partially grid-based, partially continuous line of varying thickness that extends across the page. Underneath this grid, he "set out schematically the qualitative (rhythmic groupings and dynamics) and the quantitative (the measured rhythm) structure of the bar, whereby the former varies as the dynamics change and the latter marks the regular structure (metre) of the piece."[62]

Klee's practice, then, traded between graphically articulating measurable quantities, which can be represented notationally and digitally, and qualities that would seem to escape quantification, those which are ambiguous, continuously variable, and thus perhaps solely available to analog inscription. As Hajo Düchting has underscored, while Klee was deeply interested in discovering what aspects of pictoriality could, like musical notation, be quantified and reliably replicated, color was for him "the 'imponderable' and thus irreducible element in the picture. While it is possible to quantify line and light/dark—as it is pitch and duration of note—the coloring of the image is not quantifiable; it corresponds to the expressive content of the musical tone."[63] Klee himself wrote that color is "secretive" and "hard to grasp," that colors are "the most irrational elements in painting" and possess "a suggestive power."[64] As we will see in his later paintings, Klee ultimately extended his experimentations beyond the broader framework of notation into a specifically digital format in which individuated, discrete, and articulated modules provide the architectural system in which "imponderables" could be contained and set off to their greatest expressive advantage. Again, similarly to the example of Seurat's *Eiffel Tower*, the digital here does not foreclose or narrow the range of aesthetic impressions but rather becomes the condition of possibility for both digital and analog intuitions to be experienced.

In 1953, Vasarely wrote, "All true art is artificial, as opposed to natural."[65] Paul Klee's distinction between "natural" and "artificial" does not conform perfectly to the digital/analog distinction, which is based on discreteness and disjunctness as opposed to continuous correlation. However, it is related to showing, rather than masking, the necessarily (partially) disjunct, definite acts of marking that comprise the act of pictorial composition. In his notebooks, Klee wrote that natural order is "the concept of illumination in nature (light form)."[66] It is the "natural unorganized crescendo or diminuendo. The innumerably subtle tones between white and black."[67]Artificial order, on the other hand, is an "analytical sub-division to make light and dark measurable."[68] The middle steps of the scale must become "perceptible and measurable," and the division of light and dark occurs on a "scale of regulated tonal mixture."[69] Artificial order is characterized by articulation and is fixed in a definite scale. Klee, however, does not champion this depictive mode absolutely or exclusively, writing first that "to obtain greater precision you must become the poorer," and again later that is it "impoverished, but clearer and more comprehensible."[70] While experimenting with fixative, notational or quasi-notational strategies, Klee does not set out to fully digitize his visual alphabet in the manner of Vasarely, as we will demonstrate in chapter 3. Instead, Klee argues that an understanding of natural laws, and laws of depiction, must achieve a compensatory balance between the precise but impoverished artificial order and the "richness" of natural order, where richness is identifiable in movement, illumination, and, most importantly, infinite gradation. Klee's verbal account is accompanied by diagrams that arrange, for example, the gradation between black and white, and the "concept" of black and white, in a stepped chart, whose *y*-axis—the gradation from top to bottom—is evenly divided into strips, labeled not numerically but alphanumerically, with letters ranging from *a* to *l*. The *x* or left-right axis gives little indication of metric division; two adjacent stepped pyramids extend down from the *a* line—from left to right extending from white (left) to the "concept of white" (right), and a mirror image of these pyramids reaches upward from the *l* line, which represents black or the concept of black. While the top "block" of each pyramid suggests a modular unit, there is neither a key nor a numeric or corresponding alphanumeric register running from left to right that would define individual increments.

In the subsequent section of his notebooks, Klee moves from the concept of "order" to the graphic visualization of what he names "natural and artificial measurement." In natural movement, expansion and detraction are represented as continuous—a pen-and-ink curve, as narrow as the width of a stylus at each end thickens as it reaches its indeterminate midpoint, smoothly, with no visible means of assessing regular "steps" in its growth and diminution. This, for Klee, is natural measurement. Artificial measurement, as a function of the imposition of artificial order, "attaches exact numerical values to the steps and so gives us a synthetic method of representing the scale of tone values."[71] The graphical index of these "exact numerical values," however, appears not in Arabic numerals but rather in a series of tallying marks, also pyramidal in form. Numeric exactitude, then, is not of the order of abstract computational function but of tabulation. This tallying method deploys the accumulation of marks for the construction of recognizable, geometric forms, such as a row of cathedral-like architectural configurations in his 1927 pen-and-ink drawing *City of Cathedrals*, displayed in his notebooks in the section on natural and artificial measurement.[72] For Klee, form in its most "natural" or numerical/modular/notational manifestation exists in service of "function"—where function is a force of production and creation, the proliferation of vitality and life itself.

Klee's obsession with units—the building blocks of science, plastic arts, music, and nature—manifests itself sensibly in his paintings but is also outlined programmatically in his writings. His notebooks contain not only his musings on translating musical notation to pictorial depiction but also numerous formulae for textural effects achieved through tiling that experiment with black and white checkerboard patterns. His schemas assign numeric values to white and black, thus imparting a calculating function to the pattern of blacks and whites.[73] Klee's construction is explicitly numerical, tending toward binary representation and highlighting the digital aspect of his work, identifiable in his assignation of a specific structural, rhythmic, and numerical value to his symbol systems, which are reiterated throughout his practice. Later in the notebooks, he evaluates rhythm again from the perspective of a black to white variation in tonality, but here, the description itself of white—the quality of white—approaches the digital in an even more explicit manner than we have seen thus far. For Klee, "scales, whether divided into small intervals or large, of equal size or sub-divided, all belong to the sphere of structural articulation."[74] His intervals are described as discrete units with a distinct color standard from which there are regularized degrees of variation.

In 1932, Paul Klee painted *Ad Parnassum*, a work that represents the culmination of his "magic squares" phase and initiates a divisionist compositional strategy in which his paintings appear morphologically similar to finely tiled mosaics. Klee's magic squares are conceived as a means of achieving a musical polyphony of color. Much larger than the pointillist dot, these colored squares are paired, in *Ad Parnassum*, with a much smaller array of painted "tiles," creating two separate layers of individuated elements that, together, produce an almost hallucinatory shimmer of color and texture. Klee's divisionist approach to *Ad Parnassum* actualizes the properties of mosaics—their disjoint, articulate surface—without relying on individuated brushstrokes (as in pointillism) or "bits" of tile to create a deviation between the smoothness and continuity of the image and the disjoint, aggregate surface of the piecemeal construction. Just as a "painting," conceived as a form or material configuration, is distinct from the specific content contained within the "image" or the "picture," the status of the mosaic as artifact must be considered separately from the existence of the picture or image communicated by the internal arrangement constituting the subject of the mosaic. But whereas mosaic tiles or Klee's magic squares become part of the visible structure, and thus inform our perceptual experience of, the image-object, pixels are generally intended to be hidden from view. The visibility of pixels typically indicates technological failure—the inability of the computer program to effectively *re*construct in its continuous density the digitized image translated into computer code from its original analog state. As William Mitchell has written, "Usually we try to produce images that are of sufficient resolution to render the individual pixels imperceptible, but seeing pixels is not *necessarily* a bad thing. Prominent pixels call attention to the process by which a digital image is actually put together, in the same way that photographic grain or painters' brushstrokes can, and this may be an important part of an image's point."[75] Klee's magic squares prefigure Mitchell's assertion here, one that might seem most readily applicable to the digital formalism of Angela Bulloch, jodi, and other artists. In the legacy of high modernism and Conceptual Art (two systems not altogether opposed in their propensity to interrogate the limits of the artistic medium), these contemporary artists deploy electronic computers to increase the visibility of the discrete structural elements of digital artifacts rather than simulating analog density and continuity.

In a more overt sense than his divisionist method, which similarly to Seurat's pointillism invokes the contemporary notion of resolution to play between the digital application of "points" or "tiles" and the smoothing of these units into an almost foglike texture, Klee's magic squares technique places the tiling effect at the forefront of the viewing experience. But in both Klee's "magic squares" and his divisionist works, the structural, textural, and color-based harmonic effects of the picture all derive from his adoption of a modular schema. Modularity, according to Manovich, can be called the "fractal structure of new media."[76] Manovich writes, "Media elements, be they images, sounds, shapes, or behaviors, are represented as collections of discrete samples (pixels, polygons, voxels, characters, scripts). These elements are assembled into larger-scale objects but continue to maintain their separate identities. . . . [The] modular structure of new media makes . . . deletion and substitution of parts particularly easy."[77] The module, in Manovich's description, exhibits digital qualities of discontinuity and interchangeability. In Klee's painting, which generates a quasi-digital, modular schema utilizing a traditionally analog medium, any colored module could notionally be substituted for any other, creating different perceptual effects without changing the overall structure of the composition.

Both Klee and Seurat could be said to have worked against Impressionism by becoming more formally "algorithmic." Indeed, moments of collusion between art and science, from antiquity forward, seem to have facilitated or to have prompted the adaptation of scientific-experimental models to image-making practices. But the primary difference between Klee and Seurat is that while Seurat created a digital system, a technique that could be used to reliably generate aesthetic and perceptual effects based on scientific principles, Klee's notational system, his charts and metric scales, are eminently concerned with the dynamic exchange between the module/particle and its capacity to activate or catalyze movement. In his notebooks, he writes that "a particle . . . must be shaped in such a way as to lend itself to movement and conduction."[78] Particles "mediate—they are the middle links that receive and transmit."[79] But even as he views particles as generative (feedback-producing) units, he seeks, atomistically, to create elemental schemas and to identify the smallest structural unit in a grid so that "any reduction or abstraction is barely possible. Each structural particle has the same value."[80] Particles with interchangeable values closely approach the description of digitality I have been proposing. But whereas Seurat's digital method produces an ostensible rigidity, Klee's goal is to activate the image by creating an interplay between digital particles.

Klee's charts and metric scales track, quantify, and make graphically legible the relationships between light and dark, dynamism and stasis, nature and artifice, and opacity and transparency. Instead of creating a deep division between a dynamic, Romantic, or vitalist conception of nature and its systematic, rigidifying quantification in a metric, notational system, Klee attempts to find aspects of reality that would otherwise remain hidden by imposing a digital veil over the visible world. He deploys digitality in a manner that potentially reshapes our thinking about the relationship between structure and vitality. Marcoulesco describes Klee's process of dividing and digitizing the world, taught in his courses at the Bauhaus, as follows: "Take the fish as a whole; find a principle of dividing it—for instance, its own scales; make a grid of it; spread this grid over the whole surface of the painting. The fish and its environment will still be visible through the grid, but the whole will be completely and differently 'illumined' by the grid."[81] Seurat's partition of matter into digital units, which are subsequently utilized as the building blocks for his pictorial compositions, is viewed with suspicion for freezing the rhythms of life in to static geometries. Klee, on the other hand, adopts a notational vocabulary that references music, a time-based phenomenon. System, then, for Klee does not foreclose movement and dynamism but rather catalyzes it. Consequently, he uses the "particle" and the notational symbol to inject his pictorial surfaces with the rhythmic dynamism of music.[82] In a different mode than Seurat, Klee uses systematization against rigidity, deploying a notational symbol system to express the dynamic, vital energies of the natural world.[83] However, while he exhibits a clear fascination with musicality and dynamism, Klee indirectly sets himself against the Impressionist quest to capture the effluvium of immediate optical perception and transfer it onto the canvas. In his 1923 essay "Ways of Nature Study," Klee encapsulates, with some irony, the Impressionist agenda: "In this way excellent pictures were obtained of the object's surface filtered by the air; the art of optical sight was developed, while the art of contemplating unoptical impressions and representations and making them visible was neglected."[84] Klee's own ideas about what art should do are encapsulated most concisely in his earlier "Creative Credo" of 1920: "Art does not reproduce the visible; rather, it makes visible."[85] In other words, art's mission is to actively reveal facets of the world and of experience that are not otherwise directly apprehensible. To merely reproduce is to foreclose the revelatory and world-shaping capacity of art. Ultimately, Klee's method, like Seurat's, carries the potential to help us observe an architectonics of the material world that is not immediately available to quotidian perceptual habits.

As we will see in chapter 5, contemporary, electronically computational practices of information visualization echo Klee's credo in attempting to graphically render large data sets, effectively setting about to visualize the invisible. If we subscribe to the notion that digital devices are measuring machines, then Paul Klee's praxis—his technique and its supporting theoretical armature—fulfills the characteristics of a proto-digital representational model that is pushed to a logical and visible conclusion in contemporary information visualization. To provide a point of reference and contrast to Klee's model, Paul Cézanne has been cited as a painter whose system might initially appear to have digital tendencies. He is read as a precursor of cubism due to the incorporation of juxtaposed shards or facets into his color-blocked compositions, so that even "surfaceless" or atmospheric spatial fields resemble the tessellated surface of mosaics.[86] Cézanne, like Klee, employs basic geometrical elements—most famously the sphere, cone, and cylinder—in his image-constructions in order to emphasize the constructedness of paintings, their status not as imitations of the natural world but as structures that parallel nature by revealing its most essential forms in relationship to one another.

Klee, like Cézanne, works toward an understanding of essential forms, but whereas Cézanne's concerns remain more prominently pictorial, Klee conducts robust analyses of notational, non-pictorial elements. Thus, not only does he expose the ontology of painting as a constructed amalgamation of parts, but he also explores a range of symbol systems that extend beyond pictorial representation. Klee sets out to interrogate the limits of notational, (non-electronically) computational systems. In comparison, neither Cézanne's practice, nor that of the cubists after him, is digital, or proto-digital in the manner of Klee or Seurat. The use of pared-down geometrical form is endemic to modernism, but not all of modernism is inherently digital. Cubism, constructivism, suprematism, even futurism mobilize geometrical abstraction to interrogate traditional representational strategies and to push the limits of painting. But their geometrical units are only very loosely modular, and too invested in exploring specific properties of form (shape, volume, depth) to be identified as notational, discrete, or aggregative (where the aggregate refers not just to the characteristics of the individual "digit" or unit but to the performative *act* of unit-based construction).

After Cézanne, Cubists seek to rectify the shortcomings of depicting three-dimensional objects on a two-dimensional surface by presenting all faces, angles, and possible points of view of their object simultaneously; the Cubist painting "opens up" its object and projects it on the canvas just as a Mercator projection renders the globe on a planar surface, but its facets are not metric, and they are far from regular.

In Cézanne's painting "the process of deliberation surrounding the application of every single dot of paint seems to postpone the picture's completion indefinitely."[87] But this is an application of paint that is more invested in the notion of durational extension, via incompletion, than in a truly digital structural analysis. When set alongside the notion of time as a series of fixed, crystallized instants, figured in the immobile "points" on the path of travel of Zeno's arrow, we see that Henri Bergson's interest in the richness, density, and plenitude of duration works even against the concept of analog signal processing. For Bergson, there is no "measurement" possible in duration, because it contains the potential for compression and extension—an infinity of intermediary steps—to develop *within* moments or measured temporal units. Ultimately, the presence of the "dot" in Cézanne's painting does not necessarily connote digitality, nor does it indicate the cultural-historical presence of a digital unconscious or a digital world-imagination. Cézanne's "vibration of painted flecks and areas of colour distributed over the whole surface of the canvas" do not correlate to Seurat's procedural, systematic, and eminently *technological* divisionist program, not least because Cézanne's approach to "the empty canvas onto which nature is gradually and fragmentarily brought to light" registers a deep desire to reveal the harmony of natural form in an integrated and overlapping (vitalist) fashion, which is too much concerned with variable internal relationships to fulfill the characteristics of digital system.[88] To return to the beginnings of this chapter, Cézanne's painting seems markedly *anti*technological in comparison to Seurat's practice, which eschews poetry in favor of technique. If Seurat's practice is about nature, it is a nature that can be expressed within a verifiable, repeatable scientific system.

Digital Structure and Computer Art

With the advent of bitmapping, *Pong*, *Tetris*, and *Tron*, the grid of pixels became an easy trope by which to identify the "digital." Early digital images resembled the notational characteristics of the EKG, in which only the apex and base represent the significant, information-bearing points on the graphic schema. Whereas in classical *disegno* every subtle modulation of a line adds layers of phenomenological and symbolic valence to the figure, highly pixilated images function similarly to the EKG insofar as each pixel contains a finite amount of differentiated information, such as brightness or color, and is demarcated by a precise boundary. The pixel meets Nelson Goodman's definition of a digital scheme because it is syntactically and semantically differentiated or disjoint. Similarly to Goodman's digital pressure gauge, each pixel in a bitmapped screen is internally uniform and is recognizably separated from adjacent pixels due to the highly articulated "edge" of each square. In an analog system, there is no upper limit to the fineness with which we can read the position of a pointer, or for that matter the fineness of modulation in a line. In the analog pressure gauge the position of the pointer is variable and subject to the discriminatory ability of a reader/observer. A digital pressure gauge contains a finite amount of information, so there is an upper limit past which a greater degree of discrimination will become meaningless. The gauge counts as a digital system if "each dot [is] taken as marking the center of a region such that any appearance of the pointer within that region counts as an inscription of the same character."[89] This means that there is no variable information within the character and there exists a definite line demarcating the "inside" and "outside" of the character.

If we replace the pressure gauge with the grid of pixels as our digital exemplar, it becomes easy to see how digital systems seem to fall outside the traditional parameters of aesthetic success. The technological limitations of early bitmapping precluded the richness, repleteness, and ambiguity (at least as they have been recognized in the classical tradition, not just in the West but perhaps even more pronouncedly in Eastern graphesis) that confer aesthetic value on classical art objects.[90] This meant that early computer-generated art is either relegated to a position of technological primitivism, where judgment of the computer's potential to produce fine art is to be withheld until the density of pixels in a grid becomes great enough to yield an impression of indeterminate fineness, or deemed a "conceptual" practice insofar as it uses a technological tool to critique traditional aesthetic values and ideologies.[91]

jodi, for example, an artist duo formed by Joan Hemskeerk and Dirk Paesmans in the mid-1990s, became a pioneering figure in the critical/activist practice that became known as net.art. jodi is the one example within a number of artists whose work foregrounds the primary graphical elements of digital structure, most recognizably the pixel. These artists' motivation for performatively engaging this digital aesthetic varies widely, and they foreground a number of issues ranging from tactical assaults on political and ideological formations to cooler meditations on the computer as artistic medium. Yet each of these artists chooses not to obfuscate but to place at a premium the viewer/user's sensory relationship to the building blocks of digital depiction.

From the inception of their collective, jodi's artworks have focused on dismantling the illusion of transparency that occupies the forefront of mainstream interface design. Together with other net.artists including Vuk Cosic, Olia Lialina, Alexei Shulgin, Jon Ippolito, and Heath Bunting, jodi launched conceptual investigations into the structure of interface design, turning the interface inside out by replacing pictures with code. These seemingly impenetrable landscapes, comprised of scrolling lines of text; rough-hewn, heavily pixilated geometric shapes; or blocky ASCII graphics, often contain elements of interactivity, but it is an interactivity turned against itself. Here, the primary function of the Internet, geared toward information access, is confounded. Embedded links lead to dead-end, empty web pages, leaving the user with a sense of futility, as if waiting for a stubbornly evasive informatic Godot. The website g33con.com, for example, allows the user to select a text box containing a series of URLs flashing in the top left section of the browser window. But when text box is selected, the screen goes "blank" white. All that is visible are the web-page titles—you-talking-to-me-you-talking-to-me-you-talking-to-me.com, then-who-the-hell-else-are-you-talking-to.com, you-talking-to-me.com, well-i-am-the-only-one-here.com, and who-the-fuck-do-you-think-you-are-talking-to.com—that bounce from one to the other in an absurd exchange of aggressive commentary, looping in an endless cycle.

The conceptual armature of jodi's projects, all highly critical of the slick, numbing spectacle of corporatized information transmission, lends itself to a digitized, low-tech aesthetic often associated with "Glitch" art, which exploits systemic flaws in order to create jittery, stuttering visual and sonic landscapes. Julian Stallabrass writes that net.art reverses the teleology of computer graphics, which have been playing "modernism in reverse, reaching ever-heightened levels of naturalism," by laying bare the operational principles of the Net and the mystifications at work at the level of interface.[92] In many cases of advanced computer graphics, technical operations are mystified by the application of a glossy layer of illusionistic pictorialization. Code is obscured, thus veiling the fact that, as a language, code is shot through with ideology. By extension, the net is an ideological apparatus. Net.artists set out to dismantle or at least destabilize this false naturalization, often by revealing source code or other aspects of the information structures supporting the Net, or by rupturing the thin shell of spectacle by injecting glitches into the system.

In many cases, glitch art transforms virtualized, naturalistic, and immersive environments into flattened abstractions. A notable example of this is jodi's SOD, one of several game modifications the duo has produced that strip down the figurative and representational structure of the interface to abstract, geo-

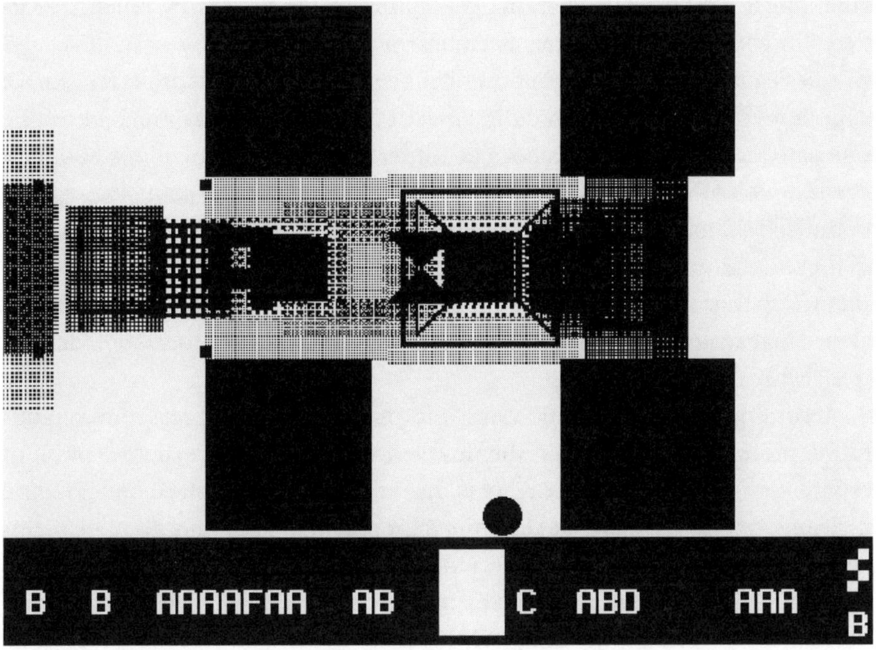

FIGURE 2.4 ▪ jodi, *SOD*, 1998 (Wolfenstein modification) game software.

metrical components. By refusing the spectacular virtualization that seems to be the imagined teleology of the gaming industry, SOD illustrates the possible alliance between a critical digital aesthetics and the technological/cultural critique initiated by net.art. Soren Pøld has argued that "net.art can be regarded as a reaction to the iconophilia of the computer industry—as some sort of digital iconoclasm."[93] In addition to framing net.art in terms of iconoclasm, it can be conceptualized in terms of interrogation of visuality or regimes of visibility. Revealing an aesthetics of digital structure, heavily digitized works such as SOD demonstrate how computational processing affects what and how we see; it gives a particular shape to and sets new possibilities and limitations for what is included in the realm of the visible.

In the noncomputational digital systems developed by Seurat and Klee, there has been no obvious presence of numbers or quantitative informational values to muddy the distinction between digits and computed numerical values. For example, pointillism assembles the image out of discrete points of color. However, the categorical disaggregation of information, numericization, digitization, and algorithm becomes a somewhat tricky business when we begin to examine the qualities of computationally generated images. All too easily and all too often, these four categories collapse into a monolithic notion of "the digital" or "the information age," described as follows by Friedrich Kittler: "In computers everything becomes number: imageless, soundless, and wordless quantity. And if the optical fiber network reduces all formerly separate data flows to one standardized digital series of numbers, any medium can be translated into another."[94] Echoes of Kittler's prophetic intonations about an age in which all forms of communication will be reduced to standardized and optimized channels of frequency and bit rate have resonated in many of the texts in the still-forming canon of media studies. In particular, one aspect of Kittler's rhetoric that has been seized upon most emphatically is the reduction to equivalence that seems to result from the quantitative notion of information derived from cybernetics.

According to the cybernetic view, information can be expressed in quantitative, probabilistic terms. But the problem with the enthusiastic reception of cybernetics and information theory is that all kinds of quantities, units, metric divisions, and so forth, are not examined for potential differences but are themselves often reduced to equivalence. Not all artists, theorists, programmers, and users/consumers of our highly mediated economy performatively engage with a potentially or actually quantitatively mediated cybernetic universe in the same way. Not all numbers, universal metrics, and units of information are necessarily perceived as belonging to the notional system of equivalences imagined by cyberneticists. In other words, even *if* ubiquitous digital technology produces an ideal digital subject that processes the world as if it is one giant computer program or algorithm, a glance at recent artifactual history reveal that all quantities are not created equal. Digits, numbers, code, and information can be taken as individuated phenomena with their own particular qualities. jodi's aggressive exposure of the pixel and the bitmapped screen provokes a meditation on the perceptual effects of digitization, but their work reads more as a critical interrogation of immersive virtualization rather than of numericization. jodi's performance of an aggressively digitized fracturing of the interface—the sensuously apprehended image surface—into digital components depends on a numeric, algorithmic process, but it is the units or modules themselves that are thrown into high relief, rather than the numeric, electronic processing system underlying the surface image.

A quick glance through the literature of the 1990s will reveal a heavily polarized set of proclamations concerning the effects of computational technology on culture. Scholars from a disparate range of fields, including literature, cultural studies, history, engineering, and computer science, projected either intensely utopian and dystopian views about the liberatory, democratizing potential of the web, or alternatively the demise of embodied, phenomenal experience that accompanies the emergence of computational technologies. To consider another commonly addressed issue that is mobilized in both favorable and unfavorable accounts of the possibilities and shortcomings of computational technology, it is now a truism that the flexibility and mutability of computational graphics shatter the promise of visual authenticity—the indexical or forensic "truth"—ostensibly afforded by analog photography and film. Both in the world of advertising and in the world of fine arts it becomes increasingly difficult to discern when photography simulates, dissimulates, or documents in an unaltered fashion the world presented in its pictorial frame.[95] Undoubtedly, this dream of visual truth in analog photographic technologies is itself illusory, but it is an ever-present issue in digital works that engage the history of film and photography.

Jim Campbell, an artist who puts into conversation digital and analog aesthetic modalities—particularly digital graphics, photography, and film—engages questions of visual clarity, resolution, memory, and knowledge. Campbell overlays analogically recorded moving images and low-resolution, computationally programmed arrays, which are both aesthetically and technologically digital, creating a perceptual and conceptual gap between analogicity and digitality. However, this gap does not hierarchize one modality over the other but rather sets out to reveal how both technical approaches to depiction can be mobilized to de-resolve the image, creating more opacity than transparency and presenting indices of technological mediation rather than an illusion of immediacy and clarity.

Jim Campbell's *Ambiguous Icons—Running Falling* (2000–2004) and *Home Movies* (2006–2008) series translate analogically recorded moving pictures, of single figures running, walking, and falling, or of family events captured by home movie cameras, into shadows that flicker across low-resolution arrays of LED nodes. Campbell performs a rejection of graphical resolution; his LED grids obscure the particularity of bodies and objects, instead conveying gestures and movements that are intuitively recognizable despite their lack of figural detail. By using digital schemata in this way, Campbell's work directly challenges Paul Virilio's estimation that "the demise of the relative and analogical character of photographic shots and sound samples in favour of the absolute, digital character of the computer, following the synthesizer, is thus also the loss of the poetics of the ephemeral. For one brief moment Impressionism—in painting and in music—was able to retrieve the flavour of the ephemeral before the nihilism of contemporary technology wiped it out once and for all."[96] What Campbell's artworks demonstrate, as have all of the works in this chapter, both those that use computers and those that don't, is that what might be thought to be the

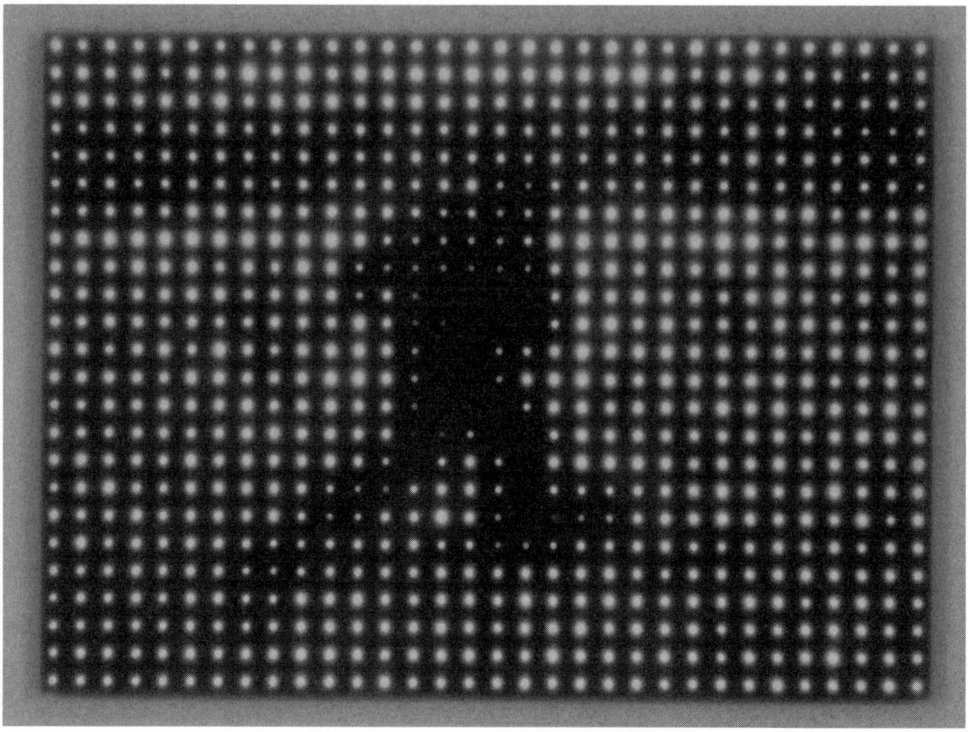

FIGURE 2.5 ▪ Jim Campbell, *Ambiguous Icon #1 (Running Falling)*, 2000. Custom electronics, 165 LEDs, treated Plexiglas, 16 x 12½ x 52 in. Collection of Naomie and Charles Kremer. Photography credit: Sarah Christianson.

"absolute character" of digital systems—their discrete, articulate, locatable position in a metrically configured universe—often raises issues about ephemerality, perceptual instability, and even semantic ambiguity.

In his *Ambiguous Icons* series, Campbell creates LED "sculptures" in which matrices of red LED nodes subject video footage of human figures moving across the frame to an overt, dedifferentiating pixilation. The number of LED nodes in the matrix varies, the intervals between each node determining the degree of resolution and the immediacy with which a viewer can identify the shapes and cadences of a running (and then falling) human figure through the digitally processed sequence. In some works, Campbell installs a sheet of treated plexiglass over the LED grid, which causes the discreteness of the individuated points to diffuse, returning to a more continuous, analog visual state. In *Home Movies*, Campbell makes the conversation between analog and digital aesthetics that is implicit in *Ambiguous Icons* directly visible by stringing a veil of wires and LED nodes that seems to either partially obscure or generate soft-focus,

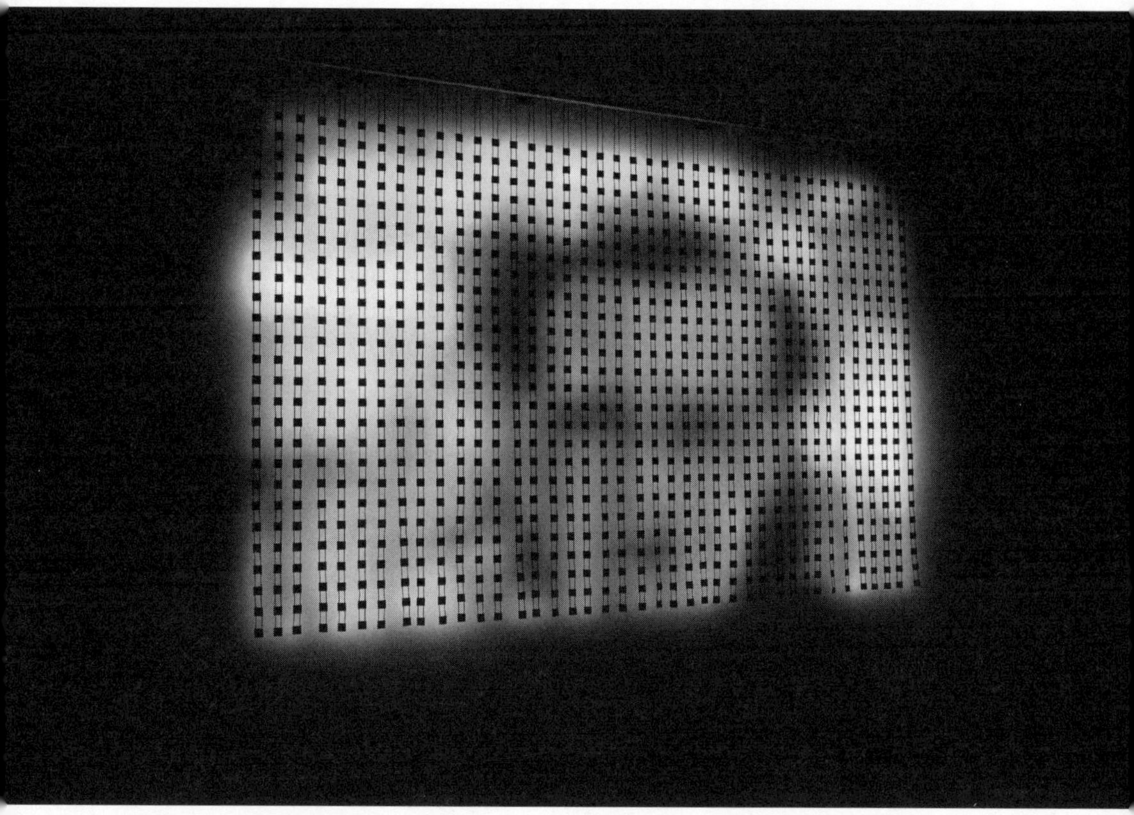

FIGURE 2.6 ▪ Jim Campbell, *Home Movies* 1040, 2008. Video installation: custom electronics, 1,040 LEDs, 120 x 84 x 3 in. Installation view, Eleanor D. Wilson Museum, Hollins University, Roanoke, VA, 2010. Photography credit: Olivia Body.

black-and-white projections of found home-movie footage. These home movies are the source material for the digitally processed semiabstractions that flicker across the grid of hundreds of LED nodes. But unlike the *Ambiguous Icons* series, which occludes the analog origins of its moving-image sources, *Home Movies* layers digital over analog picturing technologies, asserting their dialogic entanglement as the formal, aesthetic, technological, and associative center of the piece. Home movies, for a certain generation of Americans, are an immediately recognizable form that might provoke a range of responses, from sentimental nostalgia to amusement and to horror at these documents of the American suburban dream. Home movies are unabashedly about memory, but memory of a different sort than the electronically stored "memory" of digital computers. In addition to subjecting the nostalgia of captured fragments of everyday life to an *unheimlich*, abstracted digital dispersal over a heavily pixilated LED landscape, the formal construction of these layered "screens" refuses to allow the digital screen to become emblematic of an overly simplified, poetically barren, quantized worldview. Instead, Campbell seeks to show how different experiences of complexity are afforded by analog and digital systems, both separately and in conversation with one another.

The beauty of the LED screens in Campbell's work does not emerge unilaterally from likeness or proximity to an analog system—from an imitation of analog aesthetic properties. While the brightness of the lights seems to intensify and wane continuously, closer inspection reveals that the increase and decrease in brightness does not mirror the smooth ebb and flow of projected analog film. Campbell's digits might seem to flow though intermediate states to reach the extreme points of the switching device (on, brightest; and off, dark). But the variation in light intensity only indicates the presence of a multilevel device in which the intermediate levels of brightness are binary switches themselves. Thus, the variations in each light occur in distinct steps or states of intensity, so that a graph of light activity would resemble the jagged patterns of Goodman's EKG rather than a continuous line with an even, wavelike curvature. To return to Virilio, again, Campbell's LED works are about technological, perceptual, social, emotional, and biological ephemerality; here, the "absolute" systematization of the digital reveals the presence of ephemerality in both systems but a qualitative difference in each system in the way that ephemerality is manifested and defined. The analog films are about a way of life, a personal memory that may have been lost, or may have never existed, while the other is about the insubstantiality of the object, its deresolution into a grid of lights that flicker into illumination or fall into darkness. As the shadows sweep across the digitized surface of the LED nodes, it produces a different experience than do the films of swinging children or passing cars—one that is more rhythmic and musical than pictorial and more about the delicacy of this highly technological configuration than about its ability to capture the (out-of-focus) detail in the filmic projection behind it.

This process of paring down figures and gestures to the broadest, most abstracted outlines subjects the world to a metric quantization at a technical level but preserves the haunting presence of analog properties of ambiguity. Paradoxically, the apparent semantic density and open-endedness in the work is achieved precisely in the act of syntactic articulation/discretization. But Campbell refuses to suppress the digital or valorize analog aesthetic characteristics. His digital aesthetic sensibility is instantly perceptible in his foregrounding of the grid of pixels, performed by either superimposing the grid over analog photographic material or by filtering and processing the analog image through the digital matrix without revealing its analog source. His works are clearly invested in the question of visual recognition, in the ways in which patterns emerge through fields of noise. In their investigation of the properties of pixelated grids; of legibility and illegibility of form; of abstraction and figuration, individuality and collectivity, registered in the universally readable movements of nonindividuated figures; and of the cybernetic feedback loop between signal and noise, Campbell's installations extend considerations about depiction, form, and the art object that have concerned art practitioners, critics, and theorists since well before the advent of modernism. Campbell's installations deploy digital processing and digital aesthetics in a way that both embraces technology and inserts it into larger historical and aesthetic discourses concerning the role of technology in depiction, and the limits within which something can be recognized or understood as a picture.

Campbell's recombinatory "media mixing" serves, at a semantic level, to emphasize the ephemerality and instability of both analog and digital media. But even if analog and digital media bear their own distinct syntax (their own syntactical "signature"), the layering of analog film and digital LED switches disrupts, complicates, or folds onto itself the syntactical signature of each signal, making analog and digital modes not only mutually referential but also interdependent. Stephen Eisenman has described Seurat's method as a "proclamation that beauty arises from a continuous process of opposition and resolution among contrasting colors, values, and lines."[97] In the twenty-first century, Jim Campbell accesses this compelling oscillation between opposition and resolution by experimenting with the pixilation of continuous, analog images. Often, he quite literally overlays the highly discrete, pixilated surfaces of LED panels with light- or line-diffusing materials such as rice paper or smoked Plexiglas. One layer does not obscure the other; neither the "continuous," almost entropic surface of rice paper nor the low-resolution, highly discrete array of bulbs on the LED panel lends itself to instant recognition. "Digitality," or at least "pixilation," in the case of Campbell, resists the fantasy of a direct correlation between technological development and immediate (unmediated) and immersive phenomenological experience; thus, computational evolution does not work ultimately against perceptual digitality and toward smooth, aesthetically "analog" virtualization. Resolution in Campbell's work emerges slowly, or fades in and out of perceptibility. This slowness, which at once presents an obstacle to understanding and also enriches the work with precisely the kind of ambiguity and irreducibility that is posed *against* discreteness and digitality, operates in tandem with the low-resolution, discrete LED nodes to propose, simultaneously, a digital, quantized worldview and a hybrid epistemology in which the two modalities do not exist in pure form, but rather coexist with and put pressure upon one another.

While the digital realism evident in video games and cinematic special effects extends a hand to the simulacral virtuality depicted so darkly by Frederic Jameson and Jean Baudrillard, the experiments in electronically computational digital abstraction launched by jodi and Campbell work prophylactically against the end of artwork that, even if it is not painting, continues to analogize and reference painterly practice. Using Gerhard Richter as his case in point, Frank Reijnders has claimed that, in the age of technology, painting "is today *impossible*."[98] Richter's project is to show that neither photography—the realist medium par excellence—nor painting hold up a vision-enhancing, corrective lens through which to take in the truth of nature but instead that both media "give the appearance of something they are not."[99] Reijnders writes, "Painting is in a position to shatter all evidence and make all essence impossible. Painting directly confronts us with our elementary state: *nothingness*."[100]

Gerhard Richter's painting, blurred or peeled away in layers from the canvas, seems insistently analog at the same time that it reflects upon technology and the nature of mediation. His use of transmediality operates differently than Campbell's on many levels, but most importantly here, he provides a counterpoint to Campbell by engaging the relationship between technology and the handmade (specifically painting and photography), resolution and blur, and depth and surface, without ever activating perceptual digitality. In general, photorealism plays between analogy and metonymy; photorealistic painting prompts the question of whether painting is "more analog" than photography and what aesthetic or conceptual qualities are to be gained by translation between media. Photorealism also allows issues of seriality and repetition, of which Conceptual Artists are so fond, to be introjected into a multimedia framework; the iteration and reiteration of morphological doubles across media boundaries call into question the ontology of the image and its subsequent layers of pictorialization. Richter's painstaking erasure of brushstrokes in his photorealistic paintings (the mark of "fingery" or gestural digitality) and his technique of blending outlines in a way that mimics out-of-focus photographs confound the distinction between the ideal of perfected, flawless photographic indexicality and the approximating function of painterly naturalism.

Richter's photographic paintings, perhaps most famously, or at least controversially, demonstrated in the fifteen canvases comprising his *October 18, 1977* series, appear to be blurred and out of focus. These paintings take as their sources the newspaper and police photographs of the young German radicals known as the Red Army Faction (RAF) or Baader-Meinhof group, three of whom were found dead while in custody in a German prison on 18 October 1977. Although the deaths were attributed officially to suicide, speculation abounded that the young peoples' deaths had been engineered by prison workers. Being "out of focus" provokes questions about the relationship between painting and technologies of mechanical reproduction, but does so in a different way than do Campbell's LED works. Richter's photorealistic painting gestures toward relationships between technology and depiction but remains both technically and aesthetically analog. Conversely, Campbell's LED grids reduce analog plenitude into a discrete, regular array, strangely rendering the data more precise and yet more indeterminate. The blur in Richter's paintings shows the contingency and instability involved in "capturing" a moment of time, either with the instantaneous click of the shutter in an analog camera or within the extended, durational act of painting. Because it has undergone a technical transformation, and now exists as a painting, Richter's blur cannot be ascribed directly to the low-resolution capacity or a mechanical defect in the device, in contradistinction to both the home movies collected by Campbell and the photographs initially appropriated by Richter. These artists' source material becomes subject to a migration across media, which ultimately underscores rather than occludes the technical specificities these media are expected to demonstrate: for example, flatness in a painting or the indexical trace in a photograph. But in Campbell's case, it is precisely the filtering of the already "blurred" moving pictures through a computational system that makes it less precise and more ambiguous. In Campbell's pieces, a struggle ensues between the two layers of media: between the picture projected on the wall and the shadowy impressions crossing the LED grid. In reference to Richter's painted photographs, Reijnders writes, "A painting can never be out of focus because: in comparison to what would it be out of focus? The blurred effect is achieved through painterly means: strokes carried out with a dry brush remove the definition from the depicted subjects. As paintings, these photographs no longer compete with *reality*. They exist only by the grace of their own reality and are therefore, strictly speaking, abstract."[101]

Looking at Richter's painted photographs next to Campbell's *Home Movies*, we can immediately see how different media contain different possibilities for interrogating the notion of being "in focus," and how this is a distinctly technological category whose standard of "clarity" becomes more uncertain—less clear—in each multimedia iteration. One cannot say that a painting is out of focus; there is no optical or technological standard either to which a picture adheres or from which it deviates. Painters deploy more and less precise, fine-grained technique, but technologies of mechanical and digital reproduction have different expectations attached to them. The home movies from which Campbell's LED curtains sample their constantly fluctuating degrees of luminosity are blurred, clearly captured with lo-fi, obsolete technology. But instead of sharpening them, restoring them, or giving them a technologically updated appearance, the addition of computational technology interposed between the viewer and the filmic projection fractures the picture even further, so that we are no longer looking at a blurred variety of indeterminacy but instead at a more fragmented, discrete, and disjunct digital screen whose resolution is too low to give us anything more than a vague impression of movement. This "impression" is far from a finely detailed portrait, much less a mirrored reflection.

Each of these examples examines the conditions and limits of representation by foregrounding digital processes and composition, thus introducing the dynamic relationship between technology, structure, and representation as a philosophical, aesthetic, and material problem. In his discussion of the state of painting as it has advanced (temporally, not evolutionarily) through modernism into the present moment, Frank Reijnders claims that the Western, modernist tendency toward the flattening and "abstraction" of the picture plane reaches its apotheosis and decay in the mid-twentieth century with Greenburgian "pure opticality." At this time artists push up against, or collide with, the inevitability and unavoidability of "the surface," the ultimate condition of painting and the absolute barrier past which it cannot progress and still retain its identity as a medium. As such, "due to the exclusive emphasis on the inescapability of the surface, from Manet onwards the focus shifted from representation to what made representation possible in the first place."[102] Reijnders's claim indirectly emphasizes the continuing legacy of modernist reflexivity. Moreover, placed in the context of the state of painting in the contemporary technical milieu, it provokes a consideration of the ways in which digital art responds to and thus reactivates the foundational tenets of modernist art practice and criticism in the present moment.

This chapter has placed the theoretical distinctions between analog and digital in a dialog with a series of artifacts extending from the two decades preceding the turn of the twentieth century to the first decade of the twenty-first century. The artifacts in question have included paintings, installations, photographs, and screen-based computer graphics, but they all engage with the problem of the digital in individual, sometimes idiosyncratic ways. Seurat, Klee, jodi, and Campbell each import the modernist concern with surface and support into their meditations on the materiality of the computational interface, or the material effects that result from electronic computational processes. The self-reflexive tendencies of this work suggest that some principles of high modernism continue to influence some strains of digital art. If the interface is conceived as a surface, and the picture plane (now, most often, the screen) is a medium through which to visualize computational processes, digital art in this vein signifies in terms of how technology reflects upon its own generative systems and its mechanisms for the production of images. Electronic computation is thus utilized to explore its own permutational affordances and constraints. In the field of graphic production, self-reflexive artists explore how digital-computational technology reshapes, or fails to reshape, the norms and limits of representation.

Even if it is a technological possibility that the pixel-like "modules" in the exemplary cases here, both those made by hand and those produced through electronic computation, could be further and further refined to the point at which they could no longer be perceived by the human eye as individual units, artists like jodi and Campbell choose not to pursue that technological teleology and instead choose to foreground digital discreteness. Digital technology may be capable, notionally, of virtualizations that appear perfectly coextensive with the physical world. The number of calculations and speed at which they can be carried out by computers is potentially infinite, the upper limit determined only by the technical parameters of existing and, as we know, always dynamically changing memory storage and processing speeds. Nevertheless, it is important to ask what is achieved by making the digital sensorially apprehensible, by keeping it open as an aesthetic and analytic category worthy of conceptual and perceptual consideration. In each of the examples shown here, the digital has always been haunted by the specter of the analog—Seurat's dots are handmade and variable in size, and Jim Campbell's screens produce low-resolution shadows that acquire a life through the action of pixilation. In fact few artworks occupy a strictly digital or strictly analog format. Instead, they often oscillate between the two states. But in order to comprehend, and perceive, this oscillatory movement, it is necessary to have an understanding of each category, to see where artworks do or do not fulfill sufficient aesthetic conditions to belong to one or the other, or where they exist in conversation. Ultimately, to have a working definition of each aesthetic modality allows the viewer to grasp the language in which the artwork speaks, and the worldview it reflects upon and advances.

3

Vasarely, Watz, and the New Abstraction

From Op Art to Generative Art

As the technical capabilities of digital media expand, it is frequently assumed that so too will immersive and mimetically naturalistic qualities in digital graphics. The "conventions" of digital imagery have transmuted from the highly pixilated, discrete bitmapped graphics emblematized by Super Mario Brothers and jodi into a smooth, perspectival illusionism that meets or even exceeds the resolution threshold of the human eye. This trend toward illusionism has resulted in a tendency to obscure the architectonic properties of digital images, which begin life as a series of illuminated pixels, or as mathematical descriptions of one of a few basic shapes—circles, squares, and lines. But as the frenzy for digital naturalism licenses the concealment of the undergirdings of digital figures, a competing form of code-based, generative abstraction has emerged to succeed the proto-computational formalisms of artists such as Victor Vasarely and Sol LeWitt. This chapter will take works by two artists as its primary case studies. First, I will show how Victor Vasarely's experimentation with a procedural visual language closely approximates computational programming. Vasarely's own writings—his treatises and manifestos—reframe his contribution to the artistic canon, and Op Art specifically. Vasarely's approach to pictorial construction not only creates novel optical-kinetic experiences through carefully engineered, abstract visual stimuli but also configures a proto-digital visual language that circulates within and expands a burgeoning digital epistemological horizon.

Second, Norwegian Generative Artist Marius Watz's 2005 homage to Victor Vasarely, entitled *ElectroPlastique #1*, translates Vasarely's algorithmic visual language into computational generative code. Well in advance of bitmapping technology, Vasarely infused his works with a distinct computational "look" by conceptualizing the image as a field of discrete values arranged and conditioned upon their relational position within an optically activating matrix. Ultimately, Vasarely's method predicts the possibilities and limitations of encoded computational plasticity. The second part of the chapter considers the effects of adding generative, temporal computation to the static digital schemas of Vasarely's paintings. Here, Vasarely's "digital," procedural aesthetic is computationally encoded in *ElectroPlastique*. Watz's cinematic narrative of the birth, development, and eventual fragmentation of a digital landscape appropriates and intensifies the model of digital visuality announced by his predecessor. Vasarely has in this instance been taken up in the context of contemporary digital practice. His theory of abstraction can be applied to digital abstract formalism, a trend in digital art that is often marginalized, due in part to its basis in design and its concomitant affirmation of visual pleasure, and in part to the lack of a sufficiently theorized aesthetic and theoretical position from which to view it.

Vasarely, who reportedly never touched a computer in his life, produced images that bear a morphological resemblance to computer art because his creative process set into motion an exploration of the possibilities generated and limitations imposed by the application of procedural logic (what might be known now as the logic of programming) to image-making. Although they are not themselves produced with the technological aid of a computer, Vasarely's optical paintings rehearse presciently the graphical indexes of computation that become common in the early years of computer art, for example, in the films of Stan Van Der Beek, Larry Cuba, and John Whitney in the sixties and seventies.[1] But these graphics do more than merely metaphorize computation; Vasarely articulates a theory of plasticity distinct from the "already known" in its imagination of matter, form, and structure in digital terms. "As I work, I reduce all the data of my creations to invariables, so that I might retrieve identical values at the moment of re-creation."[2] For Vasarely, expressing the possible relationships between discrete elements or units unlocks the possibility of seeing through new eyes the architectonic configuration of world, universe, and even the principles guiding modern social organization. Vasarely's obsession with a cybernetics-influenced pancomputationalism manifests in his formulation of a series of notational schemata, including a decimal-based scale of color-form permutation and several instantiations of a plastic alphabet.[3] This alphabet notates discrete, articulate, and interchangeable elements out of which, often through algorithmic processes, an image or a visual field is constructed.

Although it is not electronically computational, Vasarely's experimentation with the basic units of form facilitates an understanding of why digital images look the way they do. By exposing the architectonic construction of modular forms that both reference grid structures and go beyond the static limitations of the grid, his work reveals the steps of digital construction. It shows how digital graphic output—the characteristics of the image made visible on a screen, on a continuum from mimetic lifelikeness to geometric abstraction—will vary dramatically as the image moves through various levels of processing, from raster and bitmapped graphics all the way to three-dimensional modeling. Vasarely envisioned his art as a program that, due to its notational characteristics, could be universally "computed" by both uninitiated viewers and future artists who would choose to adapt his algorithms. Those who learned the grammar of Vasarely's alphabet could use it either to produce their own works or to generate a new instance of an existing work. These new instances would be, in theory, not mere reproductions or copies of Vasarely's paintings but, as in the case of Sol LeWitt's wall drawings, an altogether new plastic manifestation of an idea. Because Vasarely's alphabet provides for permutations and reordering of constitutive elements, future iterations of his alphabet could precipitate sometimes minute, sometimes macroscopic changes to his originary frameworks and motivating concepts. In this sense, then, Vasarely builds into his practice at the outset the possibility of appropriation and refiguration, which we see performed explicitly in Watz's *ElectroPlastique*.

Vasarely's images make visible the differences between digital formatting and analog production. Pictures, as opposed to diagrams or other symbol systems, thrive on indeterminacy and ambiguity, as we see in Goodman's example of the EKG versus Katsushika Hokusai's painting of Mt. Fuji. But Vasarely's painting practice offers a model of depiction that looks computational without using computers; his paintings look like not "pictures," per se, but abstract permutations of units and modules that nevertheless posit themselves as depictive, if of an alternate and non-normative conception of matter and space. Watz's appropriation or "remix" of Vasarely's aesthetic expands upon and affirms Vasarely's vision of a digital universe through the introduction of computational processing and generative code. In one sense, it would be easy to see *ElectroPlastique* as a translation of Vasarely's analog system into digital code, and thus as a digitization of an analog work. Watz does enact a remediation or a translation between media, but his work treats Vasarely's world as an already existent and fully developed digital system, the experience of which might be both notionally and perceptually shifted by the appropriation of Vasarely's aesthetic into a computationally coded medium. Conceptualizing *ElectroPlastique* as a translation requires a determination of what "languages," or what aspects of each artist's respective visual world, are not only translated successfully but also available or more susceptible to translation at the outset.

Both Watz and Vasarely mobilize elemental modular structures in their art.

What makes them particularly exemplary of a digital ethos, however, is their treatment of these structures as part of an algorithmic, encoded system. The dialog imaginatively enacted between Vasarely and Watz—the former employing analog tools to explore the still-gestating notion of digital systems, the latter pushing digital visual language further into the domain of self-generating computational abstraction—reveals the conceptual and visual qualities of digital materiality and initiates the question of what might be learned by bringing the underlying structural principles of digital images back to a visible surface. Vasarely, and Watz after him, attempt to reveal the basic structural components of the natural/material world, envisioned through the lens of digitality. Each artist explores the conditions of possibility for a new, digital abstraction to arise and examines what this digital abstraction might communicate about the world. In what follows, I peel back the structural and historical layers from Watz's computational generative abstraction to Vasarely's vision of a plastic alphabet in order to assess whether the construction of digital abstract landscapes discloses the structural components of a digital epistemology. Ultimately, the novelty of Generative Art extends Vasarely's artistic successes and failures, first in its affirmation of the aesthetic and social possibilities latent in the notion of a programmable visual language, and second, in its obfuscation of that possibility by way of its simultaneously hedonistic and hermetic, aggressively superficial opticality.

Digitality and Proto-Computationalism in Op Art

Known as the father of Op Art, Vasarely formulated over the course of his artistic career, beginning in 1929 and continuing until his death in 1997, an optical aesthetic deeply influenced by scientific and technological innovations of the twentieth century. Trained in early adulthood as a scientist, Vasarely dropped out of medical school in Budapest to pursue a career in fine art and graphic design but continued to investigate the natural and physical sciences as well as cybernetics and technology. His ongoing amateur fascination with scientific development paralleled his effort in his professional career to achieve an artistic realization of the structural principles of materiality itself. His artistic aims were driven in part by his aspiration to understand relativity and quantum mechanics. Through his reading of Albert Einstein, Niels Bohr, Werner Heisenberg, and Norbert Wiener, he determined that it could be possible to make "scientific models [which are complex, abstract, and not necessarily given visual form] visually comprehensible" by offering these models "plastic equivalents."[4]

In 1965, the Museum of Modern Art in New York mounted an exhibition entitled *The Responsive Eye* under the curatorial expertise of William Seitz. This exhibition, initially masterminded as a grand tour of the great optical experiments in art from Impressionism forward, was ultimately narrowed in scope to showcase only contemporary art, and a very particular version of contemporary art at that. *The Responsive Eye* gathered together examples of the profusion of painterly and sculptural work focusing on "perceptual effects" that exploded onto the art scene in the 1960s.[5] Artists featured in the exhibition included Guido Molinari, Frank Stella, Larry Bell, Agam, and of course Vasarely, among many others. Seitz's historical vision became a window onto the artistic projects in the early 1960s about the relationship among technology, abstraction, and depiction. With this exhibition, Op Art rushed with tidal wave force into the art scene and then just as quickly receded.

Art has always been about perceptual effects, among other things; such an observation on its own comes as no surprise. However, the particular form of perceptual abstraction—one that activated a vertiginous sense of the physiological nature of vision[6]—that proliferated in the mid-twentieth century gave pride of place to stricter, more simplified and schematic modes of discrete inscription than even the relatively systematized methods governing neo-Impressionism discussed in chapter 2. The regularized, hard-edged illusionism of Op Art, similar to the art made with early computer graphics, lacks the "look" of fine art —the ambiguity and density, or even the negation of these qualities, visible in the aggressively purified, pared down abstraction embraced within purist avant-garde movements such as Suprematism. Op Art seems, in its subjection of the viewer to a new *trompe l'oeil*—this time not a mimetic illusion but a dizzying, physiological trick—to fall to the wrong side of the distinction between low and high art, the popular and the refined. It lacks the immediately legible indices of political, economic, and social critique that belongs to the most vigorously applauded art of the twenty-first century. As such, designated as an (implicitly distasteful) "optical" or "retinal" stylistic flash in the pan, Op Art's reputation has been mostly relegated to a niche market of tricky, gimmicky, poster art.[7]

Seitz's articulation of the interpretive dimension of Op Art deviates from the point of view taken here in its privileging of innate visual response[8] and in its concentration on the physiological impact—the "perceptual effects" that occur in the "incompletely explored region area [*sic*] between the cornea and the brain"[9]—of Op Art's depictive strategies and visual characteristics. Instead of solely attributing success or failure to Op Art on the basis of its ability to stimulate neural responses, it should be viewed instead as embedded within and experimenting with a burgeoning computational/informatic epistemology. An evaluation of Op Art that focuses primarily on its manipulation of the connective pathways between opticality/retinality and the physiological sense of disorientation is certainly valid but deviates from the reasons for addressing it here. Op Art's mode of illusionism does generate bodily and perceptual experiences of vertigo or kinesis. However, it also illustrates the intersection between an emerging computational worldview, Vasarely's own response to and innovations within this worldview, and the digitality that emerges in his depictive strategies and the resulting pictorial field.

While Op Art has been typically framed in terms of its capacity for kinetic or three-dimensional illusionism, Vasarely's artistic, theoretical, and social pursuits were only partially about vision itself and were in fact equally invested in the possibilities for a populist visual language manifested in the creation of computable structures. As we will see, a digital aesthetic is engendered by his implementation of a plastic alphabet, and alphabets can be used as a common tool to enable and to structure communication between human beings. Whereas one approach to thinking about Op Art focuses on optics as a dimension of human biology, physiology, and perception (and is thus not about the human in a humanistic sense), Vasarely's research program gives visual and textual form to an inhuman system (computation) in order to meditate on the limits of human communication, as well as on the conditions under which communication can be performed and replicated successfully. Moreover, he uses computation to consider how communicative innovations—scientific, artistic, and social—occur and to identify the conditions that provoke epistemological change.

In spite of the summary dismissal of Op Art in America, even after the Museum of Modern Art's (MOMA) *Responsive Eye* exhibition (countered by the success of a few exceptions such as Bridget Riley), some limited attempts to recuperate Vasarely's reputation and his grand artistic vision were launched in the later twentieth century. Although these efforts have not resulted in a wide-ranging valorization of Op Art, in general, or Vasarely, in particular, what is perhaps most notable about the commentary surrounding his work is the marked morphological similarity of Vasarely's imagery to early computer graphics. The question is whether or not there is anything at stake in making this formal comparison. I contend that Vasarely produced pictorial constructions that resemble computer art because his creative process set into motion an exploration of the possibilities generated and limitations imposed by the application of procedural logic to depiction. Despite the fact that they are not themselves produced with the technological aid of a computer, Vasarely's graphics rehearse the graphical indexes of computation that become common in the 1980s: blocky, Manhattan-skyline pixilation and simplified outlines of basic geometrical forms. They enact a digitally conceived creative process but lack the step into full-fledged electronic computation.[10] As such, Vasarely's paintings engage the distinction between computation, or a computational aesthetic, and digitality, or a digital aesthetic, which I have been tracing here.

In 1959, Vasarely linked art and the applied technical sciences, pointing to the fact that as scientists are building electronic chess-playing "brains," artists are also engaging with the possibility of a new model of visuality governed by binary code. Vasarely writes, "For quite a long time now, one branch of the plastic arts has been working on plastic language that can be encoded as a binary system."[11] Although his disposition toward technology is sometimes ambivalent,[12] Vasarely's insight about the preoccupations brought about by the electronic age is prescient and far ranging. Alongside artistic attempts to produce an encodable, binary, electronically storable plastic language comes a frenzy for totality, for the accelerated production of an exhaustive archive of all plastic possibilities discoverable within the breakneck computations of the electronic brain. "There are groups of young artists among whom everything happens as if they were feverishly taking inventory of all of plasticity's possibilities. This is a matter for an electronic brain, for a future plastic bank."[13]

What is notable here is not only that Vasarely envisions a stored-memory archive but also that he begins to see the profoundly inhuman quality of electronic processing and the explosion of human scale in the vastness of the electronic archive. Electronic computation is devised as a tool to aid in the constitution of new, human knowledge systems. At the most basic level it is a human construct, despite deterministic computationalist claims that such descriptions do not merely simulate nature but actually replicate and execute the laws of nature, as in the case of complexity theory.[14] However, automated computational technologies are designed to carry out calculations, find patterns, organize data, and store information at a rate and in a volume impossible to match by the human mind. The fear that computers will acquire the capability to exceed human intelligence is articulated in popular cultural artifacts such as James Cameron's *Terminator* Series (1984, 2001, in addition to two other films released in 2009 and 2015, directed by McG and Alan Taylor, respectively) and the Wachowski Brothers' *Matrix* (1999). According to the computationalist model of consciousness, if the brain is a biological computer ("wetware" to the "hardware" and "software" of the machines we call, nonspecifically, computers),[15] operating systems and hard drives become most terrifying when they surpass their function as tools—as stand-ins that ostensibly permit humans to engage themselves with higher-level problems than basic calculations by taking over menial, number-crunching tasks. They threaten not our physical strength, as in the case of industrial machines, but the aspect of humans that in the great literary and philosophical traditions has set them apart from other animals—the capacity for intellection and consciousness.[16]

The frenzy to compute and store multiple possibilities is related to the desire for total knowledge, but this also leads toward what might seem to be a fantastical or counterfactual image of an infinite pool of information whose enormity precludes the possibility of parsing or sorting. This "ideal" of a total knowledge bank in actuality presents an incalculable informatic sublime, in which the very quantity of data renders its territory too great to be conceived as a mapable, navigable world. As Jean-François Lyotard has written, "The system . . . has the consequence of causing the forgetting of what escapes it."[17] Correlatively, the system also, through its absolute calculability by machine and its utter incalculability by the limited processing speed of the human mind, causes human forgetfulness of what is inside it as well. It is to this end that Vasarely's art is valuable to humanism: paradoxically, in its very exposure of the inhuman qualities of a machine-computable informatic universe. He reminds us of the rules by which the map of this universe is constructed, and cautions that we have come to see the map *as* the territory, so that our conception and perception of the material world is both advanced and partially occluded by an overzealous application of informatics.[18] Vasarely's abstract landscapes graphically render one possible manifestation of a cyberneticist's utopia, in which the universe and all the organic and inorganic bodies and systems within it can be explained in algorithmic, digital, or computational terms. Over the course of the twentieth and into the beginning of the twenty-first century, this descriptive model becomes naturalized as the central epistemological paradigm of the contemporary world, and as such begins to demand a new modality of interpreting the architectonics of form, or even a new definition of the beautiful. For Immanuel Kant the judgments of beauty obtain from the recognition of nature in art, but if a shift occurs in our estimation of the structure and constitutive elements of nature, in other words into a computationalist perspective, then it would stand to reason that the definition of the beautiful requires extension if not a comprehensive revision. Moreover, if that which the viewer recognizes in a work of art as a constitutive aspect of nature will likely be judged as beautiful by rational consensus, an artwork that demonstrates or participates in the transition to a cyberneticist or computationalist worldview should become the new mirror of nature, and thus the new standard for judgments of artistic beauty.[19] That is to say, if Vasarely performatively engages the new epistemological model, his work will require description and evaluation in terms of this new model, rather than one governed by a preinformatic worldview. To apply terminology to his painting that might illuminate the aesthetic characteristics and social milieu of a seventeenth-century painting would be to foreclose the former instance's aesthetic, theoretical, and cultural content and context.

Despite the highly contentious status of Kant's theory of aesthetic judgment, art connoisseurship and evaluative standards within the art world have, with respect to painting, resisted, if not computational determinism, then the effects on art theory such an epistemological shift would be expected to have. Specifically, in this case, the notion that Vasarely's painting graphically depicts a new digital/computational view of nature permits a greater range of interpretative richness and breadth of signification than has been generally accorded to his work, to cybernetic art, and to Op Art in general. His painting actualizes the vision of the creative mind at work, the kinds of structures it will build, and the fictive imagination of the world it will have. It envisions a universe constructed on computational principles that give way to a digital notion of discontinuous, constitutively discrete objects, bodies, and even knowledges.

Jasia Reichardt, the curator of the *Cybernetic Serendipity* show[20] held at the Institute for Contemporary Arts in London from 2 August to 20 October 1968, writes that "the processes involved in making computer art are best suited to those who follow an analytical approach in their work, who are concerned with permutational procedures, serial techniques or the transformations of images from one finite state to another."[21] However, while celebrating the potential in digital approaches to artistic production, she also makes the concession, still common in evaluations of computationally generated art, that artistic masterpieces in the late 1960s had yet to be realized, despite the creativity and innovation generated by cross-fertilizations among art, science, and technology.[22] Seitz acknowledges that the work presented in *The Responsive Eye* occupies a tenuous position with respect to art, aligning it more strongly with design and technical practices such as scientific diagramming.[23] Vasarely is most favorably received by artists, curators, and theorists who go to the edge of what is most broadly accepted as art, to the crossover domain of art-science, to design and computer graphics, and to esoteric mid-twentieth-century theories that are propounded in artistic manifestos of a new abstraction suffused with a cybernetic spiritual idealism.

A consequence of the rise of the information society and the ever-increasing preponderance of computationalist models (for instance, cognitive science's proposal that perception and consciousness can be reduced analytically to computable neural activity)[24] in scientific, social-scientific, and even humanistic modes of inquiry has been ostensibly the narrowing of the divide between C. P. Snow's "two cultures."[25] But in actuality the determinism often found in these models relegates alternative approaches to knowledge and the lifeworld to an ever-more marginal position, both within and outside of the academy. While for some this may represent a welcome shift toward verifiable scientism within disciplines traditionally unbounded by the tenets of scientific methodologies, this also introduces a greater urgency to questions surrounding the role of humanism, and specifically the problems open to humanism that are less accessible to deterministic models, such as the role of art in formation of social attitudes and behaviors.[26]

Vasarely's digital utopia, presented in both his writings and his visual art, might prove chilling to some viewers. However, Vasarely imagined his art as a universally accessible, populist form. He viewed his plastic alphabet as a system built to encourage artistic literacy, and the formation of social communities around art reception and art practice. But if we look *only* with eyes accustomed to interpreting painting by virtue of what is contained within the frame (a habit of looking that becomes impossible later in the twentieth century with the advent of critical practices including Conceptual Art, installation, performance, and land art), Vasarely's work remains visually compelling but interpretively hermetic. Rather, the locus of significance within his work is distributed; the frame must be dismantled, allowing his work to signify as a more open-ended process, so that the "open work"[27] encompasses not only painting, sculptural artifacts, and sometimes film but also Vasarely's theoretical, cybernetically infused narrative of a society whose eyes might be collectively opened by a digital program, a new mode of visual literacy. And in turn, this narrative is enabled by the context in which his project was conceived: Vasarely's coming of age in Budapest in the 1920s and his continuous fascination for and study of cybernetics, quantum physics, and the scientific models that promulgated a worldview characterized by dynamic systems and provided the contemporary, contingent assessment of what is most human about humans.[28]

■ Programming the *Alphabet Plastique*

Educators of modern art have undoubtedly encountered with some frequency in their teaching career the protest from students, when confronted with Mark Rothko, or Kazimir Malevich, or almost any abstract expressionist, that "a child could do it." With respect to Vasarely, we encounter a different problem—that "a computer could do it." Vasarely's work looks to the twenty-first-century viewer like a trippy screen-saver application or a retro graphics program. Similar to the now quaint outdatedness of the diegetic video game space in the film *Tron*, Vasarely's art has the look of technology about it, but more precisely, it has the look of technological obsolescence.[29] It appears digital but outdated. However, Vasarely devises a digital aesthetic, and even a digital notational schema in the

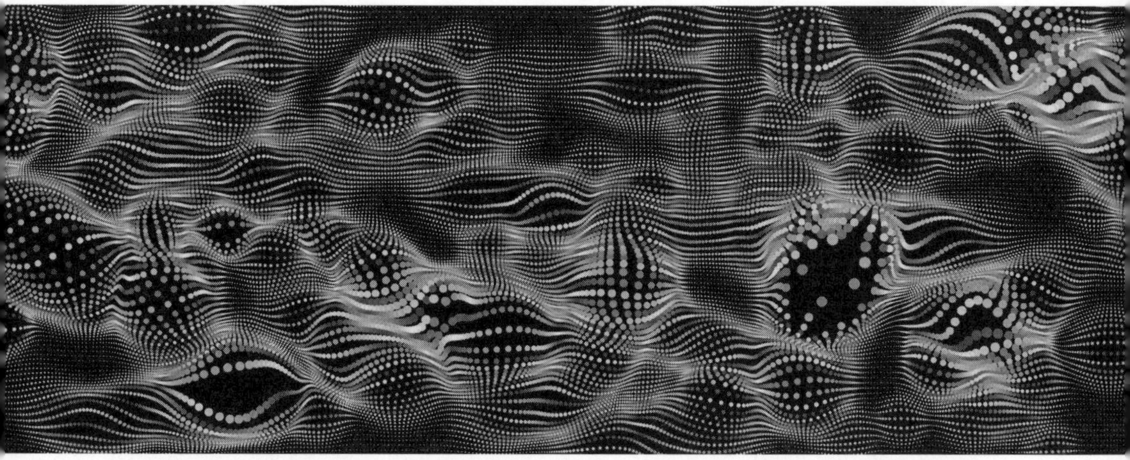

FIGURE 3.1 ▪ Marius Watz, *ElectroPlastique #1*, 2005. Generative animation, 5:00. Created with custom software developed in Processing.

form of his *Alphabet Plastique*, before personal computing was widely available to artists.

Especially when confined within the small, regular scale of printed books, which contain relatively few installation shots and thus reveal little of the variety of scales, materials, and contexts implemented in his work, Vasarely's images might appear dry, lifeless, and drained of the animated vivacity or warmth that index the empathic creativity and the capacity to infuse vibrancy and repleteness into inert materials attributed to the great masters. But such an interpretation would fail to take into account how Vasarely and, after him, Watz locate their particular brand of optical and structural beauty in the elementary stages of digital construction. Vasarely, in particular, does not utilize a pared-down (or top-down) method of abstraction but rather creates an algorithmic universe driven by individuated elements and built from the ground up, bound not to mimesis or replication of the external world but to its own exactly formulated programmatic parameters that reveal structures and patterns that would otherwise remain invisible.

According to granddaughter Michèle Vasarely, biographer and champion of her grandfather's life and artistic practice, the *Alphabet Plastique* is a theoretically functional notational system that also qualifies as digital.[30] "Vasarely acquires a singular place in the history of art as he erases the boundaries between two apparently opposite worlds, art and computer science. Following a rigorous and unrelenting path of experimentation, he arrives at the standardization of the means of creation within a small number of regular forms and color codes, a plastic alphabet, an aesthetic system of multiple combinations duly numbered and classified."[31]

The *Alphabet Plastique* brings together computing and pictorialization, and functions as a manually computed (nonautomated) visual programming language, similar to Processing, the programming language developed by Casey Reas and Ben Fry used to produce Watz's *ElectroPlastique*. The question is whether a rhetorical sleight of hand draws an artificial connection between the digital appearance of Vasarely's work and the digital processes of electronic stored-program digital computers, which render integer values as pixels on a raster grid. In both his practice and his theoretical/philosophical work, Vasarely demonstrated a consistent fascination with the notion of a systematic method of picture-making. The result bears some similarity to Paul Klee's "visual language," which bends his interest in musical notation to produce a notational "alphabet" of pictorial symbols, but Vasarely's project envisions a more finely tuned digital-programmatic system than Klee's quasi-notational schema. "The codification of these elements allows for the creation of a bank of plastic possibilities that can be stored in electronic memory. Vasarely conceives the principle of an interactive program capable of recalling millions of colored combinations that can be readily exploited as an inextinguishable source of compositions and as a reliable statistics test of aesthetic preferences."[32] For Michèle Vasarely's claim that his combinatory program is fully replicable and interchangeable to be correct, not only would Vasarely's language require the assignation of values to his modular forms but also these values would have to be regularized and specified to the extent that each symbol could stand for one character and one character only, as per Goodman's parameters for a true notational, and then digital, system. Moreover, this system would have to be available to other "programmers" as well. One aspect of Vasarely's thought that suggests the likelihood that his *Alphabet Plastique* could at least notionally fulfill this requirement is his desire to create a universally legible art form. To reach the level at which a system is truly programmable, it must be possible for that language to be both readable and writable. Legibility opens into the possibility of full literacy, wherein a notational system functions as an avenue of intersubjective communication because it is both readable and writable. To create an "art for the common man" begins in a subtle manner to integrate viewer and user. If this is truly a programming language, then it should in theory be available for future applications and reiterations.

Vasarely's own experiments with abstraction led to a collection of writings and visual art that, in a much more developed way than previous artistic forays into digital systems using analog tools, began to articulate a theory of plasticity distinct from the already known in its imagination of an understanding of matter, form, and structure in digital terms. "As I work, I reduce all the data of my creations to invariables, so that I might retrieve identical values at the moment of re-creation."[33] For Vasarely, expressing the possible relationships between discrete elements or units unlocks the possibility of seeing through new eyes the structural and architectonic principles that configure world, universe, and even social organization. His art and writing unfold from the notion that the world is fundamentally calculable, that all natural and artificial forms and all events are susceptible to calculation. There is also an assumption here that a particular system of knowledge, experience, and expression arise out of this calculability, which eventually manifests in the development of a new visuality aligned with and attributable to a digital and even numericized universe.

Vasarely's obsession with a cybernetics-influenced pancomputationalism manifests in his formulation of a series of notational schemata, including a decimal-based scale of color-form permutations and several instantiations of a "plastic alphabet." These schemata notate discrete, articulate, and interchangeable elements out of which, often through algorithmic processes, an image or a visual field is constructed. The following is Vasarely's description of the evolution of the plastic alphabet from concept to materialization.

> Once I had discovered my alphabet, I hastened to put it into material form. I selected six basic colors: a chrome yellow, an emerald green, an ultramarine, a cobalt violet, a red, and a gray. From it I obtained six scales, each with 12 or 13 nuances, ranging from light to dark, and I added colored blacks—a blue black, a red black, a green black, and so on. Then I had tens of thousands of sheets printed by the serigraphic process, and had all the units of my alphabet punched out of them. Placed in cases, like type characters, they are so many form-colors which form the surest and fastest method of realizing my programmings executed on scale paper. By simple collage I obtain exactly what I want, that is, a combination which is both formal and colored, and which I call *algorithm* or *permutation*.[34]

In his repetitive process of experimentation with digital rules for image processing, Vasarely struggled to discover the grammatical rules for a universally legible and infinitely reproducible visual language. This ambitious project, though it yielded formal results that have ghettoized Vasarely's art, helps us to understand something about first, the qualities and characteristics of contemporary computer graphics, and second, the reception of and attitude toward this type of technologically mediated imagery. In particular, the description of his process resonates with early computers in its evocation of punch-card coding, reproducibility, efficiency, discrete, interchangeable units (a necessary property of digital systems), automation, and expandable-compressible scalability.[35]

In his attempt to compile a universal language he examines the way images can be broken into grammatical units and built up in complex architectures. His is an architectonic rather than a mimetic approach, as can be seen in the development of layered spaces similar to voxels in raster-based 3-D computer modeling (which are often characterized by the stepped quality of a surface as opposed to smooth vector-based curves). In 1954, Vasarely discovered that by drawing outlines, which he called "networks," on successive, thin layers of plexiglass and then superimposing these tracings over one another, he could build "a space which no longer owned anything to Euclidean perspective, or to any other kind of perspective."[36] The process of layering enabled Vasarely to "translate real space into a plane."[37] Most importantly, this translation entailed a new disjoint, segmented, and articulate notation of individual depthless sections, which in combination would create the perception of spatiality. These two-dimensional "layers," similar to those in computer graphics, are amalgamated to produce an illusion of three-dimensionality or virtualization. However, the virtualization does not go so far as to replicate the natural world, producing instead digital landscapes whose three-dimensionality produces a world that does not correspond either to a normative mimetic visuality or to the top-down reductions of early twentieth-century avant-garde abstraction.

However, while his own form of abstraction emerges out of an elementally constructed, bottom-up method of facture, he does indeed pay homage to approaches to abstraction that do not conform to a digital schema. In response to the perhaps now prosaic observation that "to go fast is to forget fast, to retain only the information that is useful afterwards, as in 'rapid reading,'"[38] Vasarely generated his own hypothesis about how abstraction, writ large, is a condition and a consequence of the machine age.

> "The increase of speed in all sectors of our existence has necessitated a proportional enlargement of designs." This quickened pace forces us to be hurried and impatient. We are no longer given to prolonged reflection; we have lost our love for detail. Moreover, technology has left our hands unskilled and at the same time endowed us with devices—in this case, photography—that instantly provide us with detail. Our lives have become entangled and cluttered with countless tools, the appurtenances of civilized man. Instead of saving, we are losing enormous amounts of time. As a result, we try to speed up our perception; we seek out the immediate, powerful impact of the moment. This new human requirement is being met by big shapes and bold, flat colors.[39]

Vasarely appoints Malevich's square as the representative figure of this epistemology, not only of industrial acceleration, but also and most importantly of accelerated calculability. But while Malevich's abstraction does not fulfill the conditions of digitality, we still see similar aesthetic choices upheld in contemporary computational graphics. For example, in information visualization we can observe this tendency toward broad, flat, and bold color-form selection, which is an aesthetic tendency that places a premium on simplicity and almost instant legibility.[40]

From Grid to Matrix

In studies and theoretical propositions concerning moments in the history of depictive technologies from the invention of perspective to the production of 3-D computational models, the grid has often come to the forefront of discussion as an indicator of an increasingly metricized world picture. If so much has been made of the centrality of the grid, and if it has been posited as the enframing structure and the possibility condition for discrete, digital pixels to appear on the screen in computational imaging, should we then suppose that the grid is a subsidiary property of, or coextensive with, digitization? David Summers's massive study of the development of metric, "metaoptical" spatial constructions in a broad and pangeographical history of image-making tracks the rise of the particular ethos of form that has come to dominate Western theories and practices of representation. Instead of approaching the notion of form from what he calls the "pictorial imagination," or the "aesthetic-expressive definition [of art] descending principally from Immanuel Kant,"[41] Summers considers how the particular shapes of cultural artifacts—images, objects, tools, architectural constructions, and even notational devices such as maps—come into being as situated and purposeful objects with a complex relationship to their embodied human creators and their "real spatial *conditions*" and contexts.[42] Summers not only identifies emblematic features of "universal metric space of Western physics and technology" but also attempts to work out the visual, phenomenological, and social conditions that contribute to and result from the mathematical, rationalized, and metaoptical world order.[43]

Paramount to the phenomena he analyzes is the production of metric space and the coordinate plane, and the embedded, corollary properties of "homogeneity, divisibility, and infinity" that stand in contrast to the "qualitative, continuous, and unified" spaces associated with the natural, primordial world.[44] One of the primary characteristics of the transition between qualitative and quantitative systems of measurement is that while qualitative systems retain some reference to the specific qualities of the particular, situated, and enworlded object subject to measurement, purely quantitative systems are notional, abstract, and separable from the format (the size, shape, volume, and texture of the surface of inscription) on which an image is presented. A logical extension of the shift from qualitative, relational systems, such as proportion and surface, to the abstract units of measure found in quantitative, notional systems such as ration and planarity, the true grid is independent of format. That is, in Summers's analysis it is not derived from the *division* of an existing surface into halves, quarters, and so on. Instead, it preexists the format, so that it is not merely a veil of lines laid over an already existent object. Moreover, the grid provides an infrastructure, and thus the possibility of conditions for, and the mechanism that facilitates and guides, the construction of a picture. The grid is an abstract measuring system that defines the relationships between objects in any image construction, pictorial or notational. The same grid can be used to generate multiple "pictures," each of which will be generated within the quantitative parameters of a metric system.

Metric units undergird and comprise the overall structure of an arbitrarily bounded gridded sector. As such, they preexist and function independently of the configurative particularities of any given image. Like ratio, which selects its units of measure by isolating and excising one recognizable feature already present in the image or object to be depicted, a gridlike structure can appear through the division of the format into regular units. However, a "true grid" is independent of both the format and the image. In other words, a grid is formed not from the repeated division of a preexisting format into smaller and smaller components but rather from the notional and additive *extension* of a metric plane or cube infinitely into space. When subjected to the logic of the grid, space itself becomes a metricized expanse that exists independently of objects that occupy it. The metaoptical cube allows any point in space to be plotted or mapped in relation to any other point. Thus, qualitative features are subsumed under the metric, quantitative structure of the grid, and no longer function to define "place" as a qualitative realm imbued with meaning through the operations of memory and symbolic communication.[45] This additive metric system may seem familiar. It can be conceived, in fact, as a digital system. If the grid were based on top-down division rather than bottom-up unitary composition, it could not fulfill the necessary and sufficient conditions for digitality. But armed with the analytic description offered here, it becomes one thread in the discursive fabric of digitality and digital systems.

Vasarely's digital world develops out of, and then moves beyond, experiments with the grid. The grid is a figure endemic to modernist art history and theory that often overlaps with a digital worldview, but its historical ontology identifies it as a subset or a token of the overall type characterized by digital systems, which can take on numerous theoretical, formal, and perceptual physiognomies. Criticism of modernist art has frequently engaged the grid, often concluding that it figures the reductive ideologies of science and capitalism. Visually, Vasarely's oeuvre unfolds as a parade of checkerboard abstractions regulated by the logic of the grid. As his career progressed, Vasarely's style of painting moved toward a rigorous exploration of anamorphic visual properties that could be exposed by exploiting the grid, despite its ostensible function as an apparatus of totalization and as a metonymic link to a grammar of highly discrete, modular and segmented plastic units.

Although Vasarely is remembered primarily as a painter (though a painter who suppresses the markers of handmadeness such as impasto and visible brushstrokes), his practice integrates architectural and sculptural elements into an illusionistic space of two-dimensional depiction. His works take on a three-dimensional solidity achieved through a skillful manipulation of optical illusion and the construction of intricate volumetric forms built from a latticework of isometrically supported "beams." The grid, always in the midst of struggling to burst out of its flattened confines into a three-dimensional matrix, is the supporting mechanism of Vasarely's abstract pictorial structures. In this way Vasarely's painting addresses the relationship between the grid—commonly understood as a tool that aids in the schematic conversion of the two-dimensional support into an illusionistic three-dimensional picture—and the matrix—a configuration related to the grid but an ostensibly more flexible, open, and indeterminate array that can be invoked to propel modernist digital schemas into more complex digital-computational operations.

In the 2006 exhibition *Grid/Matrix*, mounted at the Mildred Lane Kemper Museum in St. Louis, Sabine Eckmann and Lutz Koepnick paired works of modernist abstraction with contemporary artistic experiments using digital technologies.[46] Their curatorial selections highlight comparisons and contrast between strategies present in some instances of high modernism and the composite structure and nearly infinite malleability that comes from reducing one's referent to binary data (or at the most fundamental level, those most famous of metonyms for the digital—ones and zeros). Paintings by Piet Mondrian, Agnes Martin, Laszlo Moholy-Nagy, and Theo Van Doesburg, whose work visually engages the modernist grid, is set alongside contemporary, computationally driven installations that challenge the ostensibly static form of the grid. For example, Julius Popp's *Bit.Fall* deploys a series of valves, a water pump, and custom electronics to create a screen of falling drops of water that mimic the grid of pixels in a bitmapped screen, or even the LED "pixels" in Jim Campbell's installations. The electronics that control the valves, and thus the frequency with which drops of water are released, are connected to a computer. This computer scans web pages and selects series of words that will be "printed" in falling water droplets, illuminated by overhead lights that, as they fall, are visible to the viewer. Popp's installation transmutes the grid from a stable form into one that is radically ephemeral, so delicate that its structure will be destroyed with a single touch.

The number of works in the *Grid/Matrix* exhibition is small but places a sharp focus on the effects of digitality on pictorial structure. The worldview advanced by the collection of artworks is one in which matter is built digitally, out of discrete parts forming a fragile physical structure that threatens to decompose into an undifferentiated cloud of constituent units. The underlying argument of the exhibition is that whereas the grid mechanistically imposes order, regularity, and predictability upon the material world, the alternative format of the matrix "emancipates" the repressive regime of the grid by opening up to spatial, rather than planar, and temporal dimensions. The matrix here is conceived as an open system in contrast to the closed system of the grid. An initial definition of the concept of the matrix can be woven from several threads. Explained etymologically by Edward Casey, "Beyond its strictly anatomical sense [matrix is derived from the Latin *mater* and is used to describe the womb or ovaries] matrix means 'a place or medium in which something is bred, produced, or developed,' 'a place or point of origin or growth.'"[47] While the grid is also a generative principle not only for depictive conventions but also for the notional mathematization and mapping of space more generally, the matrix comprises a symbolic system that is less about a highly regularized configurative schema than about connectivity, metaphorized variously in terms ranging from connective tissue to numerical tables. For Eckmann, the grid is associated with analog technologies and with precomputational historical moments.[48] It connotes, in her estimation, rationality and stability, and is a product of modernity and industrialization. By contrast, the matrix emerges alongside computational technology. It is still a format that implies calculability and structuration, but it is mutable, constantly in flux. The matrix, according to Eckmann, "is unpredictable, fluid, disparate, disjunctive, ambi- and multivalent, and, importantly, frequently invisible."[49] Of course, the example of perspective painting provides evidence of the erasure of the grid despite its governing presence, and Eckmann's suggestion that it is capable of existing within "both/and" conditions contradicts the actual operations of computing devices, which, as we have seen, are switching mechanisms that function based on binary states: yes/no, on/off, and black/white. Nevertheless, it is constructive to view the grid and the matrix as tropes characterizing the sometimes-subtle shifts between the computational age and prior epistemological formations.

Thus, while her theoretical formulation is useful in the categorization of formal and social tendencies belonging to the modern and the contemporary eras, Eckmann's proposals clearly deviate from those I have set forth in previous sections of this text. I have argued that proto-digital practices coexisting with the inception of industrial practices productively inflect notional and aesthetic analyses of digital-computational practices occurring after the invention of contemporary computing devices. Industrial technology, techniques of mass production, and so forth, have certainly informed many aspects of what Eckmann deems the more fluid character of the digital age. Just as the argument can be made that facets of modernism persist within theories of postmodernism and the actualities of the present, the grid is not unilaterally superseded by the matrix or cast off with increasingly dexterous, complex technological innovations.

In other words, the grid and the matrix have a mutually constitutive relationship, in terms of both digital graphics and pictorial structure. Although the grid is a perfectly regularized system, it allows for a greater potentiality for permutation and instability than a strong claim about the totalizing, self-referential quality of grids would acknowledge.[50] And, while the matrix is defined in the broadest terms as a precondition of materiality, and etymologically as a womb, a place of creation, gestation, and genesis, it is in itself without particular form or is indeterminate in form. It is a common place out of which worlds may be birthed, but unlike a grid, with its modular, latticed divisions, the matrix is unbound by immediately recognizable structural or formal laws.[51] Consequently, it becomes difficult to describe concretely the originary underlying framework or figural characteristics of a matrix, which would in turn give digital depiction its specific graphical appearance. In colloquial, contemporary usage, the matrix is often conflated with a modular cube that extends the generalizing and predictive capacity inaugurated by the grid into three dimensions.[52] In 1999, the popular film *The Matrix* added a metaphorical dimension of temporal flux to this cube by portraying the "matrix," that is, the fictional world digitally created to entertain the minds of human bodies as they are farmed for their energy; the humans were "plugged in" but otherwise inert, kept alive by tubes and fluids in small, womblike pods.

What the *Grid/Matrix* exhibition reveals, ultimately, is a correspondence, instead of a rupture, between the grid and the digital matrix that simply extends the two-dimensional, planar grid into a three-dimensional cube. Agnes Martin's grids, rendered with tantalizing fineness in two dimensions using graphite and washes on paper, for example, are placed in dialogue with Jeffrey Shaw's early experiment with 3-D virtual reality, *the Legible City*, in which users bicycle along virtual roadways flanked by blocky, three-dimensional words that stand in for the buildings in a given city plan. The conversation between gridded and matriced formats proposed by the exhibition shows the relationship between the grid and the matrix unfolding as a pictorial strategy—and an epistemological paradigm—that was under continual negotiation in Western art from the Middle Ages forward.[53] Until the twentieth century, conventions of Western pictorialization dictated that any trace of the grid as an underlying technical support should be hidden from the viewer, leaving only an impression of seamless recession into depth. Of course this is an idealization, and paintings can offer a distinct sense of spatiality without conforming perfectly to perspectival rules.[54] But whether or not they both function as counterfactual ideals, the matrix as the support structure in which material, spatial, semantic, or numerical connections occur and the grid as the graphic configuration governing our conception and inhabitation of space facilitate the construction of a theoretical framework for digital materiality, in which digital elemental particles come together to form an image that is both regularized and also fluid and mutable.

In Vasarely's painting, the grid is not a tool that aids in the production of a mimetically virtualized universe, as in many cases of painting deploying the Cartesian perspectival grid as its underlying structural rule. Instead, the grid is itself the subject—the visible content—of his work. However, and here I agree with Eckmann, whereas in modernist painting the grid is often adamantly flat and self-referential, and submits the painting's visible world to a strict, orderly regime, as in Mondrian's black and white grids punctuated by primary color, Vasarely's grids deploy order against flatness. Rather than exploiting the flattening power of the planar grid toward a polemic refusal of depth or spatial illusionism, Vasarely's compositions swell and distort their modular array. They turn the structural regularity of the grid against itself and produce a visual and kinetic sense of form struggling beneath its configurative parameters, thus invoking the specter of the matrix in conjunction with the grid.

Part of Vasarely's oeuvre is dedicated to exploring the possibilities inherent in the grid of creating an overall unified metric system regulative of the depictive space of his paintings. He explores the capacity of the grid to build a world out of interchangeable elements that when brought together in the common fabric of a given painting create simultaneously a sense of regularized space and also reveal how distortions become more evident as disturbances in the system. Such disturbances are highlighted precisely by the fact that, as per Gilles Deleuze, differences are exposed in the process of repetition; deviations are more visible if there is a standardized system against which they can be mea-

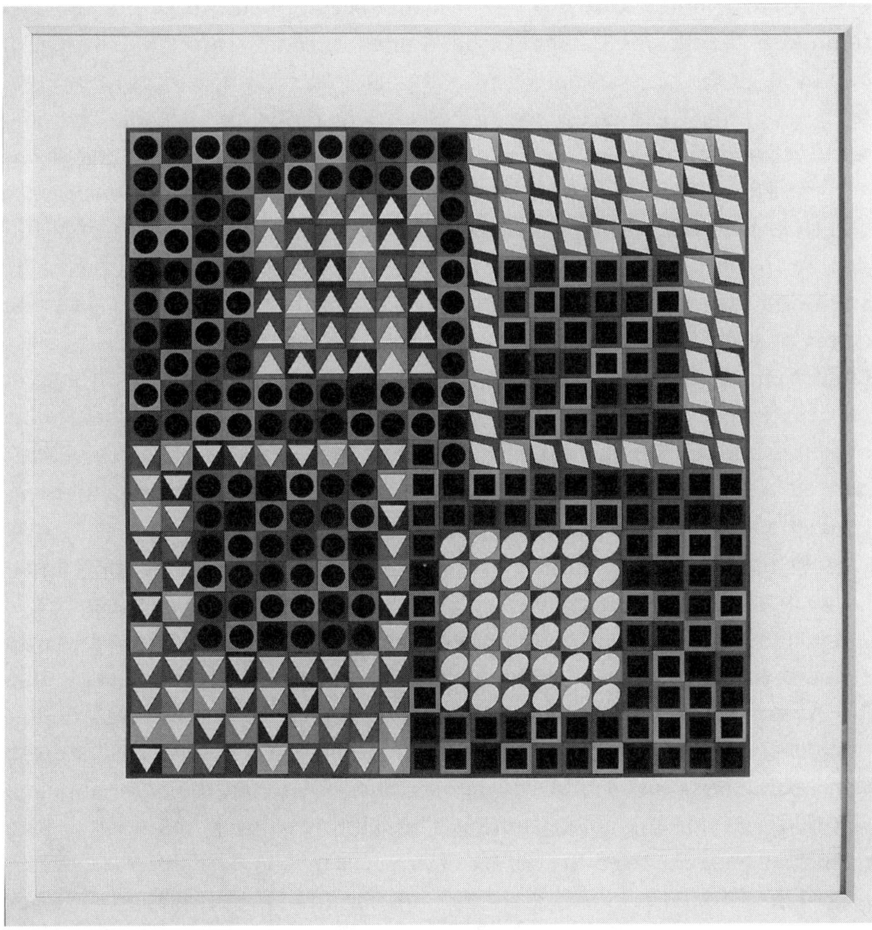

FIGURE 3.2 ▪ Victory Vasarely, *Alphabet Plastique—Our-MC*, 1965. Serigraph. © 2016 Artists Rights Society (ARS), New York / ADAGP, Paris.

sured. If one imagines the grid as a delicate web generating a terrain (marked with topographical features), the web, composed of perfectly regular squares if viewed as a plane from a direct, frontal perspective, will lose its appearance of regularity as underlying shapes appear to stretch and compress its otherwise perfect flatness. In Vasarely's 1935 painting *Harlequin*, he has begun to explore how distortions manifest when a grid is subjected to the pressure of forms swelling beneath it. The regularized grid of floor tiles ubiquitous in perspective paintings transforms into drapery and becomes subject to quite a different set of laws than in traditional three-dimensional representation ruled by laws of recession. The units in this painting do not lead the eye back to a notional horizon or vanishing point but now supply a planar surface that can be manipulated to produce the illusion of a humanoid figure protruding through it. The grid, and its ability to act as a mobile, twisting material surface, is thus the subject of the painting. The figure of the Harlequin is instantly recognizable, seeming to stretch and distend the black and white grid as it pushes through the planar surface. The transmogrification of the grid facilitate the perceptible emergence of distinct volumetric forms without the use of outline to define shape and without the application of shading or modeling to produce the effect of the figure swelling away from the picture plane. In other words, the grid subjected to the forces of stretching and compression supplies the sufficient conditions for a figure to become apprehensible, rejecting outline and modulation as strategies for defining the limits of a form. The possibilities for the shape and gesturality of figure are regulated by the gridded picture plane, but Vasarely exploits the morphologically dynamic properties of the grid to cancel out flatness and stasis (two terms often mobilized in critiques of the modernist grid).

Both *Harlequin* and a simpler 1937 drawing, *Martian*, reveal Vasarely's preoccupation with the morphogenetic qualities of the grid-turned-matrix, a fascination that will eventually be replaced by a series of experiments with encoded color-form permutations in his *Alphabet Plastique* and planetary folklore paintings. In *Planetary Folklore, Number 3* of 1964, Vasarely works through a number of such color-form permutations in order to lay out one possible set of visual parameters that would evidence a new aesthetic sensibility for a digital, algorithmically programmed painting. The painting is structured along a strict, rectilinear grid. However, the eye is drawn not as much to the structural principles of the grid itself, as in the case of *Harlequin* and *Martian*, than to the black to grey gradations delimiting a different value for each square and the array of colored shapes, ranging from ovoid to circular and small and to large, painted in widely varying, often clashing hues, interspersed between the squares. This painting has a mathematical look to it—it is immediately apparent that, even if the system cannot be readily detected, the composition follows a set of rules. Its aesthetic is digital, coded, and ordered within a grid but is not fundamentally *about* the grid in the manner of his earlier explorations. *Planetary Folklore* instead institutes a visual system based on discrete elements, and as such represents the development in Vasarely's method from a reliance on the grid as the unifying system underlying depiction to a novel invention of a syntactically and semantically discrete, digital configurative system. This system advances the digitality present in Georges Seurat's painting, by introducing a conceptual practice whose aesthetic digitality is matched by not only a programmatic but also a mathematical and indeed proto-computational systematicity. This in-

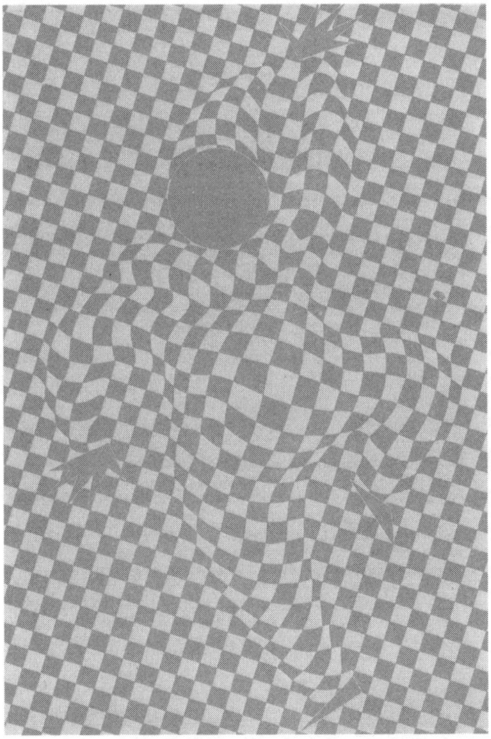

FIGURE 3.3 ▪ Victor Vasarely, *Harlequin*, 1935. Gouache. 60 x 40 cm (23⅝ x 15¾ in) © 2016 Artists Rights Society (ARS), New York / ADAGP, Paris.

vention of a digital, programmatic, and algorithmic method pushes Vasarely's practice closer to the electronic-computational image-making technologies of the twentieth century, but rather than using his technique as a means toward a mimetic end he chooses to resist virtualization and to foreground the digital elements that reveal the graphical composition as a notational schema rather than a depiction, normatively conceived.

Vasarely's paintings such as *Harlequin* and *Martian* break through the barrier of the grid and into the zone of the matrix. The overall structure of the grid in these pieces, insofar as it can be viewed in terms of both interchangeable units and an integrated fabric, does not fully develop the disjointness and articulation that we see in the seriated experimentations of his planetary folklore or *Alphabet Plastique*. While both approaches reflect upon the relationship between part and whole, and between elemental units and modulation, over a spatial expanse, the latter example more fully executes the operations necessary to define a system as interchangeably discrete and, by extension, digital. In his later visual systems—the *Alphabet Plastique* and planetary folklore—whose conceptualization begins to emerge in the late 1950s and comes to fruition in 1963 with the exhibition

The Plastic Unit at the Musée des Art Décoratifs in Paris, his digital worldview evolves into what might be identified as a programming language. Conceived as an alphabet of basic elements or building blocks, possessing their own structural limitations that in turn govern the array of possible outcome for the image, Vasarely's systems, both the "planetary folklore" and the *Alphabet Plastique*, were the product of a career-long goal to compose a formal language of pure, irreducible units of shape and color upon whose principles would develop a universally legible (because it is based on an algorithmic notation system) and infinitely permutable visual program.

■ The New Abstraction

In 1954, Victor Vasarely summed up the current state of abstract art and pointed to the future of abstraction with his statement that "the term abstract in painting refers not to an established fact, but to an irresistible trend toward plastic creation different from the kind we already know."[55] Around this time high modernism was reaching its apogee of medium-specificity, hermetic self-referentiality, and worst of all, threatened the etiolation and utter banalization of some of its most revolutionary discoveries, inciting denunciations of high modernist artifacts, which seemed to provide nothing more than a "visual muzak" resulting in bland decorativeness.[56] While visionary at its outset, Clement Greenberg's pronouncements about the ideal function of painting had initiated a monolithic form of abstraction, abrogating the possibility that abstraction might act outside a closed circuit of flatness and pure opticality. In the above quotation, Vasarely advocates a new trend in plastic creation—a new method of imagination and construction, and even a new model of semiosis—distinct from what we know, that is, the existing norms that had relegated avant-garde abstraction into a diminished conventionality. Vasarely's technics would encompass new technologies but also new ideas about what abstraction is good for: how and what it is capable of communicating and that Greenberg's pure opticality covers over or forecloses. What we are looking at, here in Vasarely's modular plastic landscape, is a new kind of abstraction. But this new abstraction is not Abstract Expressionism, with its overtones of spirituality, totemism, and the externalization of an interior emotional life buried deep by the machinic pressures of modern life. The new abstraction repeats neither the spiritualist purisms of Kazimir Malevich and the Suprematists, and Wassily Kandinsky and the Blaue Reiter, nor Jackson Pollock's secrets of the deep. Thus the new abstraction is not "pure" at all but rather about technics, that is, about the kinds of intuitive, yet quantifiable, discoveries provoked and made possible by the particularities of the technical means and mechanisms developed in the twentieth century and beyond.

The properties and combinatory possibilities latent in the programmatic, discrete model of color-form developed by Vasarely in the mid-1950s find coherence under the rubric of the new abstraction described above. Vasarely proposes a new basis on which to evaluate abstract art, one that works against a false assumption that previous models of abstraction were stable and monolithic. Whether the abstract is formulated as a pathway to the unconscious, a conduit for pure expression, or a purifying dissociation of structure and figuration (a way to show that the communication of meaning is independent of figuration), abstraction is often conceived as a means of uncovering, laying bare, or revealing something fundamental about nature, human expression, or experience by removing the false trappings of illusionistic imitation. The new evaluative framework proposed by Vasarely's art and writing pushes beyond a high modernist theory of abstract painting, which fails to account for the specific relationship between abstract form and the computationalist worldview that begins to gain momentum in the mid-twentieth century.

Vasarely's approach to digital plasticity revises the expectations about what abstraction is supposed to do; before, it accessed the unconscious, expressed emotion and played with color, the pure qualities of medium. Now art is not about the painterly medium at all, and not about expression, but about ecological and informational systems, which reengineers understanding about the constitutive features of humanity and life in general. The supremacy of inhuman systems and technologies is cemented by the substitution of a phenomenologically direct experiential model—the lifeworld—for the new cybernetically influenced picture of a fully informatic universe, in which the human is no more central in a universe shot through by information than was the earth after the heliocentric revolution. If the stuff of the world is all reducible to informatic patterns, humans are no different than any other living organism that is also animated by informatic impulses. And, moreover, what is more inhuman than fully automated computation, carried out at greater speeds and stored in vastly larger quantities than is possible in the human mind? If there is a fascination here with the relationship between computation and life, it is not primarily human life that is to be explored and understood but rather an all-encompassing knowledge of the systematic principles underlying form and matter that Vasarely hopes to achieve. His visual programming languages, in other words, are composed not simply of the goal of arranging pleasing combinations but also with the intention to explore the physical structure of organic life as well as its animating energies. This is less a style than a series of conceptual propositions that also lead into a clear formulation of the larger significance of digital aesthetics. Likewise, the relationship that will be developed between Vasarely and Marius

Watz should be envisioned not in terms of perfect stylistic continuity but rather in terms of programmatic iteration and execution: iteration, first, of the socially distributed digital method heralded by Vasarely as a democratized language of form, and second, of potential developments of new linguistic turns that occur when Vasarely's rubric is applied in a digital-computational system.

To flesh out his idea that abstraction is a "trend"—a way of thinking and seeing—that moves inexorably and dynamically toward new, undiscovered, or as-yet-inarticulate figurations of the plastic/material world, Vasarely traces five phases through which he predicts abstraction will pass if it is permitted to fulfill its transformative potential. "(1) The plastic unit becomes unidentifiable (that is, non-representational); (2) exterior vision is transformed into interior vision (early abstract phase); (3) abandonment of the conventional workmanship of painting—touch, glazes, materials, and other elements—for pure color, pure composition; (4) abandonment of all inherited techniques—canvases, pigments, brushes—and the advent of new materials; (5) abandonment of the two-dimensional plane surface as an end in itself, thus opening up the supra-dimensions of space-movement-time."[57] These stages in a progression toward the last, still struggling to be attained, transitional fifth step are visible in the modernist trajectory beginning with Manet and reaching an ostensible apotheosis and decay with the likes of Pollock, Barnet Newman, Rothko, and finally Jules Olitski. Late nineteenth-century painting begins to collapse the perspectival illusionism of picture plane that dominated Western art from the fifteenth century onward. In so doing, artworks begin to straddle figuration and abstraction and gravitate toward an interest in locating the basic elements or minimum units by which meaning can be expressed.[58] The first phase finds solid ground and moves into the second with Paul Cézanne and Henri Matisse. Kandinsky, Malevich, and Mondrian, each in their particular location in time and space, develop third-phase, nonidentical theories of pure composition and pure color. Robert Rauschenberg, Dan Flavin, Joseph Beuys, Claes Oldenburg, and Joseph Kosuth all represent the abandonment of traditional materials that heralds growing inapplicability of the title "painter." While Vasarely imagined his phases as subject to continuous revisitation and reworking, many of the most notable instances in the latter phase (that including Rauschenberg et al.) occurred later chronologically than Vasarely's initial conceptualization of these phases, indicating a rather visionary ability to analyze developmental trends in visual art. Stopping short of claiming Vasarely's status as a techno-aesthetic prophet, it is important to note that he views his own work as a progressive marker and catalyst for future innovation but not the pinnacle of abstraction; in fact, his primary aim is to establish the latent potential in abstraction for ongoing experimentation in order to counteract rather morbid predictions about high abstraction signaling the end of art.

Thus, in rethinking the function of abstraction, Vasarely develops a mode of art practice (primarily but not solely issued through the medium of painting) that is not merely a style but presents a new conceptualization of the possibilities inherent in using digital units to rethink the underlying structure of the material and ideational universe. His creation of a new abstract language not only metaphorizes but also imparts aesthetic (apprehensible) tangibility to a radically reconfigured notion of worldly architectonics. At a purely stylistic level, Vasarely's painting, and Watz's generative computational art after him, might both fall into a loose category of geometric, as opposed to expressive or lyrical, abstraction. But geometric simplicity does not capture the complex theoretical propositions contained within Vasarely's paintings. If the question arises, of why he must work within the framework of abstraction, the answer brings us back to the imperative to discover not the outlines of particular shapes or bodies but rather the building blocks of a digital epistemology and a method of image production that can be iterated and reiterated by any artists who choose to adopt his algorithmic programming language.

For Vasarely, mimetic particularity and figuration (traditional visuality) will ultimately yield to a new model of abstract essentialism. In other words, figuration lends itself to particularity, while abstraction lends itself to the presentation of essences. To make an initial generalization, the new abstraction revises principles of materiality and its representation. It is about not just compositional strategy for pictorialization but a more general consideration of the composition of structure itself prior to and after the fact of picturing. However, whereas the essentialism of the expressionists was primarily emotional and spiritual, Vasarely's vision of the abstract-essential is conceptual and technological. "Whereas the Art of yesterday strived to *feel* and *make*, today it has the capacity to *conceive* and *cause to be made*. If the conservation of the work previously resided in the excellence of materials, their technical perfection, and the mastery of the hand, today it lies in an awareness of the possibility of *re-creation*, *multiplication*, and *expansion*."[59] Yesterday's art, extending backward well beyond the threshold of abstraction, was an art of feeling. Artistic genius could be measured by how successfully an artist combined technical skill with a delicacy and quickness of feeling to produce an overall sense of emotional and technical dexterity in his craft. When painting moves into an abstract modality, the logical extension of this art of feeling would become an expressive abstraction, in which painting now conveys a purified and essential emotional charge without remaining beholden to figuration. Moreover, if art in the past was a transmission of genius, it also represented an originary moment of creation, of *techne* in the Platonic sense of making, and making as a direct conduit of presence and expression from artist to viewer.

Vasarely's causal construction is much more in line with the evolutionary algorithms set into motion by computational Generative Art. *To cause to make* is to build a machine that will carry out the act of making; to cause to make is to start a process that will continue to change and to build on itself even with the removal from the picture of the artist's hand. The mark is no longer a conductor of genius but one switch in a living, dynamically changing circuit. Thus, technique and form become part of an aesthetics that is eminently social and emphatically political. "Technique has evolved from manual to industrial; language, from personal to universal; morality, from egocentric to communal."[60] In addition to building the technical device of a digital, algorithmic visual language, Vasarely dreams of an art that utilizes his new aesthetic parameters toward social and communal ends. Technology exists to make art universally practicable and universally accessible, a sentiment echoed in pronouncements about the democratizing potential of digital art, which can be rendered *ad infinitum* and distributed widely, unlike the unique, auratic object.

In the same breath, Vasarely is both suspicious of and celebratory about technology: "Only works endowed with great informative strength shall victoriously withstand depreciation cause by mechanical transposition."[61] He is championing not merely mechanical reproduction but also the inauguration of an art of "*re-creation, multiplication*, and *expansion*."[62] He envisions not a machine that transposes the art of yesterday into a cheap, easily disseminated form of today but rather the machine that at the outset produces a new communicative modality. This novel model announces a digital worldview that is intended not to remain hermetic or closed within the imaginative realm of the artist but to circulate and multiply, to expand through the execution of new algorithms and the evolution of coded machine-language systems that can be exchanged, appropriated, read, and rewritten. Originality and uniqueness are no longer to be sealed and safeguarded but to be made available to diffusion, translation, and mutation. Recall that a defining characteristic of digital systems is the identicality and interchangeability of units. The moment of re-creation is not reproduction, in a mechanical sense, but a new instance of a self-similar element. Whether or not he is able to create actual interchangeability or to determine a truly invariable metricized system for nonmetric values, such as color, the very fact that Vasarely theorizes this translation of nondigital values into a digital schema indicates his desire to discover the poetic and structural potentialities within a digital system.

Vasarely's images engender a palpable tension between the conceptual and the visual. His clear examination of the relationship between the notion of structure, individual structural components, and the properties of a digital universe are deeply conceptual and heavily invested in the question about a contemporary worldview, upon which scientific and technological innovations exert a profound influence. The peculiar way in which Vasarely blends concepts, materials, and visuality has afforded a rather fecund comparison between his own practice and Art Concret, a mechanical, exact, and anti-impressionistic artistic movement that rejected association with practices of abstraction insofar as abstraction refers to, simplifies, or deconstructs a preexisting world, remaining in this sense mimetic and reductive. In other words, Art Concret does not re-present a material reality but constructs visualizations of abstract thought. A term coined by Theo Van Doesburg in 1930, *l'art concret* is intended to characterize a nonfigurative approach to art distinct from abstract art in its commitment to unify materiality and intellection. Unlike Conceptual Art, which, ostensibly, discards the image or places it in a secondary position to the primacy of the "idea," Art Concret resists an ontological separation between idea and image, and suggests that the image uses pictorial mechanisms, such as color line and shape, not to dissimulate the external world but to render direct visualizations of intellectual activity. The theory expounded by proponents and practitioners of Art Concret about the sensibility of concepts realized through visualization provides a comparative framework from which to examine Vasarely's peculiar abstract modality and ultimately argues against a false distantiation between concept and form, and ideation and visuality.

The similarity to Art Concret in Vasarely's thought issues from his exploration of the possibilities within and parameters of abstraction itself without mimetic reference to the external world. Abstraction, for both concrete artists and Vasarely, occupies a dimension separate from the physical world, a dimension that is constructivist and architectonic in its examination of basic structures but abandons figuration and direct reference to forms observed in nature. Vasarely's fabrication of an architecture of elemental replication facilitates his nomination not only as the father of Op Art but also as a progenitor of digital-computational art. Digital graphics are fundamentally constructivist in the sense that they build architectonic models from unitary, elemental units of form. As Siegfried Kracauer noted about the difference between painting and photography, painting gives meaning a spatial form, but photography tries to make meaning out of an indexically captured fragment of space.[63] Likewise, Vasarely's constructivist, concrete images search for the way that structure in-forms meaning: they attempt to uncover, by depicting structure itself, the semiotic territory, such as the topographical features, or natural and artificial borders, of form without the shackles of mimetic attachment. While Robert Morgan has described Vasarely's work as "dematerialized pictorial spaces," these paintings are eminently material insofar as they render imagistically the possibility of materializing semiosis.[64] Vasarely depicts both the infrastructure of materiality and the way that material arrangements can reveal the process underlying the composition of communicative sequences. For this reason his paintings and mosaics seem to exhibit simultaneously a conceptual retreat from familiar real-spatial conditions and a hyper-materiality similar to the uncanny density of certain digital imaging techniques.[65]

Proponents of mid-twentieth-century technological abstraction mark another instance of the emergence of an increasingly ubiquitous cultural and artistic fascination with *transformation*—of material to information, of discrete parts into overall fields and vice versa, and of continuous line and volume into aggregated pixels, beams, and electrons. In an article exposing a formative presence of abstraction in early television art, Christine Mehring cites early TV artist K. O. Götz: "The most extreme consequence of the dissolution of classical form principles in painting . . . to me appeared to be the statistically programmed electronic pixel painting."[66] Classical principles provide the beams and trusses supporting the structure of classical visuality, and by extension, aspects of classical epistemology. If the greatest consequence of the dissolution of these principles is the inception of a digital image-world, the consequences of this emergence must also necessarily come under close examination. Vasarely, like Götz, views his invention of a digital programming language for painting, which I have been calling the new abstraction, as a transformative agent in the formation of cultural knowledge systems. He includes his paintings in a complex interrelated network of discrete systems, including "strata," "crystals," "interstellar clusters," "microscopic beings," "electrons," and "suns," that in conjunction with one another comprise the universe and all the activity within it.[67] However, Vasarely does not insist that he is the prime mover or the sole initiator of this worldview and draws analogies between his "linear networks," whose formal shapes draw their influence from various sources including woven fabric, maps, and the lines and grids of modern physics, and the drawing systems of the futurists and Paul Klee. For Vasarely, there are two types of art, one based on "genetic heredity" and a current type, exemplified by Klee and the futurists, that is based on information and its transformation into visual color-form. Thus, "only world endowed with great informative strength shall victoriously withstand depreciation caused by mechanical transposition."[68]

Vasarely's writings and his images combine a populist ideology and a view of art invested in and informed by science and mathematics. His desire to create a universal language of art (manifested in his algorithmic, notational *Alphabet Plastique*) manifests aesthetically in the highly discrete, digital surfaces that characterize his art practice. After Walter Benjamin, the phenomenon of mechanical reproduction is most frequently aligned with populist image-making strategies, leaving painting behind as a medium redolent of outmoded, aristocratic, or ritualistic attachments to auratic uniqueness. Vasarely's invocation of the futurists, who attempted to change the face of painting by incorporating visual citations of mechanization and industrial technology, does speak to an interest in the look of machine-made imagery. But note that in the nineteenth century, Seurat preserved the handmadeness of painting despite his goal to create (similar to Vasarely) a regularized and systematic painterly technique. Technologies existed at this time for mechanical color printing, but notably, Seurat did not avail himself of them in his artistic practice. It was only when art practitioners sought the near-total destruction of mimetic pictorialization that a truly allographic art (i.e., one that replaced the artist's signature with mechanical and chemical processes) began tenuously, as in the case of photography, to claim a place in the artistic canon as a counterbalance to the "destructive" impulse in other depictive practices. Historians of the visual traditions in art and science have since focused extensively on the deep imbrication of art and technologies of representation not just beginning with the origin of modern technics but also receding well past the horizon of written history. Whether we think of art as *techne*, as making, or if we ascribe to the eighteenth-century (Kantian) definition of art—divorced from utility and segregated from everyday life—it is a brute fact that art is always-already technological.[69] But the question at hand is about the degree to which technology is indexed in the artifact, or whether the role of technology is suppressed in service of the excision of utilitarian characteristics.

Pertinent to this issue, which is ultimately about whether "art," to be so named, must suppress its technological mechanisms, is the cultural disimbrication of art from decoration, design, ornamentation, and entertainment, to say nothing of notation, information visualization, or other types of (traditionally) nonart depiction. Innovations in visual technologies, such as the panorama, photography, and cinema, were at their inception frequently allied with a "media of attractions" that exerts a influence-by-proximity on the history of art but whose context of exhibition and reception is dissociated from fine art proper.[70] Consequently, a history of fine arts image construction and reception cannot mute populist voices nor fully distantiate visually democratized innovations from fine art traditions, despite resistance to such practices that might surface among some proponents of a fine art elite, especially given the increase in scholarly research on popular entertainment media such as video games and trash cinema.

Part of the reason Vasarely's oeuvre warrants closer examination in the context of a newly inflected aesthetic discourse is precisely because it operates outside of the normative tropes of art history. Taking from my earlier investigation of analog and digital systems, the criteria for the attribution of artistic success have been determined on the basis of properties circulating exclusively within the domain of analog systems. The ambiguity, density, and determinacy of analog systems derive from the necessary transition through indeterminate states. Although the absolute discreteness of digital signals is a theoretical proposition not borne out in actual practice (digital systems in fact may exhibit indeterminate conditions, as in the case of pixel artifacting, in which the leftover traces of illuminated pixels may be burned into a screen subjected to prolonged exposure of a static image), the facility of digital processing in producing mathematically calculated, discretely compiled images is anathema to the standards by which aesthetic achievement is traditionally measured in the history of art. Vasarely's practice is particularly interesting insofar as it posits a new aesthetic system, and in so doing also advocates for the creation, first, of a greatly democratized program for artistic production, and second, for a much broader shift in social economic and political organization leaning toward equity across a variety of intersubjective and collective practices.

■ *ElectroPlastique*: A Generative Appropriation of Op Art

Thus far, the foregoing analysis has been about a model of image production that looks computational without using computers. Now, a thread will be drawn into an examination of a particular branch of contemporary digital picture-making. Marius Watz's 2005 "remix" of Vasarely's aesthetic extends Vasarely's ideas through the introduction of computational processing and generative code. In Watz's work we are seeing no longer simply computational and programmatic metaphors but rather the execution of commands via generative code, which leads to the question, what new information or phenomenal experience is yielded by the refiguration of Vasarely's aesthetic into a computationally coded medium?

In 2005, Watz, a Norwegian digital artist and graphic designer, created *ElectroPlastique #1*, a "temporal composition" built with the programming languages Processing and Java for the electronic arts festival Territoires électroniques, held at the Fondation Vasarely in Aix-en-Provence. Over a duration of five minutes, an uncannily organic landscape of abstract moving images blooms and decays

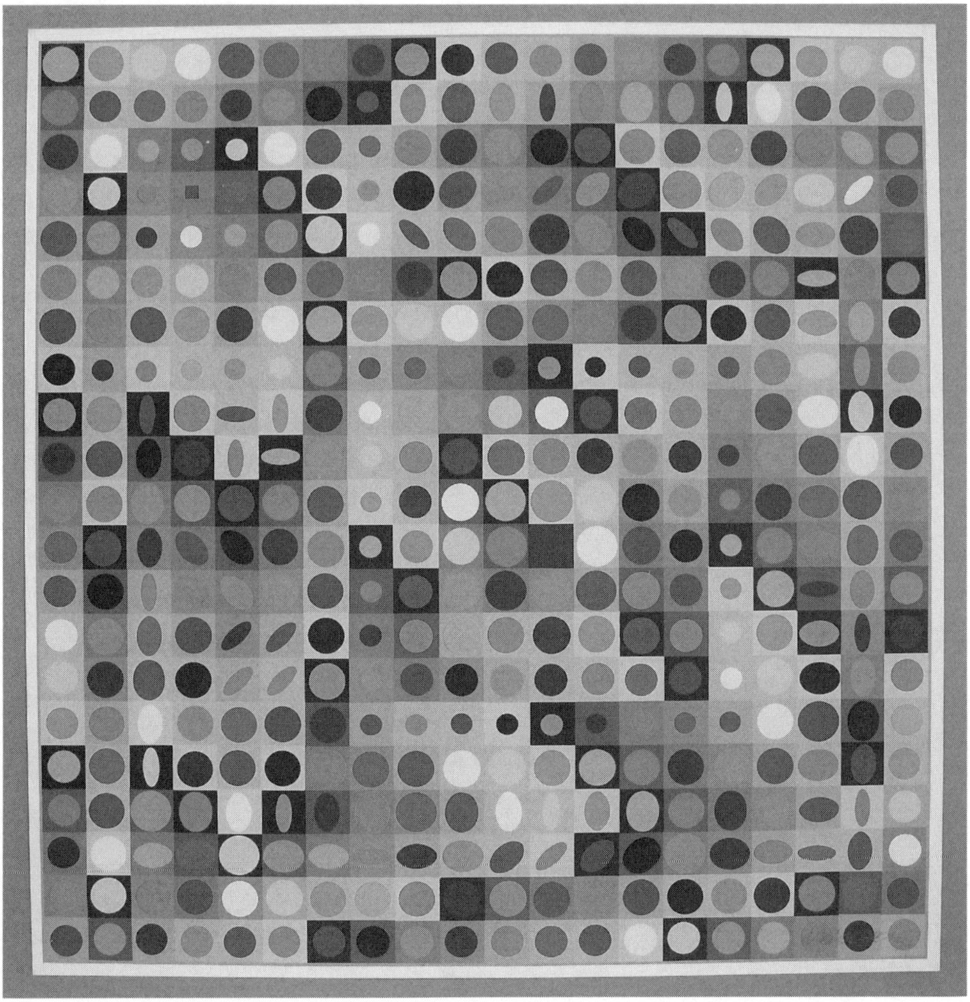

FIGURE 3.4 ▪ Victor Vasarely, *Planetary Folklore, Number 3*, 1964. © 2016 Artists Rights Society (ARS), New York / ADAGP, Paris.

across four screens, accompanied by an electronic soundtrack composed by James Welburn. Taking as his inspiration the work of Op Art progenitor Victor Vasarely, Watz's *ElectroPlastique #1* pays tribute to Vasarely's intricate, transformational abstract landscapes whose contours are dictated by a grammatical alphabet of basic geometrical, modular forms. According to Watz's description of the work, "in *ElectroPlastique #1* a regular grid is deformed and then used as the basis of a series of organic abstract systems that evolve over time. Due to the panoramic format of the 4-screen projection, the impression is much like a landscape. In the end the grid is exploded and disappears, hinting at a non-Cartesian vector space."[71]

Watz creatively and professionally identifies with a group of young artist-programmers who utilize the productive constraints of software to produce algorithmically evolving code-based abstractions called "Generative Art." Put simply, a work of Generative Art comes into being when an artist defines a set of rules that set into motion a process or series of processes resulting in a "complete" work of art. Algorithmic, generative strategies have existed in art production for centuries and do not inherently require the aid of electronic computers; in 1787, Mozart designed his *Musikalisches Würfelspiel*, a generative musical composition whose operative mechanism was a set of dice and a 177 measure score. Chance, instrumentalized through a toss of the dice, determined the order in which the measures would be played and thus superseded authorial control as the primary organizing principle of the aleatoric musical piece. That Mozart supplies an early example of algorithmically unfolding art is not accidental—the history of generativity in the visual arts has been inextricably linked musical composition, particularly to experimental avant-garde composition, on one side, and to the hedonistic rave scene of the 1990s one the other. Interestingly, the distance between these two musical genres has collapsed, to a certain degree, as the popularity of raves has dissipated and video jockey (VJ) culture has begun to align itself with the experimental art scene.

Generative Art is a term that applies to a compositional strategy rather than to a particular style or genre and does not necessarily rely on electronic computation for its success. Most often, however, it describes a computer-based trend in software art in which randomness is built into a chain of executable, coded commands to introduce unpredictable results into the "final" work of art. Influenced by the conceptual, algorithmic practices of artists such as Sol LeWitt, Victor Vasarely, the Algorists, Jean Tinguely, Jean-Pierre Hébert, the early digital artist Manfred Mohr, and Roman Verostko, Generative Artists are deeply invested in the questions of (1) how code and algorithmic proceduralism can shape the final outcome of artworks and (2) whether code bears a specific materiality that imprints itself on the face of the artwork. In short, Watz, Casey Reas (whose work is examined in chapter 4), and many of the self-identified group of Generative Artists take principle of structure and form as their central conceptual and aesthetic material.

Some reservations about the historicization of Generative Art have led Watz to comment that "uncritical use of the term [generative] risks conflating artists from different periods and assuming that their artistic interests are the same, when in fact the contexts in which they produce their works are very different."[72] Nevertheless, Watz in *ElectroPlastique* creates a necessary and explicit link to Vasarely's earlier investigations by performing a series of formal permutations of Vasarely's basic elements of structure. Watz suggests ultimately that his optical surfaces contain a latent multidimensionality that reveals itself when the structure is subjected to stretching and compression both spatially and durationally. In other words, while Vasarely's optical constructions can gesture toward spatial play and dynamism, there is also a sense in which their kinetic energy becomes frozen or dormant on the canvas, forcing the viewer's attention to the static format of Vasarely's depictions rather than to their dynamic potentiality. Rewriting Vasarely's interest in kineticism into the context of generative code, Watz adds actual instead of virtual duration and dynamism to the image. In so doing, he echoes Vasarely's fascination with the optical possibilities in kineticism, which he believed could supply the activating element that would "engender a humanistic and philosophical concept of the plastic arts" by encouraging a conceptual, technological, aesthetic realm that placed mutation at the center of thought and experience.[73]

ElectroPlastique is not a direct reiteration of Vasarely's plastic alphabet, or a straightforward performance of his visual language. Rather, it explores in an associative manner the visible and physical properties of Vasarely's plastic universe. Vasarely's Op Art canvases might be said to create a kind of virtual space with different physical rules than the ones belonging to the space occupied by the viewer. In *ElectroPlastique*, Watz similarly seeks to build a fictional digital space with its own physical properties and parameters. But this fictional space would be, for Watz, kinetic instead of static, in order to test how the system would develop within its parameters if given the added dimensions of time and movement. Beginning with the grid, the original form of computational graphic space, Watz's composition progressively distorts that perfect originary order, not destroying it but subjecting it to a slow, ongoing series of permutations from a perfectly regular to a more anamorphic or even potentially chaotic form, which represents a different concept of the nature of order. Thus, we must consider Watz's project not only as a transfer of Vasarelian optical schemas into a computational, kinetic form but also as a test case of what experiential dimensions can be added by the dynamic visualization of growth, change, and decay.

Just as painting is more adept at expressing certain kinds of emotions, concepts, and experiences (or is more adept at expressing certain aspects of these varieties of experience) than poetry and vice versa, computers have a certain range and domain of expression that they are best at as well. It is not just a fuzzy humanistic bias to claim that art based on code is a product of programmatic logic. It is a truism that the language used to convey information conditions the kind of information that can be conveyed. Thus, legal language will convey different information about a civil dispute than would a novel or a newspaper article, to say nothing of the complexities and opacities that arise in translation between French and English or Spanish and Japanese. Artist Peter Bentley has joked that coding is literal and unambiguous, and tends to produce literal, unambiguous thinking in human programmers. After all, if what computers are best at is efficient calculation, then the artifacts they make best must be about, reference, or be comprised of calculations. But another less tangible effect of the development of procedural computer programming languages is that the methodical nature of code restructures the way we conceive of and perceive the world by reaching to the bare bones of structure itself. Given the compositional and procedural organization of digital images, then, it seems quite natural that digital structure and abstraction should go hand in hand.

Looking again at the specific characteristics of Vasarely's oeuvre and the issue of translation and appropriation introduced by *ElectroPlastique*, it is important to take into account how both of these artistic models respond to and deviate from representational norms pertaining to both abstraction and figuration. If we examine the kinds of imagery that have shaped the popular perception of digital graphics, it is immediately noticeable that the spare, pixilated, and geometric abstraction of *Pong*, *Space Wars*, and *Tron* has given way to an immersive cinematic experience interwoven with a nearly unquestioning faith in the mimetic naturalism made possible by 3-D modeling. Graphics subscribing to this newly possible and ever-increasing digital naturalism ask that viewers or users—even as they interact with the moving images on the screen with the aid of technological prostheses such as pushbutton, and now motion-sensing, controllers or touchpads—think of these figures as not merely lifelike but also imbued with real vitality. The most mimetically accurate, computer-generated imagery asks us, in short, not to think about computers at all. The designer's success in constructing and programming digital figures is measured by the disappearance of any signs of its digital ontology; in a digital universe, every object begins its existence as a simulated sculptural amalgamation of balls, grids, and squares, only later acquiring the layers of tissue, hair, and fabric that guarantee its lifelike effect.

For example, recall Disney's Pinocchio, who prior to his transformation into a "real boy" by a beneficent fairy is marked as literally and symbolically "unreal" by the presence of hinge-and-screw joints and squared-off wooden limbs. After his transformation, those limbs take on the rounded contours of flesh and the "hinges" of his joints are hidden under implied layers of organic tissue. Of course, the technique of hand-painted cell animation disappeared from Disney's production model before the turn of the twenty-first century, in an industry-wide echo of Pinocchio's own neurotic complex that he is not real enough. Computer-generated imagery (CGI) animation ups the ante one step further, so that Pinocchio's cell-animated, real-boy body remains too closely lashed to tradition of line drawing instead of the new, more mathematically complex technology of 3-D modeling. But for all this appearance of reality, a digitally modeled world still seems too clean and frictionless to be fully organic. Even a head of hair, each strand of which undulates according to a perfectly calculated and calibrated probabilistic motion curve, cannot seem completely natural precisely because it is numerically calculated. In a computational universe, even randomness is a probabilistic value calculated into an equation and thus does not seem up to the task of the unpredictable surprise of the phenomenon known as *chance*.

This brief discussion of digital naturalism illustrates that digital producers attempt to disguise the tools and procedures of the act of digital composition. If underlying every digital graphic is a pixel, a vector, a raster, a grid, and a bitmap, the illusionistic impulse of digital naturalism covers over and disguises the structural principles of the image. The architecture of digital images is anchored by and initiated from the foundational geometries of the point, line, and grid. In their nascent state, like the not-yet-real Pinocchio marionette, most digital figures look more like precarious stacks of cones, spheres, and cubes than the uncannily organic characters they eventually become. Even the most naturalistic animations begin as roughshod wire-frame or geometrical models, only gradually acquiring the layers of mathematically modeled tissue—the muscle, skin, hair, and fabric—that complete their illusionistic circuit.

In contrast to the illusionism pursued by digital naturalists, the artists I call digital formalists, including Watz, and their predecessors, in this case Vasarely, foreground the tools and the technical means of production. Digital formalists are interested in the particular revelations made uniquely possible by digital tools, and they bare the formal properties of digital structure in an unashamed and even celebratory nakedness. While most computational images obscure the tools of their production, and strive for a complete illusionism, both Watz and Vasarely obsessively reiterate the properties elementary structures, and in so doing effectively reverse the illusionist teleology that seems to have taken hold in many areas of digital image production. In their continual presentation of basic forms, such as circles, squares, spheres, and cubes, Watz and Vasarely rehearse the process of digital fabrication from the ground up. Thus, while most makers of digital artifacts attempt to conceal evidence of the tools of production, such as pixilation, Watz and Vasarely announce a finished product at the point where most digital craftspeople begin.

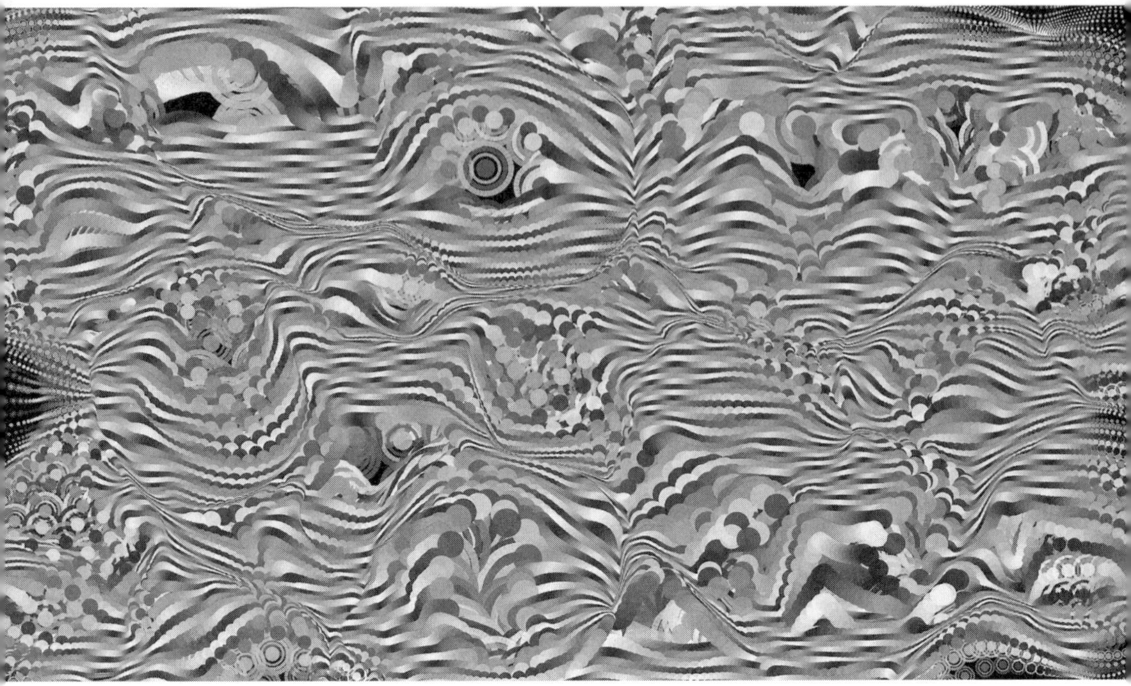

FIGURE 3.5 ▪ Marius Watz, *ElectroPlastique #1*, 2005, generative animation, 5:00. Created with custom software developed in Processing.

This does not mean that their works imitate the ostensibly "antiaesthetic" procedures associated with Conceptual Artists. Conceptual Art self-reflexively interrogates the ideological, aesthetic, and philosophical underpinnings of art but most often does so in a decidedly ascetic manner that branded it as embodying a sometimes parodic, sometimes deadpan exposure of the architecture of bureaucracy that Benjamin Buchloh has named the "aesthetic of administration."[74] The digital formalism exhibited by Watz and Vasarely, on the other hand, displays a visual hedonism that blossoms, somewhat paradoxically, within the constraints of pared-down modular forms. Both Watz and Vasarely subject the grid to anamorphic shifts, either in the temporally extended realm of moving images or in a synchronic, static form. But in both cases, the two-dimensional grid is imbued with a sense of organicity as spheres, cubes, or other volumetric shapes push against the fabric of the grid—distending, compressing, and distorting its perfect regularity, and in so doing exploring the experiential possibilities latent in a mathematically computed visual terrain.

Watz's appropriation, alteration, and intensification of Vasarely's "software" transforms Vasarely's creation of something "like software" or "like a program" into the technological phenomenon—a computationally executable, binary machine language—that Vasarely can only imagine and describe. The incorporation of generative change and the replacement of intention with algorithm make this art even less humanistic than Vasarely's but more about the form, movement, and actions of an antihumanistic, perhaps even vitalist, organic force. We are dealing with a paradoxical organicity here, precisely because the works are generated by a computational language and epistemology within an enclosed computational universe. The unfurling of branchlike structures and the growth and decay of forms does not, contrary to discourses surrounding artificial life, need to mimic biological life to evoke poetic associations with biological processes; we might anthropomorphize computational output, seeing them as shapes bubbling on the screen, or even invent associations between computational and biological processes that are reinscribed within the code, but there is nevertheless a sense of the alien, of synthetic artificiality, to the graphic output of computational processes that makes them seem too smooth and our interactions too frictionless, ultimately calling into question the veracity of the organic metaphors that are too easily applied to digital graphics.

But this uniform quality of digital space is another (paradoxical) artifact of its discrete ontology. The very fact of digital particulate composition enables each particle to be filtered, engineered, cleaned up, and perfected. In analog snapshots of the earth from space, the surface of the earth is marbled with cloud cover, and these swirls of white over the glowing blue surface have conditioned the way in which we imagine the earth's surface to appear. In contrast, an image of the earth (whose ontology is computationally generated) from which all traces of cloud cover have been erased, through the amalgamation of cloud-free pixels drawn from many digital photographs, loses the sense of multilayered complexity and density we get from the analog photograph and instead becomes too smooth, too frictionless. It lacks the indeterminacy, the density, and the repleteness that characterizes analog images. This does not mean the digitally compiled photograph is not beautiful but that it is both qualitatively and quantitatively a different artifact than the one captured by the analog camera.

Rewriting Vasarely's interest in kineticism into the performative context of generative code, Watz adds actual instead of virtual duration and dynamism to the image. Vasarely saw more than just optical possibilities in kineticism and believed that it could supply an activating element that would "engender a humanistic and philosophical concept of the plastic arts" by encouraging a conceptual, technological, aesthetic realm that placed mutation at the center of thought and experience.[75] While echoes reverberate between Watz and Vasarely in the relationship between conceptual and visual elements in their work, there

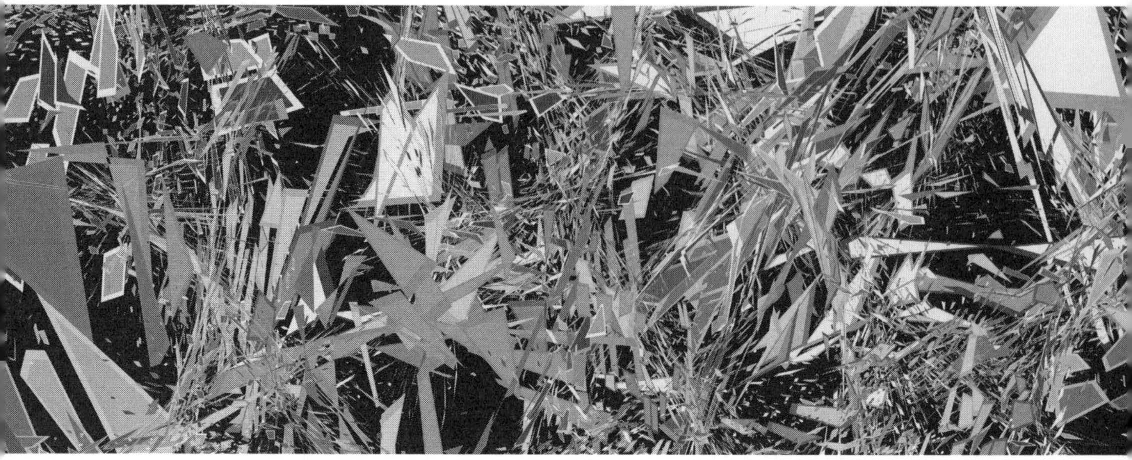

FIGURE 3.6 ▪ Marius Watz, *ElectroPlastique #1*, 2005, generative animation, 5:00. Created with custom software developed in Processing.

are also some notable differences between them. While Vasarely painstakingly devised a "toolbox" of units that would take the first steps toward the realization of algorithmic, programmed pictorializations, for Watz the programmatic basis for his pieces is already a given. He is therefore able to initiate his work from a different starting point, which pulls his focus toward a different set of artistic concerns than the ones central to his pioneering predecessor. Vasarely's conceptual goal, to prove that it is possible to invent a reiterable system for producing graphical models, has already been demonstrated by the very fact of computational programming. Op Artists set themselves the constraint of working largely (though not exclusively) within static frameworks, but within this constraint they want to elicit a sense of pulsating dynamism.[76]

There is thus a preoccupation with virtual perceptual effects in Op Art that fades in *ElectroPlastique* because the dynamism is made actual. Moreover, Watz's graphical schemas act quite differently upon the viewer's sensorium than does Vasarely's, whose constructions produce their illusory kinetic effects by using optical patterns to generate a sense of physiological instability in the viewer. Viewer space and pictorial space, then, are magnetically pulled toward one another but are then revealed as radically incongruous as the viewer struggles and fails and struggles again to cut through the visual disorientation effected by the pictorial schema. Watz's lugubriously morphing visual field, on the other hand, is less aggressively confrontational and more harmonious in its otherness. It seems content to uphold the distinctions between the parameters of computationally generated space and that of cardinal viewer space without resorting to the dizzying oscillations of Vasarely's earlier paintings.

Watz sets himself to a different experimental task, not to trick the eye but to construct a world with its own physical forces, actions, and reactions. This world is less dependent on employing its underlying system to "trick" the viewer's sensorial apparatus into seeing movement and change where none exists. Vasarely's work is, both conceptually and aesthetically, more about a system of interacting and interlocking discrete parts. Watz's formal strategy, in this instance, is concerned to a greater extent with creating an overall field that becomes susceptible to topographical distortion. Where Vasarely's schemas are composed of individual units or elements, the spatiality of *ElectroPlastique* begins with a virtual webbed "sheet" under which solid forms pass, producing protrusions and distortions in the otherwise flat plane.

Both twentieth-century Op Art and twenty-first-century Generative Art fight to uphold the retinal as a viable aesthetic characteristic. Vasarely sought to explode the overvaluation of expressionism in the fine arts by experimenting with the visual possibilities latent in systems and algorithmic permutations. Watz's generative compositions work to redeem the retinal from its summary dismissal after Conceptualism by meshing the theoretical richness of dynamic systems with the visual hedonism of his screen-based moving abstractions. Often in analysis a greater emphasis is placed on the introjection of randomness and chance into time-based systems, but less attention is granted to visual and other sensory elements of the pieces, as though these qualities are either self-evident or perhaps resistant to language. It seems crucial, however, for the theory and criticism of both Op Art and Generative Art, not to privilege either side, the conceptual and the aesthetic, as if they are independent entities, but rather to find a vocabulary to articulate the inextricable relationship between system and surface, and to realize their symbiotic support, without which the underlying structure and the raison d'être for these visual fields breaks apart and dissipates from view, like the bits of color sliding from the screen in the final moments of *ElectroPlastique*.

4

Spectral Analogies

From Wall Drawing to the Art of Programming

Thus far, the chapters of this book have presented theories and artworks that make the distinction between analog and digital systems readily perceptible if not absolute. The preceding analyses have largely supported the idea that there is a striking difference in the phenomenological experience of digital and analog notational and depictive strategies, and a resulting variance in the way we must conceptualize both the nature of digital and analog artifacts and the worldviews they propound. But this penultimate chapter foregrounds the work of an artist who operates in a more indeterminate range of picture-making, one that is fundamentally tied to the specific functions made possible by a digital computer but whose morphological structures are dense, continuous, and remarkably and markedly painterly. Many of the works discussed thus far, from Georges Seurat to Victor Vasarely, are palpably discrete, programmatic, and digital, foregrounding the digital at the level of interface. But the "programmed paintings" of Casey Reas are technologically digital, insofar as they are derived from the processing of discrete units, but aesthetically appear to be analog. Reas treats the digital as a primarily technological category, rather than an aesthetic one. As such, his work only occasionally and tentatively reveals the digital architectonics underlying his graphic schemas; most often his work is suffused with the analog properties of continuity, smoothness, and gesturality. As such, Reas's work might be considered in terms of a hybridization of analog and digital. The incorporation of technological digitality and phenomenological analogicity gives rise to what I will call a *computational* aesthetic. The computational thus blends elements of discreteness and continuity not merely to dissimulate analogicity but also to hybridize properties belonging to digital and analog structural modalities. Unlike other works in this book, which are identified as analog or digital independently of their reliance on computers, this computational aesthetic necessitates electronic computational processing. This new type is introduced toward the close of this book because the categories of analog and digital must be initially disaggregated and their aesthetic properties and effects evaluated before their constitutive roles within a computational aesthetic can most productively reveal themselves.

In his essay on his 2004 project *{Software} Structures*, commissioned for the Whitney Museum of American Art's Artport, Casey Reas describes his creative process: he wants "programming to be as immediate and fluid as drawing" and he "work[s] with software in a way that minimizes the technical aspects."[1] Reas is perhaps best known for designing the programming language Processing, for which he and coauthor Ben Fry won the Golden Nica award at Ars Electronica in 2004. For an artist who so explicitly and emphatically values immediacy, fluidity, and organicity in his own artistic production, it might seem curious that he made computational programming his medium of choice. It might also seem odd to select Reas's work in a book theorizing a sensorially apprehensible digital aesthetic, predicated on discreteness and syntactic and semantic disjunctness. Indeed, the digital structure of Reas's conceptual and instrumental process reveals itself only furtively and more often cloaks the digital in dense, continuous, and analog surface effects. The final output of his work, in other words, is not heavily discretized in the manner of Vasarely or Marius Watz; Reas's pictorial schema does not overtly embrace the pixel as a fundamental expressive unit, as in the case of John Maeda, Reas's teacher, or John F. Simon. Rather, the works bring to light an aesthetic of emergence, or a computational aesthetic, by emphasizing the aesthetic possibilities of algorithmic variation within a given visual system without necessarily revealing the unitary elements undergirding the structure of the artifact.

Reas's desire to "minimize the technical aspects" of his work and to make working with software as fluid as drawing underscores the resistance to the determinate properties of computational media exhibited in his "Processes." In his introduction to the *Processing* handbook, Reas offers a brief account of his transition from traditional analog media into the experimental use of software as an artistic medium. Despite an early exposure to early personal computing programs such as BASIC and Logo, Reas relates that he preferred drawing and set computers aside for many years. During his training in design at the University of Cincinnati, Reas reconnected to computers and began to use Illustrator and Photoshop. But in light of his interest in the fluidity and immediacy of drawing, Reas's reasons for continuing to pursue computer-aided design are particularly illuminating: "As I shifted my work from paper to screen, static grids and information hierarchies evolved into kinetic, modular systems with variable resolutions and compositions. The time and energy once spent devoted to details of materials and static composition shirted to details of motion and response."[2] What is suggested here is that while the construction of informatic systems is possible in LeWitt's realm of linguistic algorithm, digital systems change information from a spatial category into a temporal one. Other time-based media, such as film, performance, or video, are interested in other aspects of time—duration, extension, acceleration and deceleration, and continuous and fragmented narrativity—but Reas addresses the question of what happens to information when it becomes dynamic. He wants to know what shape information takes, what interactions can take place between modules, and how these interactions change the overall form of the information-based structure. Information—conceived here very differently than in the instance of information visualization, here taking on the sense of the "material" of digital systems—becomes a living organism, not trying to *copy* life or liveliness as in the case of artificial life (AL) projects, but becoming an entity in itself whose transformational capacities are revealed in the computational, performative execution of code.

While Reas's prints, given their intentionally painterly character, are not obviously computationally generated, his screen-based installations are clearly rendered with the aid of software processes and are situated in the context of multimedia installation. Even his prints are often placed in juxtaposition with streamlined hardware configurations on which moving images bloom, swirl, decay, and disappear in ongoing cyclic sequences. And yet, despite the presence of screens and screen-based, nonphotographic animations, his work often seems to conform to the evaluative criteria of analog pictorialization. The underlying processes generating this work are electronically computational, and thus technologically comprised of digital units, but even if the overall piece is comprised of individuated elements, it is notable that properties of discreteness and disjunctness are frequently occluded in Reas's surfaces, drawing the character of his work closer to an analog aesthetic despite its computational ontology.

Reas's pictorial schemata set into motion a complex series of analogies between the digital and analog, and between the organic and the technological. The digital becomes the hidden infrastructure, the causal mechanism of the graphic configuration that in the end is made invisible by a proliferation of painterly layers of texture and color. Reas's production uses electronic-digital computation to "analogize" the analog.[3] On the one hand, he is deeply invested in a digital, proceduralist logic, which undergirds his installations and sets in motion the generative systems that yield a given visual result. On the other hand, the richness, ambiguity, and organic harmony of the graphic output of these generative programs revel in painterly abstraction. His choice of a programmatically constructed medium is not accidental and can be construed as a manifestation of a post-Conceptualist investment in the notion of information conceived as an active processing of discrete functions that resolves into a complex informational architecture. However, this is not merely an anesthetic programmatic approach but one that also yields an aesthetically rich visual landscape. If Reas's use of digital technology is haunted by the specter of analog painting practices, by a desire for the spontaneity and gestural contact that is traditionally associated with painting, this tension that arises in his work makes him an ideal springboard from which to see how the analytic category of the "digital" can be disaggregated from electronic-computational machines not only, this time, to clarify differences between the features of an analog and a digital worldview but also to set up, first, a theory of analogico-digital aesthetic hybridity and, second, a theory of a computational aesthetic. Reas underscores these various and complex modalities to demonstrate how artists can utilize computational technology in a multitude of ways: to highlight the properties of digital graphic composition by foregrounding pixels or other structural building blocks, or to occlude the picture's digital infrastructure, leaving only indirect clues, or none at all, to its digital ontology.

Reas, LeWitt, and the Legacy of Conceptual Art

Reas's painterly aesthetic sensibility commingles with his fascination for the history, legacy, and contemporary computational application of Conceptual Art. In 2004, Reas produced a multilayered, collaborative, textual, and visual project entitled *{Software} Structures*, commissioned by the Whitney Museum for the Whitney Artport, an online exhibition space showcasing Internet-based art projects by prominent artists working within the nebulous field of "new media." Reas envisioned this project as an assessment of the relevance of Conceptual Art to contemporary software-based art practice. *{Software} Structures* addresses Conceptualism by testing the possibility of importing the strategy, philosophy, and aesthetic of Sol LeWitt's wall drawings into a computational, software-driven form. The project begins, as Reas avers, from "a simple question: 'Is the history of Conceptual Art relevant to the idea of software as art?'"[4] In the following section, I will begin to formulate an answer to this question through a consideration of the seductiveness of Conceptual Art for both digital artists and theorists of digital art practice. Specifically, I will examine Reas's conceptual indebtedness to LeWitt, whose influence suffuses the work of the younger artist. Sometimes referenced explicitly in Reas's practice, sometimes only peripherally, LeWitt's deeply nuanced ideas about the primacy of "process" nevertheless provide the conceptual ground from which Reas's art unfolds.

The relationship between the computational, the digital, the analog, and the "conceptual"—more specifically, Conceptual Art of the 1960s and 1970s—is a complex terrain, especially with respect to existing tropes in media studies. Media theorists such as Edward Shanken, Eve Meltzer, and Warren Sack have drawn important connections specifically between Conceptual Art and software art, gesturing to the "information world" that emerges with the birth of cybernetics and information theory in the mid-twentieth century.[5] Cyberneticists in this period described a world comprised not of solid matter but rather of impulses, of continuous feedback loops between signals and noise. Most importantly, both signals and noise are themselves composed of individual "bits," a number of elements that can be measured and computed. Information again becomes defined as a measurable quantity. If the world is made up of information, all systems, from biology to consciousness and to electricity, are also quantifiable, measurable, and calculable.

In the 1960s and 1970s Conceptual Art launched rigorous critiques of the technological and bureaucratic systems at work in shaping the cultural imagination and social practices in the burgeoning information age. For the 1970 information show at the New York Museum of Modern Art (MOMA), curated by Kynaston McShine, Hans Haacke created the participatory work *MOMA Poll*, asking museumgoers to respond to the question, "Would the fact that Governor Rockefeller has not denounced President Nixon's Indochina policy be a reason for you not to vote for him in November?" Participants were asked to register their response by voting yes or no, and to drop their ballot in a clear plexiglass box in which the collected results would be volumetrically visible. Governor Nelson Rockefeller was at the time a prominent member of the board of trustees of the MOMA. Two-thirds of those who chose to vote dropped their ballots in the yes box. This work was conceived by Haacke as an algorithmic system concretizing the abstract notion of "feedback" in a quasi-sculptural, dynamic, and politically charged form. Although the work does not use computers, it is often viewed as exhibiting a parallel logic to the procedural, programmatic systems at work in electronic computers.

Conceptual Artists interrogated bureaucratic and statistical systems of social order and control by applying a proceduralist logic to their art practice. The link between bureaucratic proceduralism and contemporary software art is made on the basis of the strict logic of programming. Software is a tool that can only be activated, and its procedures executed, if it follows a causal progression or chain of command. However, just because a work is procedural—because it presents the "rigorous," "axiomatic" "look of thought" that critic Donald Kuspit associated with Conceptual Art—does not mean it is digital in the manner I have described.[6] A work of Conceptual Art such as MOMA *Poll* participates in the new epistemological horizon characterized by technological developments in computing and information science, but its aesthetic sensibility is vastly different from that of a strictly digital work, characterized by discreteness and interchangeability. The exemplary cases of Conceptual Art's "systems aesthetic" lead their charge in a text-based, antivisual rebellion against what they perceived as the soporific, normatively constrained domain of academic pictorialism, a rebellion that might seem to be attuned—in its interest in tearing down normative visual and epistemological frameworks, for example—to the aesthetic and theoretical concerns of the artists practicing a digital method. But in fact, the pieces by Reas that announce themselves as most strongly indebted to Conceptual Art turn out not only to preserve the centrality of the visual but also to be no more aesthetically "digital" than their supposedly more painterly or "organic" counterparts.

Consequently, the answer to Reas's question about whether the legacy of Conceptual Art is relevant to contemporary software-based practice seems to be an obvious yes, but the manifestation of Conceptual Art's primary preoccupations transmogrifies, taking on a new valence, within Reas's rather unique, even idiosyncratic approach to software art. Reas follows the Conceptual Artists' lead in applying a proceduralist logic to his art practice and in engaging in a series of rigorous experimentations with and reflections upon specific objects and themes similar to those of the Conceptual Artists of the sixties and seventies (which range from, on the largest scale, cultural processes of making meaning to aesthetics and the more deceptively narrow issues such as local mayoral elections, as in the case of Haacke's MOMA *Poll*). But upon further inspection a monolithic affirmation of a perfect congruence between not just twenty-first-century software art and Conceptual Art in the sixties and seventies but also more specifically Reas's software art and Conceptual Art becomes less feasible. Both Conceptual Art and computationally generated software art display a certain similitude in their participation in and critical interrogation of their status as artifacts of the information age. But most emphatically in the exemplary cases of Reas and LeWitt, the frigid, machinic application of procedure is shot through an almost romantic aesthetic sensibility—what has been identified as mysticism in LeWitt's work and thought—and what in Reas's art leads to a suppression of a digital aesthetic in favor of an investigation of analog traits, such as fluidity and organicity. To this end, Reas's practice must be read both with and against the grain whilst building a genealogy of software art whose path joins that of Conceptual Art, at least for a time. As we will see, his projects do not speak univocally, instead exploring the multivalent possibilities inherent in software, some of which celebrate a vernacular model clearly influenced by Conceptual practices, others of which revel in a postpainterly aesthetic profusion, and still others of which weave hybrid worlds, demonstrating the compossibility of the painterly and the conceptual, and the digital and the analog.

The generative framework that fostered the rapid growth, flowering, and (apparent) decay of Conceptual Art, and the slower but inexorable unfurling of computational technology, was the postcybernetic figure of information, and the accompanying fantasy of a total "information world," a worldview in which all matter, phenomena, and movement—anything and everything—can be explained in terms of information science or "informatics."[7] An "information world" is a world seen as consisting of an interlocking system of relations, in which the behavior and transformations of its parts are dictated by its architectonic parameters.[8] Information, defined as unstructured data organized into a coherent, significance-bearing pattern, becomes the trope according to which the underlying structural order of the universe is understood. If it is possible to reduce and process phenomena into their constituent parts, and grasp their operational principles by observing interactions and relationships between these parts, the world is hypothetically knowable as a totalized system. This notion of information links Conceptual Art and digital computing, resulting in a computational aesthetic; both construe information in terms of binary structure—in terms of ones and zeros and patterned data.

For Conceptual Artists of the 1960s as well as for contemporary artists such as Ben Rubin and Mark Hansen, whose piece *Listening Post* (2002) displays data-mined information from conversations in Internet chat rooms on a grid of LED screens, information is combinatory, aggregating into series of lists and endlessly scrolling, infinitely permutable combinations of letters and numbers. In the 1990s the scientific practice of information visualization, which shapes raw numerical data into pictorial form, begins from the premise that information is not an inherently visible quantity but must be actively configured (and thus selectively interpreted) by human designers to be apprehended sensorially. In *Index* (1972), the group known as Art and Language shuts what are presumed to be printed ledgers away in closed file cabinets, thus rendering visual knowledge, or information acquisition, literally inaccessible. As we have seen, the figure of the grid is one trope associated with a "scientistic claim to reason,"[9] but in its strongest case, reason conceptualized through the lens of information theory becomes most reasonable, most like itself, when it escapes the visual register altogether.

Reas, echoing the argument for a "computational method" that functions independently of the technical specificities of computer hardware and software, affirms that the history of "software art" begins with two groups of progenitors that emerged in the 1960s.[10] One of these groups contains the small number of artists whose experiments with the graphic possibilities of early digital computer are only recently receiving scholarly attention.[11] The other group is comprised of artists who explored procedural thinking and algorithmic processes without directly accessing computational technology, namely, Conceptual Artists and members of Fluxus. Ironically for an artist whose production is so emphatically visual, Reas bolsters the connection between software and Conceptual Art (which we recall, for Donald Kuspit,[12] exhibits "the look of thought") by asserting that "software is an immaterial medium, much like thought."[13] While electronic processes may be conceptualized as immaterial, art is most often realized as a visible or sensible quantity/entity. Consequently, it must be asked how this immateriality inflects the sensible, aesthetic qualities of the resulting artifact.

Johanna Drucker has argued for a critical interrogation of the rhetorical equation "between the idea of 'data' and the actual materiality of its existence in digital form."[14] According to Drucker, the materiality of digital form is often elided in the "rhetoric of electronic cyberspeak, where data has somehow mistakenly come to carry an aura of immateriality as a feature of its fundamental identity."[15] Borrowing from Theodor Adorno, Drucker claims that a sinister effect of the rhetorical maneuver of enclosing information in self-referential or self-identical loop is the negation of the possibility of seeing this equation as anything other than inevitable, self-evident, or natural. Correlatively, then, the view that graphic output is "merely" epiphenomenal or "merely" contingent on interface design is to fail to account to for the ideological nature of the images resulting from computational processing. In contrast, a software art model privileging critical code production is supposed in contrast to be more philosophically or conceptually replete precisely because it interrogates both the structure of the code undergirding the graphical rendering as well as that of the graphics themselves. Reas's statement that "the software implementation is closest to the concept" underscores any allegiance he might have not just to software art but also, perhaps most prominently, to LeWitt, who maintained that the artistic core of his wall drawings lay not in the inscription of lines or the application of paint to the wall's surface but instead in the written instructions for the drawing. The success of LeWitt's wall drawing practice, and perhaps in one facet of Reas's software art production, is in large part due to the incommensurability between the visual and the nonvisual, their inability to overlap seamlessly and signify congruently.

▪ Software Art: Computing Conceptual Critique

Because the operations of computational machines are hidden, it might be said that computation notionally escapes or exceeds the possibility of imagistic representation. Electronic computational processing, in which vast numbers of invisible calculations are carried out at the speed of light, far beyond the human sensorial threshold, is in one sense emphatically opaque. As proposed a moment ago, one way to approach the graphic interface is as merely an epiphenomenon of the blackboxed operatics of computational processing. Consequently, the computationally rendered depiction might be said to mislead the viewer, to lull him or her into contemplation of a false idol or a weak shadow of technical operations. For this reason, some artists have made the focus of their work not images but the hidden processes undergirding graphical representation. By refusing to cloak the form of code in the spectacular garb of pictorialization, these artists, often sited as the torchbearers of an updated Conceptual Art, seek to show the ideological nature of code that functions beneath but ultimately structures the visible layer of representation that appears on screens and monitors.

Placing Conceptual Art outside the sphere of the visual arts and analyzing its properties using the tropes made available with the advent of the information sciences, aligns it with many of the impulses driving software art. Such an unholy alliance is not farfetched. Jack Burnham's *Software* show, Kynaston McShine's *Information*, and the London Institute of Contemporary Arts' (ICA) *Cybernetic Serendipity*, among other exhibitions, along with the formation of the *Radical Software* group/journal, all occurred within a narrow historical window, around the years 1968–1970. Software, as a concept, captured the cultural imagination long before personal computing became a reality in American households.[16] Conceptual Artists, including LeWitt, became interested in the proceduralist logic of software and the cybernetic and systems-theory-based notion of information in part because these models offered a distinct method for abrogating subjectivity from the process of artistic creation. LeWitt and his allies, aware of the subject-shaping power of ideology and its incursion into the criteria by which art and artists are included in and excluded from the artistic canon, began to expound upon the possibilities opened up by automating the creative process, imagining that such automation would permit new qualities to manifest that would have otherwise remained outside the socially-historically constructed realm of imaginative possibility.

Due to its bent toward aggressively self-reflexive ideological critique, which smacks roundly of sixties and seventies Conceptual practices, software art has carved out a niche of digital art production commonly linked to the precepts of Conceptual Art. In its emphasis on the reflexive and critical examination of the software processes underlying the final graphic output, and its sometimes violent admonitions that software is shot through by ideology, its primary activities are clearly invested in interrogations of and interventions into the politics of computational technology. Whereas one might assume that computer programs and interfaces act as a blank screen on which we imprint or project intellectual/conceptual and social/communicative output, the systems we use have been designed to excel in specific capacities. But while it is clear to a user not literate in programming that each application is limited in the type and tasks it can carry out, it is less obvious that each programming language also has a specific range of communicative aptitude. Reas and other artists choose software as their medium in order to make transparent the fact that individual programs are not neutral, and that therefore the selection of one language will produce a different kind of result than another program. For Larry Cuba, a pioneer of early computer-driven abstract animation, using computers to generate abstract, mathematically structured landscapes "affects your vocabulary."[17] This is especially true of abstraction; the mathematics and algorithms executed by computational technology will create a particular visual dimension and set of visual parameters that are most clearly perceptible in an approach to graphic configuration that exposes and foregrounds the structural principles underlying pictorial construction. While this realization should perhaps come as no surprise in the light of art historical arguments about medium specificity, software artists have based a good part of their inquiries on the idea that the ideological underpinnings of programming languages and software applications have been obscured by a rash of illiteracy amongst the general populace (whether an illiteracy imposed willfully or through accidental pitfalls in the educational system) if by not outright acts of suppression.

Starting from the premise that software art examines the processes underlying the pictorial/graphic output visible on the computer screen, it is easy to see how a theoretical-historical bridge forms between the "dematerialized" Conceptual Art practices of the 1960s and 1970s and the software art at the turn of the twenty-first century. Software art frequently allies itself with the antiaesthetic tendencies of Conceptual Art and specifically orients its critical and reflexive processes along the trajectories of the performance art, the art-and-technology movement, and the critique of information, systems theory, and the aesthetic of administration introduced by Benjamin Buchloh in reference to Robert Morris, Hans Haacke, Mel Bochner, and Joseph Kosuth, among others.[18] As in software art, which sets itself not to the task of creating visually compelling works of art but rather to the ideological critique of power/knowledge networks supported by software, according to Buchloh, "beginning with the readymade. . . . in the absence of any specifically visual qualities and due to the manifest lack of any (artistic) manual competence as a criterion of distinction, all the traditional criteria of aesthetic judgment—of taste and of connoisseurship—have been programmatically voided. The result of this is that the definition of the aesthetic becomes on the one hand a matter of linguistic convention and on the other the function of both a legal contract and an institutional discourse (a discourse of power rather than taste)."[19]

Art after Marcel Duchamp, then, opens itself to reflexivity, tautology, and both internal and external (cultural, ideological) critique, because it becomes incorporated into the same social, political, and economic systems from which it is excluded by a Kantian viewpoint. In other words, art becomes a product of institutional discourse and subject to evaluation based not on its universal legibility as an object of beauty but on its eminently contingent linguistic, juridical, and ideological definitions.

The crucial part of the argument proposed above is the turn away from a traditional model of aesthetics derived from *aesthesis*, or sense perception, and toward an aesthetics of governance, in which visualizations index the operations of power/knowledge systems but relegate visuality to a mere placeholder for an alternate order of communication. The aesthetic of governance, bureaucracy, or administration establishes Conceptual Art and the visual arts as distinct zones bearing a common ontology but divergent evolutionary tracks. Nevertheless, despite the fact that Conceptual Art's critical reflection upon the history of ideologies embedded within traditional aesthetic systems has earned Conceptualism a reputation for being antiaesthetic, Conceptual Art remains intertwined with the visual arts, even if many of its constitutive practices seem to reject or at least to problematize traditional pathways to visual pleasure. Delimiting a new aesthetic of bureaucracy and control isolates Conceptualism from the domain of traditional aesthetics, placing it instead within the realm of language games or other procedural systems such as mathematics, cryptography, or "programming" as it was known prior to the advent of personal computing.[20]

Warren Sack has argued that given the entanglement of computation with bureaucratic organization and systems of control, politics and economics provide more apposite analytic reference points for computational systems and computational culture than does Kantian aesthetic philosophy. Sack assesses visualization practices in terms of an "aesthetic of governance," to determine "what sorts of governance they support or reflect": government via the *demos*, the people, or the *bureau* (the office).[21] By extension, Sack diagnoses artistic visualizations, such as those produced with Radical Software Group's Carnivore Client software, which allows artists to interpret and visualize network traffic, in terms of an "appropriation and *détournement* of bureaucracy."[22] In other words, to make his link between mid- to late-century Conceptual Artists and computational practitioners, Sack focuses on the Conceptualists' reflexive critique of bureaucracy (often achieved by incorporation of the material signs of bureaucracy into their artwork, such as the filing cabinets in *Index* or Robert Morris's 1963 *Statement of Aesthetic Withdrawal*) paralleled with the demonstrable claim that "metaphorically and literally, computers are an outgrowth of bureaucracy."[23] While LeWitt performs the role of the bureaucratized subject in his open modular cubes, carrying out repetitive duties with the same cadence as an industrial factory machine,[24] computers are designed to function exclusively according to the rules of procedural logic. Computer technology can therefore be understood as both an effect and a re-producer of bureaucratic ideology.[25] Given that Conceptual Art critiques traditional aesthetics by way of embracing an administrative antiaesthetic (mobilizing metaphors of tables, graphs, maps, files, lists, and so forth), it seems to integrate seamlessly with a mode of computer-based art practice that exploits the practical and technical uses of a tallying, numericizing, and statistical media. Art that reflects upon the invention of the computer as a bureaucratic tool—an aid to a frictionless dispensation of bureaucratic tasks—would relate closely to Conceptual Art, which places under a microscope the various administrative forces at play in social, cultural, economic, political, scientific, and urban systems.[26]

While reception of Conceptual Art has turned largely on the premise, whether applauded or derided, that the movement as a whole was self-reflexively critical, aggressively programmatic, vehemently antiaesthetic, and consequently visually dry, there is also another way of seeing it as struggling to develop an aesthetic appropriate to the times. Where a surfeit of subjectivity could only tie the artist to the dead and dying traditions of the past, automation stood a chance at yielding something truly new because the processes would allow the development of the as yet unimaginable. While the dream of the information world imagined by Conceptual Artists has undoubtedly exerted a strong influence on artists now working with computational software, this link is neither absolute nor perfect, as other tensions and nuances in the art reveal themselves. A one-to-one correlation between software and Conceptual Art not only limits software art to a derivative position but also fails to account for the complex relationship between aesthetics and computation within these works. Moreover, the all-too-easy categorization of software art as an immaterial medium binds its somewhat glibly to the older Conceptual territory of "dematerialization," missing many nuances of the more recent practice in the equation.

If Benjamin Buchloh and Sack are correct that Conceptual Art resists a card-carrying membership within what are traditionally labeled "visual arts," the analogical relationship between computational and Conceptual Art becomes more tenuous when the computational practice under study—in this case, Reas's—is resolutely visual. Even within the subgenres of computational media, Reas has remained, again like LeWitt, difficult to classify. Aspects of various genres appear in threads of his work but no firmly woven fabric results that would ventriloquize or reject the (sometimes outspoken, sometimes implicit) tenets of militant interpretations of the ideological and bureaucratic underpinnings of software particularly and computational media more generally. For example, Reas treats software as his primary medium,[27] but he cannot be called a software artist *tout court* given his outspoken interest in textures and surfaces—in aesthetic principles. Software art, as Inke Arns has argued, while related to Generative Art—another genre with which Reas is frequently associated—in its use of predefined processes and rules used in the service of a "negation of intentionality"[28]—cannot be equated with the pure exploration of generative processes, insofar as software art is fueled by the premise that "the medium—or rather: the material—of software allows for a critical reflection of software (and its cultural impact)."[29] Software art sidelines visible results and critiques or even denigrates the visible in a similar fashion to Conceptual Artists of the sixties and seventies. Software artists view code through the lens of ideology and examine coded processes as a form of cultural production whose potential to act as a system of control is often obscured. Software artists perform a technological and cultural critique, whereas Generative Artists more often use the software medium to explore possibilities of emergence and dynamic change without necessarily regarding the facilities and constraints of software through an overtly political frame/lens. For this reason, Generative Art has been viewed with some suspicion as an overly aestheticizing or depoliticizing strain in digital art, whereas software art adheres more closely with brands of activist art that has received more attention in the field of media studies.

From Wall Drawings to Processes

It was in 1968 at the Paula Cooper Gallery in New York City that Sol LeWitt for the first time drew on the wall and called it an artwork. This simple enough act carried enormous ramifications for the contemporary art world and resonated strongly with many of the issues occupying the front lines of the Conceptual avant-garde. Not only did the practice of wall drawing eliminate completely the problematic "support," already under critical investigation by the likes of Frank Stella with his shaped canvases and *Irregular Polygon* series (the latter beginning in 1967), but it also undercut the commercial viability of the work by

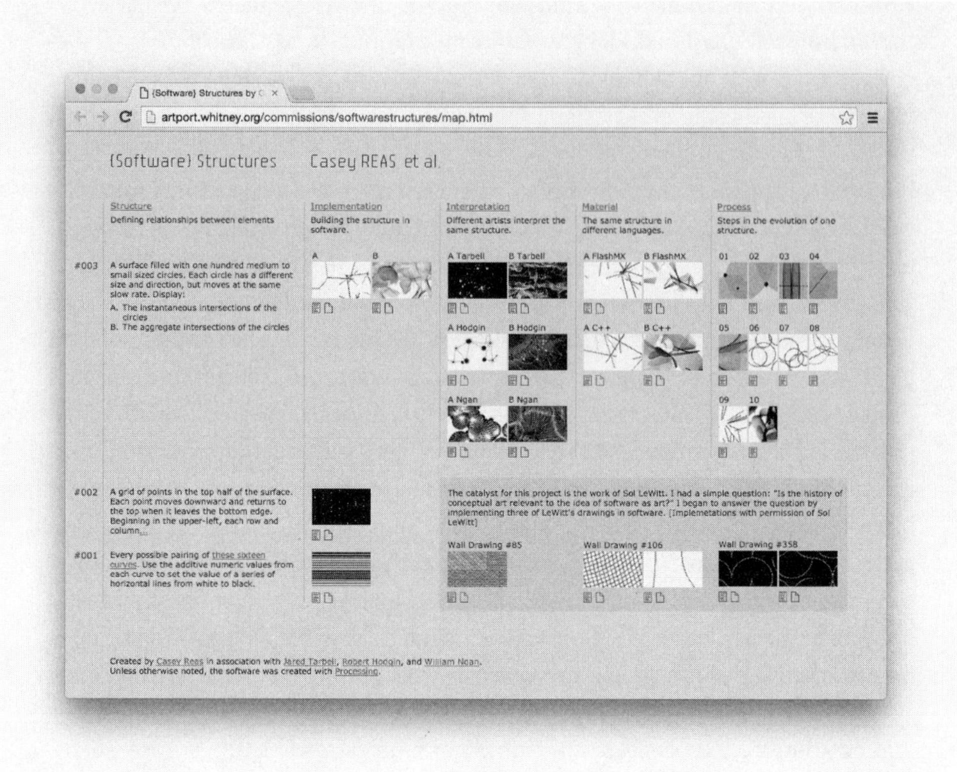

FIGURE 4.1 ▪ Casey Reas, *{Software} Structures*, 2004. © Casey Reas.

refusing to produce a clearly defined object of exchange. Later his practice of hiring draughtspeople to realize his sometimes vague, interpretively resistant instructions also called into question the primacy of the singular authorial hand and fractured the linearity of attribution.

One of the most significant aspects of LeWitt's wall drawing practice, the facet of his work that continues to resonate with Reas and other computational artists, was his built-in distantiation of drawing from instruction, or graphic rendering from code. LeWitt's method separated the Idea—what he considered the core of the artwork—from a set of written instructions that he would pass on to a selected draughtsperson or draughtspeople to be drawn at a given site. The signifying capacity of the work was ultimately located somewhere *among* the drawing, the instructions, and the elusively immaterial, even nonlinguistic "Idea."[30] The effect of this procedure was the disentanglement of the creative act into an array of constitutive elements. Where any temptation to conflate inspiration and realization had existed, LeWitt replaced it with the assertion that multiple, or perhaps infinite, channels for the manifestation of a concept open themselves materially against the backdrop of a single idea.[31]

Wall Drawing #51 (1970) is one of LeWitt's most didactic experiments in the relationship between built, architectural space (the "immaterial" dimension of the concept) and the practice of drawing as an inscription of a two-dimensional pictorial schema upon or within an architectonic configuration. The instructions for the piece are remarkably simple: "All architectural points connected by straight lines," but the visible results demonstrate the rule far more appreciably than some of his more obfuscating works. Whereas the grid and a simple catalog of linear elements, rather than real spatial features, govern the visual logic of *Wall Drawing #146* (1972), in which a wall is covered loosely by a series of arcs, straight lines, broken lines, and not straight lines,[32] *Wall Drawing #51* illustrates the principle of site specificity by calling attention to architectural points of interruption, including light switch plates and electrical sockets or irregular angles in the intersection of walls and ceiling. In *Wall Drawing #146*, the grid dictating the length of lines and arcs remains visible, but the arrangement of the line fragments within the modules—the order in which arcs, straight lines, broken lines, and not straight lines appear, their meeting point with the edge of their modular constraint—appears more vulnerable to the draughtsperson's interpretation, more contingent on decision rather than the immovable contingencies built into the architectural parameters of the site.

In 2008, net-based artist Benjamin Bruneau demonstrated the multiple configurative possibilities for *Wall Drawing #136* in an online work that, without textual commentary, presents a photograph of a white gallery wall and its brick floor. The only link on the page is the word "another" printed in unassuming typeface on the left-hand side of the screen that, when selected, cycles through different possible renditions of the drawing, graphically conveyed in blue lines on the surface of the gallery wall presented in the photograph. Like *{Software} Structures*, Bruneau playfully activates LeWitt's natural language algorithms in code in order to explore the combinatory possibilities latent within them. However, whereas Reas is more interested in the differences between media that come to light in the process of implementing the instructions, or in other words is more invested in testing LeWitt's claim that the "idea" is the core of the work and that its actualization is secondary, Bruneau's rendering engages the liminal zone between the immateriality of code structures and the materiality of wall drawing in a more literal fashion.

Thus, Reas's *{Software} Structures* offers a more complex view of the processes involved. If LeWitt's wall drawings depend for their conceptual success on the gap between instruction and execution, there is an analogous moment in Reas's

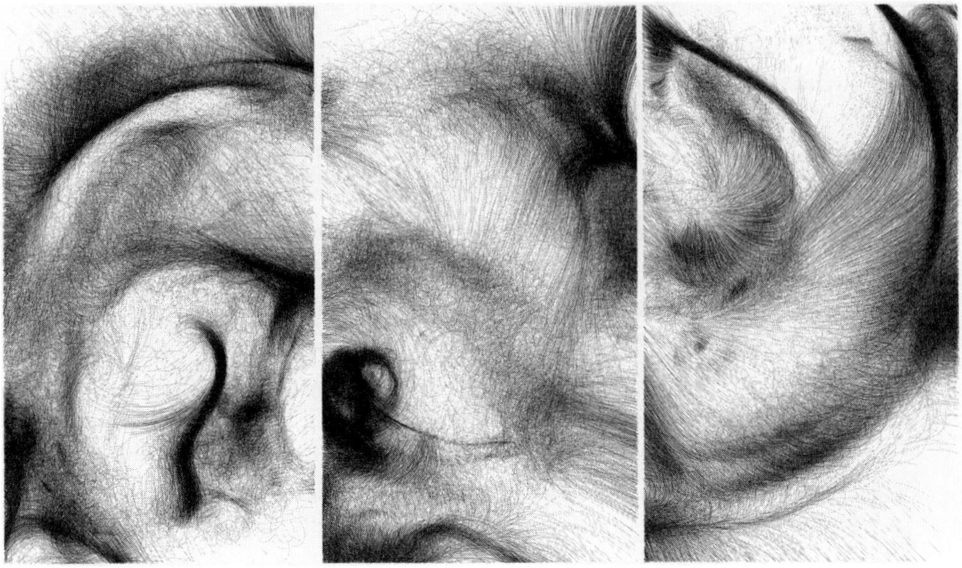

FIGURE 4.2 ▪ Casey Reas, *MicroImage*, 2001–2003. © Casey Reas.

project, whether the screen-based visualizations are direct adaptations of LeWitt's algorithms or are part of the series of more indirect homages entitled "Processes." Reas continued interest in the appellation "process," instead of drawing or programming, in his post-2004 work follows from a dual interest in principles of emergence and LeWitt's mystical proceduralism.[33] Beginning with *{Software} Structures* and continuing onward, Reas began to call his works "Processes" in order to reveal their open-endedness and availability to realization across multimedia platforms; a "Process" "defines rules and instructions which describe a relation between Elements outside of a specific physical media."[34]

In *{Software} Structures*, Reas begins by implementing three of LeWitt's wall drawings—#85, #106, and #358—in order to explore deviations between the products of physical and computational media. The primary and the most immediately apparent distinction between these computational implementations and their realization in real architectural space is, first, their coarseness—the slight pixilation of the lines indexes their discrete digital composition—and second, the facility of computational systems to subjecting structures to expansion, multiplication, and magnification, or conversely contraction, attenuation, and diminution. This trait is most visible in Reas's adaptation of *Wall Drawing #106*, in the original instance of which arcs are drawn in black pencil from the midpoint of a wall. Unlike his screen-based rendition of *Wall Drawing #85*,[35] which remains static and alters the optical properties only in the sense that the low resolution and the lighting conditions given by the screen interface cause a slight sensation of pixilation and of a rainbow "ghosting" in the cross-hatched squares, Reas's software implementation of *Wall Drawing #106* opens the work to user interaction and to the temporal dimension. As the user drags a mouse to the left over the surface of the software-driven "drawing," the density of arcing lines multiplies rapidly, far surpassing the number of intersections of the original, until the delimited area is covered by a screen of fine black lines, revealing a pattern reminiscent of the concentric wave effects produced by the warp and weave of synthetic fabrics, of a jaggedly stylized Op Art, or of John Whitney's early experiments with the cinematic possibilities in computer-generated abstraction. The simple level of interactivity introduced here transforms LeWitt's process, in which a single instance presents one of many possible interpretations, into a more determinate demonstration of all possible graphic renderings of the idea compressed into a single, interactively animated frame.

In the following step of *{Software} Structures*, presented on the web page in several columns or "sections," entitled "Structure," "Implementation," "Interpretation," "Material," and "Process," Reas no longer draws his structural support from LeWitt's existing wall drawings but instead generates twenty-six individual implementations of three primary "software structures." These three sets of natural-language-based instructions imitating LeWitt's instructional approximations of a core "Idea" isolate and put pressure on different facets of the foundational notion of a computationally derived structure. Reas employs several related strategies for highlighting possible indeterminacies, inconsistencies, and flexibilities in computational processing, and for duplicating the collaborative unfolding from conceptualization to inscription enacted by LeWitt and his draughtspeople. As LeWitt asserts with respect to his own practice, Reas's work begins as a vague idea that requires a second level of linguistic articulation to take form.

Similar to LeWitt's translation of Idea into Text into physically implemented wall drawing with the aid of a draughtsperson or draughtspeople, the initial step of Reas's process defines a text-based software structure whose source text is written in English. *Structure 003*, for example, is described as follows: "A surface filled with one hundred medium to small sized circles. Each circle has a different size and direction, but moves at the same slow rate. Display: A. The instantaneous intersections of the circles B. The aggregate intersections of the circles."[36] The second step enacts the translation of the structure into computational software. In *Structure 003*, when Reas translates code—the computational software—into graphical output, he creates two instantiations of the process, one of which is more aesthetically digital, the second of which approaches a smooth, analog aesthetic. In the first graphical instance, Reas reveals lines that measure the intersections of the circles. As two circles cross one another, the distance between the two points of intersection will increase and diminish. If a line is drawn connecting these two points, it in turn will lengthen as the circles become more overlapped and shorten as they move apart. When Reas sets this system loose on a screen filled with invisible circles, it visually manifests in a field of line segments that elongate and diminish as they tumble across the screen. In the second frame, Reas shows the intersections aggregating over time, leaving warped, grey ovals whose transparency produces a layering effect as they gradually collect, like damp fallen leaves, with increasing density on the screen. With each successive step of the process, the metric character of the lines—in which pixels are added and removed like inches in a ruler—disappears. As such, the initial, digital aesthetic gives way to a smooth, continuous analogicity.

For the following "Interpretation" section, Reas commissioned three artists to implement his wall drawing software structures in the manner of LeWitt's draughtspeople, thus allowing for the openness of interpretation while experimenting with the notion that the three instantiations will prove the existence of an undergirding "deep structure that reveals the intention of the author."[37] All three interpretations, by Jared Tarbell, Robert Hodgin, and William Ngan, all built with Processing, indeed disclose an underlying structural consistency that suggests their common ideational origin. This structural logic is conveyed in a scattered, overall field; the visible surface is comprised of a distributed array of interacting or intersecting elements. These elements are clearly individuated, behaving as discrete units, but their collisions produce both immediate and residual effects that determine the overall textural quality of the animated visual schema.

In "Material," the penultimate section of the work, Reas demonstrates Larry Cuba's earlier claim, in 1986, that the capabilities of the software—the medium—will alter the visual qualities of graphic output.[38] Just as steel, wood, and oil and tempera paints will exhibit different material properties, so too do programming languages yield variant effects in the perceptual qualities of the work. Processing, a language developed at MIT by Reas and Ben Fry, was built as a platform designed for artists; Reas and Fry built it as a tool for teaching and research in graphics-based programming. Its relatively simple and minimal application makes it easy to operate as a sketchbook, a way for artists and designers to quickly and easily render their ideas visually. Although it is open source, readily accessible, and runs well on the web, it runs slower than C++/OpenGL, another programming environment tested in this section of {*Software*}

Structures that is capable of graphic rendering at far higher speed and resolution than either Processing or Flash but does not run on the Internet. C++ produces the most elegant, delicate, and continuous visual structures and is therefore most proficient in masking its limitations and the particularity (or eccentricity) of its characteristics as a tool. Flash MX, by contrast, was authored to support efficiency in web animation. It calculates more slowly than Processing, however, so a work with a high number of elements and computation demands becomes slow and fragmented, ultimately losing compositional clarity and cohesion.

Lastly, Reas includes a "Process" section to underscore the "open"—available to multiple, ongoing interpretation, iteration, and evolution—aspect of his processes. Reas begins his explanation of this section of the project by raising the specter of Hans Namuth filming Jackson Pollock at work, pointing to the extent to which the emergent, process-driven act of painting and other traditional forms of art-making have been exposed through criticism and media attention. Conversely, programming has, according to Reas, remained hermetically closed, due in part to its precision and the fragility due to that precision, as a technical language—a strictly notional system—that is not available to the same free "play" as physical materials. This section reveals intermediate steps in the development of Reas's implementation of *Software Structure #003*. Moving from the first, mouse-controlled calculations of the line resulting from the mobile overlapping of two circles to the removal of user input via automation; the erasure of the circles, displaying only the stretching and shrinking line segments and center points of the circles; to the disappearance of the center pixel; and onward to the final rendition of the software structure, this section is the most overtly didactic in the project. Whereas the previous sections focus more heavily on the openness and multiplicity inherent in the artistic-interpretive act, this addendum seems the least conceptually linked to the project as a whole, though it is pedagogically informative.

This online project as a whole is more didactic than Reas's other works, containing explanations and visual demonstrations of how a software structure transforms an aesthetically digital schema, characterized by single, moving pixels and short, spinning falling lines into a more replete painterly surface, as the screen blooms into textural richness. While one vector of influence is clear between LeWitt and Reas, and indeed between many instances of Conceptual and computational art, it is not enough to say that Reas simply ups the ante of LeWitt's linguistic algorithms by submitting them to the automation of computational processing. Not only does Reas translate linguistic programs into a form executable by digital computation machines, but he also brings the emphasis back to the visual register. Reas's programs, in all their visual richness, refuse the "dematerialized" antivisualism of Conceptual Art of the 1960s and 1970s. The influence of Conceptualism on Reas's practice is in many cases obscured and difficult to read in his screen-based animations. And, moreover, any digital properties of these animations are also hidden by the presence of continuousness and ambiguity in his graphical forms.

The Open Work

Even if only teasingly, LeWitt's drawings are accessed phenomenologically not just as regular, cold, information-ridden structures but also as networks of forms that have a life of their own. His repetition *ad absurdum* of a rationalized plan not only underscores his disdain for the notion of an expressionistic transcendence but also in a more positive sense allows for a form of sublimity achieved through the secession of authorial control and a concomitantly distinct physicality, which is a new but immediately recognizable compositional (material) structure, born of the world of concepts. His work operates similarly to Siah Armajani's *A Number Between Zero and One*, in which all the numbers between 0 and 1, resulting in 25,974 pages were printed out on individual sheets of paper resulting in a nine-foot stack whose sheer physicality "render[s] palpable the terrain not accounted for by the structural logic of information. . . . After all, paper's surface is the very site of our institutional practices; on it, we map the world, graph the rise and fall of the economy, certify our titles, legalise our relations. But in Armajani's nine-foot stack, paper's behaviour subverts such functionality. One sheet after another, surface abuts surface, two dimensions become three, abstract space becomes real."[39] Likewise, LeWitt's engagement with metrics, rules, and modules,[40] and his deliberate excision of artistic subjectivity, is ultimately not about signaling the end of art or the end of the subject but rather about opening up a new space of experience not bound and limited by the existing horizon of expectation.

Paralleling LeWitt, Reas works within instructional constraints to produce unpredictable results. In his comments on organic and Conceptual systems, he acknowledges the administrative function of computational technology—the fact that "computers are built to be predictable."[41] Computers, taken both within and outside of an art context, are tools constructed to facilitate regular, repeatable, and efficient calculations. LeWitt's wall drawings, despite their algorithmic design and flirtation with proceduralism, cannot be fully notational because they are indeterminate. Conversely, computers' functionality rests on their ability to make precise, accurate calculations. They cannot interpret or detect nuance. Even randomness, such a central component of Generative Art, must be simulated in a digital computer, so that the chance operations that defined LeWitt's "algorithmic" processes possess a different quality of indeterminacy than do the generative functions carried out by digital programs. Digital computers and human decision making each impose different constraints on the ostensible open-endedness of chance. Of course, "pure chance" is always mitigated by the system in which it acts, so as Reas, as well as many Generative Artists and pioneers in the simulations known as "Artificial Life" have shown, it is also wrong to assume that the determinacy of computers forecloses the possibility of truly aleatory experiments.[42]

In an attempt to combine the indeterminacy inherent to LeWitt's natural-language-based "programs" and the dynamism made possible by computational systems, Reas builds into his processes a degree of open-endedness, couched as a guard against technical obsolescence, that enables them to more closely mirror the play between ambiguity and procedural determinism set into motion by LeWitt's instructions. Granting primacy to natural language rather than a programming language enables the "idea"—the principles of structure and interaction between parts within the work—to migrate across platforms, and mitigates the problems that occur when software becomes obsolete and no longer runs on ever-newer, ever-more-powerful machines. But additionally, the replacement of a precision-dependent programming language with English natural-language phrasing injects ambiguity and multiplies possibility into an otherwise determinate system.[43]

In 1962, Umberto Eco published *Opera Aperta (The Open Work)* in which he proposed a model of the work of art comprised of discrete structural elements that can be moved, recombined, and recontextualized to create differentiated works.[44] Intrigued by Eco's notion of "openness," practiced by the likes of John Cage contemporaneously to but independently of Eco's publication, Reas adapts it to his own art production, realized across multiple media platforms including ink and 3-D printing in addition to screen projection and monitor-dependent interfaces. Conceptualized within the framework of Eco's open work, Reas's multimedia processes can be seen as working against computational determinism. Paralleling LeWitt's wall drawings, which for their material instantiation must adapt to the technical, spatial specificities of the installation site, Reas's processes preserve their vulnerability to constantly shifting technological parameters as a fundamental aspect of their "openness"; in Reas's appraisal, "an open work presents a field of possibilities where the material form as well as the semantic content is open."[45] Despite their surface appearance of dry, even bureaucratic proceduralism, LeWitt's wall drawings thrive on radical contingency—the eccentricities of draughtspeople, irregularities within the installation site, and the uneven texture of walls or materials used to mark their surfaces.

It is here that an unexpected tension appears between the determinacy of code and computational processing, between the contingency and ambiguity of natural language, and to an even greater extent, between unsystematized, analog drawing and precisely and unambiguously mapped digital graphics. For Reas's adaptations of LeWitt's natural language instructions to preserve the openness and ambiguity present in the earlier linguistic algorithms, they must attempt to subvert some of the characteristics of computational technology. Accordingly, he writes one layer of instructions for his Processes in English, so that they may be adapted to new programming languages or adopted and reinterpreted by different artists.

Despite computers' inability to handle ambiguity, they are also tools that allow vigorous change to occur within their programmatic constraints; hence, Reas takes advantage of the dynamics of computational systems to generate "incongruous results which I find more satisfactory than randomness."[46] In this statement Reas gestures to the concept of emergence, a frequent referent for theorists of not only A-Life but also Generative Art.[47] Later in the interview, he expands on this idea, giving a more thorough explanation of emergence as it relates to his work: "The concept of 'emergence' refers to the generation of structures that are not specified or intentionally programmed. Instead of consciously designing the entire structure, I write simple programs to define the interactions between elements. Structure emerges from the discreet movements of each organism as it modifies itself in relation to the environment. The structures generated through this process cannot be anticipated and evolves through continual iterations involving alterations to the programs and exploring the changes through interacting with the software."[48]

Reas explains in 2006, "My work in the past year has synthesized ideas explored in *{Software} Structures* with my previous explorations into emergence. Each new work is called a Process and defines rules and instructions which describe a relation between Elements outside of a specific physical media."[49] As opposed to a model of abstraction that is about smooth, all-over color fields or stark monochromes, Reas's approach is friendly to theories about artificial life, which posit AL systems as relational (and of course narrative, which is peripheral to the discussion here) and digital in the sense that AL is at its core about the dynamic relationships between elements in a system and the pressures these individual elements can exert upon one another in real time and within systemic parameters to direct movement and behavior in unexpected ways. Part of Reas's rationale for using software is that relationality is not static; software creates elements that interact and develop through interactions over time. And the use of multimedia magnifies certain facets of the work, that is, each medium provides a different perspective on the various kinds of interactions the work produces, whether between bodies and spaces, states of the system, actors within the system, and so forth.

Consequently, it is particularly compelling for Reas, as an artist using computational software in *{Software} Structures* to adapt LeWitt's algorithmically produced, exported, and graphically rendered natural-language-based "software," that some kind of processing must occur to translate among the levels of LeWitt's wall drawings, from the concept to the instructions, the draughtsperson, and the specific spatial and material parameters of the installation site. Reas's acts of re-coding and implementing LeWitt's instructions as computational programs necessitates that the original work have an original "source code" that is open to interpretation, retooling, and transmedial implementation. The capacity of LeWitt's instructions to be subjected to restructuring at the level of the base code but to remain, at the level of concept, the same work is a property of the openness of "software"—whether based on natural language or computationally driven—to transformation and realization in multiple media formats.

The critical approach to digital ideology taken by software artists advocates or even requires interpretation of computational processing as a programmatic exploration of the permutational possibilities generated from the interactions of digital parts rather than as a rich, continuous aestheticism based on analog principles. Given the multilayered visual richness of Reas's graphics, that at times display a kind of organic hedonism, it is striking for Reas to claim that "the most important element of each process is the text."[50] Moments such as this are evidence of a fundamental struggle in his practice between the visual and the conceptual, a tension that obtains in several modal dialectics; between algorithmically encoded emergence and drawing; between hardware and software; and between text and image. Reas's transmedial experiments do not unilaterally mobilize critical reflections about software but instead conduct complex appraisals of aesthetic deviations occurring between differential uses of material (and electronic) substrates. In *{Software} Structures*, for example, a new possible iteration of analogico-digital aesthetic hybridity manifests each time a different programming language implements the same set of instructions, revealing the disparities in what these languages can disclose, visually, conceptually, and experientially. Reas's practice can then be viewed as a playful exposition of the revelatory, world-disclosing properties of computation in its relation to materials and media.

To expand, now, the discussion of Reas's projects beyond *{Software} Structures*, like LeWitt, Reas argues that the concept underlying each of his many multimedia projects stands regardless of the medium in which it is realized (screen based, print, etc.). Thus, Reas regards software as a conduit that can translate the generative structural principles of the work—the computational construct—into a variety of media. Specific media highlight specific features of the work. So, for example, in *MicroImage* (2001–2003), Reas employs several "platforms" as follows: "I work in print to reveal the resolution of the system, I work with animation to have complete control of how the image unfolds over time, and I implement the structure in software so it's possible to interact with it. The software implementation is closest to my actual concept, but the other media provide additional views into the structure."[51] In general, computer screens do not possess the same capacity as prints to highlight the delicacy and complexity (or, indeed, multiplicity) of Reas's imagery, demonstrating that although both artifacts are fundamentally software driven, they yield differing aesthetic properties at the back end. Likewise, animations show the dynamic properties of his systems, but the cadences, sequence, duration, and variety of processes visible in any given slice of time are drastically altered given the programming language used to execute the animation. Many of Reas's choices of physical media have to do with resolution: whether to render a print or produce a screen-based image, for example. Some of his aesthetic choices pertain also to his goal of creating "painterly" images; in some of his animations he will bypass limitations in processor speeds, which normally permit only a certain number of lines to be drawn in a given frame. Reas's intervention here produces a greater degree of density of lines in the frame and thus a greater sense of density and repleteness in the picture itself.

Thinking across the limitations and affordances of specific media, in general, broadens the range of perceptual interaction one might have with an artwork. For Reas, presenting his work not just in a multimedia context but also as an active negotiation of the aesthetic parameters normatively exerted by specific technological configurations permits a way of thinking about computational design that thinks hard about what it means to be a medium without giving in to essentialism or reductivism, so that his work can effectively engage in internal dialog about analogicity and digitality, computation, and hybridity. Given cultural expectations about what makes a work more phenomenologically dense and rich (the use of analog technologies), computationally generated or assisted artworks easily run the risk of appearing "flat" or dimensionless, given that they are generated by digital mechanisms, which might seem too simple or atomized to achieve the repleteness and ambiguity we expect of works of fine art. But Reas circumvents the appearance of unidimensionality by employing several different physical media in many of his projects, devising installations that utilize multimedia to underscore the density of his "Processes." Recall that density is a term used to describe and, more importantly, to evaluate the merit of analog pictorial techniques. Consequently, the operative question remains whether Reas's technical choices, while embedded in a digital substrate, attempt to cover over the digital foundations of his processes in favor of promoting an aesthetic based on painterly abstraction.

Printing, for example, does not negate the computational ontogenesis of Reas's "Processes." The print represents only one possible form of the process, so that even in this apparently "closed," unalterable, noninteractive form of presentation, there is always inherently embedded another possible way of seeing. In some senses, this open-ended space of multiple graphic possibilities encourages one to interpret Reas's work as simultaneously, and quite paradoxically, formalist (painterly and object driven) and Conceptualist (placing idea over materiality and process driven). Each interface (paper or screen) makes visible different details. Each sets up its own visual world, its own points of access to the diverse array of latently visible details. Thus, on the one hand this fostering of the visible seems to promote a formalist visuality in which the viewer derives meaning by seeking subtle cues in the visible register. On the other hand, the formal result, similar to LeWitt's wall drawings, can be viewed as an epiphenomenon of the underlying "concept," or more specifically the underlying, driving mechanism, which is of course the computational software itself. Overall, this yields a computational aesthetic that can be identified neither as analog nor as digital.

One important difference to note between Reas and LeWitt is that a central aspect of LeWitt's innovation depended on his abrogation of "painting," where painting signifies handmadeness, contingency, and the authorial mark. His "formulation of a predetermined system" precluded easy classification of his wall drawings into medium-determined categories such as drawing or painting.[52] Here, the medium itself becomes a mirage, shimmering in and out of visible clarity and refusing to cohere in a singular, stable physical form. In his most thoroughly conceptual mode Sol LeWitt advocates for a model of administratively executed art in which the artist plays a clerical role rather than one of a genius master craftsman.[53] But his work seems to perform a series of contradictions as it makes its way into a visual format; LeWitt's argument that the final form is incidental is belied by its adamant, albeit shapeshifting, presence. Ranging from delicate webs of graphite to bold, almost alarming bars of saturated color, LeWitt's wall drawings, as well as many of his modular structures (such as *Serial Project #1*), are visually compelling with or without the accompanying conceptual armature of text/instruction.[54]

Visibility thus remains at the heart of LeWitt's wall drawing practice but

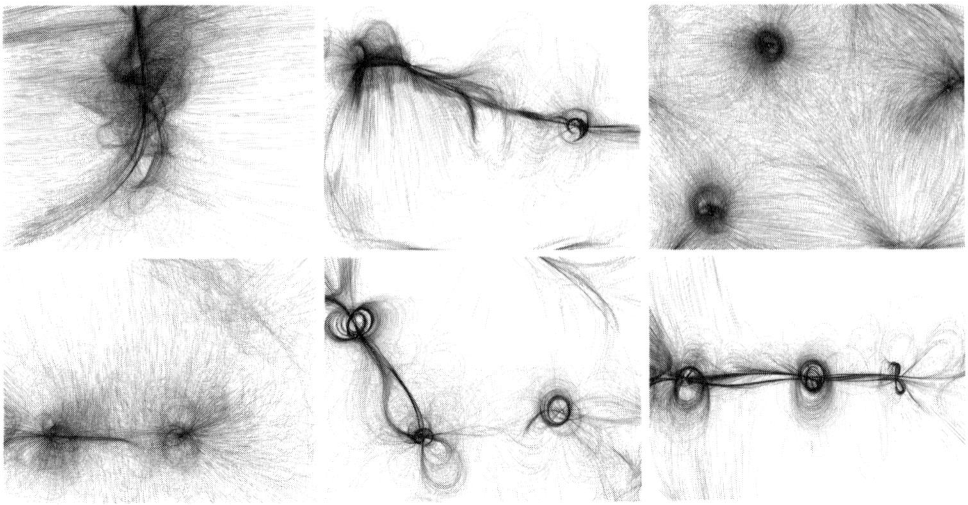

FIGURE 4.3 ▪ Casey Reas, *Tissue*, 2002. © Casey Reas.

coyly, ironically, and often coolly. Even when his drawings emblazon walls with broad, dizzying swaths of saturated color, LeWitt often maintains an aesthetic of mechanization, of a graphic simplicity that conjures the figure of mass production. Reas, on the other hand, makes an about-face back to the painterly, even as he claims that the "core" of his work is "about creating processes and not images."[55] If computational technology is founded upon bureaucratic principles, and if many day-to-day human-computer interactions retain ties to a particular model of utility, Reas turns the ruthless, exhaustive, and exhausting logic of John Simon's *Every Icon*, which we shall visit presently, against itself and toward the multiplicity of entities, tracelines, transparencies, and filaments that compose the painterly surfaces of many Processing sketches.

Reas's *MicroImage* and *Tissue* (2002) series, for example, layer fragile, transparent webs of spindly lines, creating dense, continuous, and replete painterly surfaces, which would seem to position this work at odds with the constitutive features of digital aesthetics. The lines in these pieces themselves are generated by the movements across the screen of small bots or vehicles that leave trails of line and color behind them. While the technical, procedural, and programmatic constraints of computers make them unable to process or deal in ambiguity, *Tissue* and *MicroImage* mobilize the programmatic logic of computation toward an ambiguous end.

The characteristics in *MicroImage* and *Tissue* do not appear to be aesthetically digital. However, the elements that produce the analog, painterly, ambiguous surfaces in these works turn out *not* index the gestural immediacy implied in the act of drawing, as we may have thought. Even though the surface appears to be aesthetically analog, it is in fact a set of digital elements that drive the graphic output of the piece. As I have indicated, the lines extending across the screen or the print are created by digital "vehicles," elements that mimic the mechanical sensors in neuroanatomist Valentino Braitenburg's studies of nervous systems in the 1980s. Reas's simulation of Braitenburg's "vehicles," each containing two sensors to detect environmental conditions and two actuators to propel the machine, are the discrete elements governing the compositional structure of the piece. Rules for the vehicles' interaction—the behavior they will exhibit if they come into contact—control the movement and location of the vehicular agents. What the viewer sees, however, is not the vehicles themselves but their path of travel.

In an electrocardiogram, only the ordinates and abscissas are informationally relevant—the lines connecting them are insignificant. *Tissue*, on the other hand, privileges the connecting lines: what would be, in a notational system such as the EKG, secondary "information." What the viewer observes, instead of the digital units themselves, as in the case of Vasarely's *Alphabet Plastique*, are the tracelines extending behind the elements, similar to the line of frozen vapor trailing an airplane in the sky. In a time-based version of the piece, after a period of scrutinizing the lines as they loop and intersect in seemingly random patterns across the screen, the intently watchful viewer might glean relationships between elements, and even potentially their position on the screen. One might think, then, of this moment of revelation as an instance of the digital furtively showing itself, coming into a partial visibility, but remaining camouflaged by analogicity. Rather than directly observing the simulated mechanisms, one gathers their information secondhand. One can guess at their level of activity and the length of their simulated life-span as drawing agents from the complex curvatures of the lines and the density of their entanglement. These knotted skeins become the sensorially apprehensible effect of the setting-into-motion of a digital system. What is revealed is a painterly, seemingly analog, visual world that is actually a visualization of the byproducts of a digital system in the act of calculation and computation, but it is not itself aesthetically digital. This is an area in which a potential divide between "computational" aesthetic and "digital" aesthetic reveals itself. What the viewer discerns, more than digitality itself, is the area *between* the disjunct units constituting the digital system. Insofar as the system operates computationally, we can nominally classify the continuously unfolding loops of multicolored lines as exhibiting a computational aesthetic. As graphic output of computational processing proliferates before our eyes, the "digital" both stubbornly conceals itself within the tangle of lines and provides the driving mechanism by which the tangle is produced. As such, the computational aesthetic, here, proves to be none other than a hybrid aesthetic combining an analogico-digital sensibility.

In this example, the "digital" acts as a world-building force but does not lay itself bare by foregrounding its compositional discreteness. Relationships between elements, their behaviors gleaned from, notably, the emergent complexity of lines, or their length and density of entanglement become the sensorially apprehensible *effect* of the setting-into-motion of a digital system. The visual domain implied by this depictive schema is about the digital system in the act of calculation and computation. The fibrous mass that results from this experiment signifies a world picture—not necessarily one that imitates our own but a horizon of temporality, event, and exchange that belies the work's outward aspect of decorative abstraction. Discreteness and disjunctness operate as the underlying logic that gives rise to a hybrid, computational aesthetic inflected by complexity and multiplicity, two prominent tropes in media studies that suffuse, in particular, Reas's "organically" inclined works.

Aesthetics of Multiplicity

In 2007 on their respective blogs, Mitchell Whitelaw and Douglas Edric Stanley began, but never pursued, a debate about the aesthetics of Reas and Fry's programming environment, Processing, addressed through the rhetorical figures of complexity and gestalt. Whitelaw engages a comment by Stanley about the preponderance of delicate, often densely interwoven filaments in Processing sketches, suggesting that Processing produces structures of a certain aesthetic nature and by extension that "simple code structures contribute to the formation of gestalts."[56] Stanley writes,

> I'm interested in the nature of all those lovely spindly lines we see populating so many Processing sketches, and how they relate with code structures. Complex forms come cheap in code; all you need is an iterator: it costs almost nothing—from the programmer's perspective—to draw 1 line and n lines, especially when you take performance out of the equation. But beyond the economy of drawing hundreds of thousands of millions of bajillions of lines, what about the perceptive field that emerges from this code? If there is a machinic relationship between the visual forms and the code forms (one our basic tenets), what do these code structures generate in terms of perceptive structures? And does computer code—if treated as a series of recursive abstractions (at least in practice)—form new perception-fields at each stratum of abstraction, synchronized to the code abstraction layers?[57]

Stanley considers not only how to account for the fact that Processing seems to have a particular set of aesthetic properties and how to articulate what those properties are but also how to understand what this aesthetic means.

The aesthetic nature of made objects is a product of the kinds of depictions that are facilitated by the material properties of the medium/tool. In sketches created with Processing, it is just as easy for the program to generate many lines as it is for it to generate one line. But this does not suffice to explain why an artist would want to avail himself or herself of this programmatic capacity, which leaves open the issue of what artistic reason exists to make use of this technological function. Unlike software art that abrogates or challenges human-computer interaction at the surface level of the graphic interface, Processing is a graphics-oriented language written for visual artists and consequently privileges visual thinking. However, the operative problem here is what particular visual idiom is most easily produced from working in Processing and what kind of "perceptual field" results from this complex linear configuration. A medium operates most effectively within a particular perceptual modality: it appeals to one or more senses in a specific way. But this line of reasoning in turn leads to a further question concerning the relationship between the structure of code and the formal/material structure of the resultant pictorialization. Does the structure of the computer code yield not only new (perceptible) kinds of images but also a new way of perceiving the nature of abstract, computer-generated depictions? Is there a gestalt of Processing, and if so, what characterizes it?

Stanley suggests that this gestalt is defined by complexity in a one-line comment inserted between two long passages quoted from Italo Calvino's *Mr. Palomar*, a novel that performs complexity in a formal, stylistic, and conceptual performance of fractallic unfurlings from microscopic to cosmic scale.[58] Stanley's provocative but undeveloped statement, that "ultimately, all of these questions of abstraction and gestalt are in fact questions about our relationship to complexity and the role algorithmic machines (will inevitably) play in negotiating our increasing *complexity malaise*," is decidedly less utopian than Lev Manovich's take on abstraction and complexity, in which modernist reduction gives way to an exuberant proliferation of shapeshifting arabesques in contemporary software-driven abstraction.[59]

Manovich articulates the distinction between the aesthetic properties of modernist and computational abstraction in terms of reduction and complexity, respectively. Reduction, as the governing paradigm of modernist abstraction, has been frequently linked to the development of modern science. Examples of this modernist reduction are found, of course, everywhere from Piet Mondrian's gridded reductions to the essence of a tree, Wassily Kandinsky's visual notations of the essences of musical compositions, and the Cubists' de- and recomposition of volumetric forms into faceted planes. The complexity-based abstraction that emerges alongside electronic computational technology accompanies, responds to, and is inspired by later twentieth-century approaches to science and technology. Whereas the modernist model is fairly one to one, linear, and deterministic—for example, three moving parts will comprise a mechanical whole with predictable behaviors—a complexity-driven aesthetic focuses on emergence, or unpredictable results garnered by chaos and randomness within or across systems. Manovich's definition of an aesthetic of complexity relies heavily on the dynamism and organic curvatures of the systems, mostly pulled from the online portion of the Kunstlerhaus Wien's 2003 exhibition *Abstraction Now*, which he takes as his primary examples. In each instance, the graphic presentation of algorithmic processes yields "dense and intricate fields" that "are never static, symmetrical, or simple—instead they constantly mutate, shift and evolve."[60]

The issue of complexity is one frequently referenced with respect to digital art and new media. John Maeda, Reas's mentor at the MIT media lab, in his book *The Laws of Simplicity*, acknowledges his contribution to the prevalence of visual complexity in computer graphics but simultaneously disowns this trend, dismissing it as a mere "unrelenting stream of 'eye candy' littering the information landscape."[61] Similarly, in Stanley's brief post, which, as Whitelaw points out, introduces questions rather than proposing definitive answers, he concludes that "all of these questions of abstraction and gestalt are in fact questions about our relationship to complexity and the role algorithmic machines (will inevitably) play in negotiating our increasing complexity malaise."[62] Here, Stanley recognizes that a problem that seems formal, or even more precisely technological, is actually a cultural one insofar as it speaks to the ways in which we encounter, interpret, and make meaning (or fail to make meaning) of the images that constitute what might interchangeably be called our world picture or our information landscape. This information landscape is the reflection we give back to ourselves of our lifeworld—the epistemological conditions of possibility for both contextual and situated experience to occur.

A rhetoric of complexity, infused heavily with metaphors of biology, evolution, and organicity, has become nearly endemic in the (albeit relatively small collection of) criticism of computational abstraction. Whereas the trope of reduction in modernist art follows the scientific "deconstruction of the inanimate, biological and psychological realms into simple, further indivisible elements, governed by simple and universal laws," an aesthetic of complexity emerges in response to a new scientific paradigm.[63] The contemporary scientific view, radically different from the classical model of the clockwork universe, produces chaos theory, artificial life, and network theory. Here, simple elements may combine, but their combination results in behaviors that emerge in unpredictable, nonlinear fashion, as they do in Reas's programmed paintings. Both scientifically and metaphorically, in the popular imagination and in artistic interpretation, complexity tends to apply easily to a huge percentage of contemporary cultural production, from the social networking sites endemic to the Web 2.0 to increasingly esoteric branches of physics and the parallel study of biological and information systems. As such, complexity is an appealing trope for the computational age. But it is also a term that becomes quickly monolithic and artificially stabilized.

An absolute division between "modernist" reduction and "contemporary" complexity in itself oversimplifies the artworks in question, given both that the "complex" aesthetic yielded by Reas's computational programming results from a definitive, pared-down number of elements and that, for example, any interpretation of Wassily Kandinsky's musical complexity is severely limited when viewed through the lens of reduction. Moreover, compulsive use of the term "complexity" limits works such as Reas's to mere demonstrations of the fundamental principles of emergence, a fine exercise but not conducive to the discovery of finely tuned observations about individual works of art. Multiplicity, another term that is perhaps less compartmentalized in a particular and somewhat esoteric branch of technoscience, also applies to the aesthetic sensibility—the phenomenal encounter—proffered by Processing's, and particularly Reas's, software-driven abstraction. Both complexity and multiplicity are terms that have been attached, if not indiscriminately, often interchangeably, to digital, code-based artwork. While it is difficult when looking through a collection of work made with Processing to "find an image that isn't some kind of swarm, cloud, cluster, bunch, array or aggregate,"[64] to equate the array of depictions made with Processing by dismissively calling them the inevitable result of using a system that is designed to generate multiples fails to account, first, for the reasons the program is designed this way and, second, for specificities in unique applications of the programming language.

Whitelaw concludes that the aesthetic of multiplicity is "a way to get a perceptual grasp on something quite abstract—that space of possibility. We get a visual 'feel' for that space, but also a sense of its vastness, a sense of what lies beyond the visualisation."[65] The fundamental characteristic of computational systems is their open-endedness—their ability to create spaces of inexhaustible potential that are not "virtual" in the mimetic sense but fundamentally about ongoing transformation. Similar to LeWitt's wall-drawing instructions,

Processing launches simple linear algorithms and recursive functions—redrawing (aggregation), overlay, accumulation, and compression—to gesture toward the fundamental mutability and expansiveness of rule-based systems. Generative, computational systems and spaces are thus, in principle, inexhaustible. By creating sets of constraints and letting the system play itself out within those constraints, they visualize the vast possibilities for mutation and transformation even within closed systems, thus adding the dimensions of complexity and multiplicity to a hybrid, computational aesthetic.

From Conceptual to Organic Systems

Launched at 9:42 a.m. on 27 January 1997, *Every Icon* is an online computational/conceptual artwork that artist John F. Simon claims he envisioned in response to the 1980s' postmodernist intonations about the death of art and the end of images. In this work, every possible combination of black and white squares runs sequentially within the parameters of a thirty-two-by-thirty-two grid (enclosing 1,024 squares). Although Simon's (who, in an interview with Reas acknowledges his own deep indebtedness to Sol LeWitt's algorithmic imagination) *Every Icon* falls more neatly into the grid-based aesthetic of early computer art, this work provides an interesting point of comparison to the seemingly organic proliferations of Processing sketches.

In 1997, with Pentium processor speeds capable of generating one hundred combinations per second, Simon estimated that all possible combinations in the top line—about 4.3 billion variations—could be completed in sixteen months. But given the exponential expansion of these combinatorial possibilities, it would take about six billion years to complete the second line. For the grid to reach its final state, in which every square turns to black, it would take several hundred trillion years—an ungraspable number that Simon asks us to consider as a "human perceptual limit."[66] In 1997 he offered the *New York Times* the following explanation: "Because there's no word for that amount of time and no word for that large a number, several hundred trillion years is my way of making you think about a very, very long time."[67] And even if processor speeds increased enough to shorten that time span, the speed of transformation would vastly exceed the capacity of the human eye to stabilize the field of black and white squares into an image.

Every Icon falls much more heavily to the side of conceptual generative systems than organic systems such as *Tissue* (a distinction Reas offers with respect to his own work). Whereas the multiplicity of "spindly lines" executed so frequently by Processing gives a sense of biological proliferation, *Every Icon* recalls much more strongly the strictly rectilinear organization of the grid that so intrigued modern artists spanning the twentieth century. *Every Icon*'s digital aesthetic, in the strict sense of the word, in which each unit is discrete, regular, and interchangeable, is tied intrinsically to the conceptual framework of the piece, which is built on the permutational possibilities of computation itself. In addition, the work is constructed not only on an idea of the computational sublime, on the massive computing power of the machine, but also on its fundamental situatedness in time. Although the system is designed on the basis of a successive algorithmic process, the sheer number of calculations necessary to achieve its end point and the span of time it would require to do so make the program practically if not theoretically (or experientially if not mathematically) open ended and indeterminate. While the piece makes itself available to the viewer through a graphical interface, the built-in possibility that the grid will reveal something like a picture —a face, a landscape, or even a triangle—is in practice only a counterfactual dream, as even the second horizontal line will never run through all its possible combinations in ten, twenty, or fifty generations.

Thus, the aesthetic in *Every Icon* simultaneously engages sense perception and refuses to grant visual resolution or completion. It initially calls upon the viewer's sensorium only to render the senses impotent in grasping the aim of the work. In contrast, what Whitelaw calls elsewhere the "system story" of the more sensorially rich aesthetic of Processing is less confrontationally conceptual. *Every Icon* evokes Conceptualist dematerialization by promising eventual pictorialization but ultimately frustrating that desire. In opposition to this rather pugnacious (or, alternatively, intriguingly elusive) digitized Conceptualism, the rich, painterly abstractions tracing and unfolding themselves in Reas's installations seem to offer up, as we have seen, an analogico-digital hybrid aesthetic to replace the austerity of Simon's 1997 propositional piece.

John Simon uses the digital—the way it looks, the way it behaves, and its constitutive features and properties—as a generative motor for *Every Icon*. Simon's overtly digitized interface functions as a conduit for its theoretical underpinnings. The activation of simple combinatorics references the digital sublime, its exploration of the counterfactual ideal that a "machine" can "produce every possible image," and its paradoxical combination of programmatic linearity with open-ended irresolvability. As Simon himself acknowledges, "While *Every Icon* is resolved conceptually, it is unresolvable in practice. In some ways the theoretical possibilities outdistance the time scales of both evolution and imagination. It posits a representational system where computational promise is intricately linked to extraordinary duration and momentary sensation."[68] The almost frustrating open-endedness of this piece is oddly thrown into relief by its clinical simplicity. Moreover, this simplicity does not render it anesthetic but rather discloses its resolutely *digital* aesthetic, which emerges not just from the fact that it is obviously always in the process of computing something but also from its adherence to the strict definition of the digital based on discreteness, interchangeability, and so forth.

The digital aesthetic qualities of *Every Icon*'s schematic landscape, as well as its air of rigor and (a rather laughable) efficiency, provide another genetic link between Conceptual Art's bureaucratic aesthetic and the visuality of digital-computational systems. The precision and severe simplicity of Simon's visual landscape might strengthen the perception that if digital graphics are rife with conceptual rigor due to their computational/programmatic ontology, they are also concomitantly devoid of visual nuance. *Every Icon*'s diminutive size and (lack of) color scheme bespeak an attitude toward the art object similar to that of the Conceptual Artists of the 1960s and 1970s. However, while the "look of thought" as rigorous, axiomatic, and "digital" is the calling card of Conceptual Art, the majority of Reas's production shifts the graphic simplicity of *{Software} Structures* to an analogy between digital systems and organic life.

Reas has claimed that his art production falls into two distinct types of systems. He applies the terms "organic" and "Conceptual" to these systems—terms that bear a (somewhat unstable and problematic) relationship to analog and digital. He repeats aspects of the distinction made by Manovich between modernist reduction and contemporary complexity in his own differentiation between "Conceptual" systems, which "are more formal and explore the nature of software, representation, notation, and process" and "organic" systems, which explore "the phenomenon of emergence," a notion often applied to the simulation of biological processes using computational means.[69] While Reas sees these trends developing separately in his work, both trends stage visual explorations of software, representation, notation, and process. And while we might suppose that one graphic mode would appear more digital than the other, both combine digital and analog aesthetic elements, thus demonstrating that computational technology does not necessarily result in a digital aesthetic.

At first, Reas's distinction between "Conceptual" and "organic" seems as if it should map evenly onto the parameters of "digital" and "analog." Descriptively, the organic would appear to be differentiated from the digital because it refers to continuously unfolding processes, such as the growth of a plant. According to a noncybernetically or computationally influenced definition, organic growth, and life itself, are analog because between each two states of growth we can always locate another state between them to an indeterminate degree of fineness. Organic systems are, then, continuously variable. In digital systems, on the other hand, states are determinate—either on or off, black or white—

there are no gradations or intermediate steps between digital symbols. They are fully disjunct from one another, discrete, and articulate.

But is this organicity coextensive with analog aesthetic properties, which Reas champions in his effort to make his digitally programmed virtualizations seem as immediate and fluid as possible? Is the distinction between Conceptual and organic systems a subtly masked rejection of digital aesthetics in favor of traditional analog aesthetics? On the contrary, the aesthetic of multiplicity, or what Reas names "organicity," complicates the equivalence between a digital aesthetic sensibility and minimal graphic schemas in which discreteness and disjunctness are not only present but also enhanced (what Manovich might deem a reductive modernist machine aesthetic), as in the case of *Every Icon*. What we often find is that the most intuitively "organic" systems in the computational domain do not necessarily demonstrate the most continuous or "analog" aesthetic sensibility. We can think back to Watz's *ElectroPlastique*, which, as I argued previously, provides us with an associative adaptation of Vasarely's programmed universe, and thus a "new abstraction." But *ElectroPlastique* also renders a perceptibly digital, grid-based organicity that is both alien and phenomenologically intuitive. What *ElectroPlastique* quite efficiently discloses to the viewer is that although neither the notions of digitality nor organicity should be adopted with uncritical abandon, digital systems can maintain digital aesthetic properties while successfully rendering more complex, multiple, and even spectacular depictive schemas that redefine the normative visual parameters of organicity.

Conceptual systems do not embody the immediacy or the qualities of handmadeness, perceptual density, and fluidity that Reas seeks in his organic systems. One approach seems much more about the facilities of computational technology itself; the Conceptual area focuses on foregrounding the particularities of technological systems. His 2003 project, *Ora*, for example, shows the compositional/foundational substrate—the building blocks—of digital pictures. Unlike Jason Salavon's mottled Rothkoesque color fields, which will be examined more thoroughly in the next chapter, *Ora* attempts to make perceptible the fact that digital images are comprised of individual "signals" or numeric sequences that contain the information for specific color values by presenting the signal as layered, sequenced "leaves" of color. *Ora*, similar to another project, *Mediation* (2002), which dissolves the representational content of the picture and rearranges it into vertical striated bands of color, echoes Salavon's painterly amalgamations and other averaging projects, revealing the way in which even the most aestheticized, painterly examples of digital abstracting are still deeply informed by the performative aspect of their medium: the ability of digital technology to calculate data and the need for objects and phenomena to be reduced to data—to be numericized—in order to be calculated. Reas describes the visual results of *Mediation*'s image processing as an "empty aesthetic surface."[70] The bands of color are certainly emptied of easily legible symbolic content, but they signify nevertheless about the inhuman processes of computation itself. Computers are devices for computation, and these various abstractions are directly and unapologetically the product of a computational process, whether that process consists of averaging, compression, or some other data-mining function.

Reas's systems, such as *MicroImage*, which do not create a sense of an overall surface but rather animate a field of parts, which through their interactions create "complex holistic structures," operate differently than *Ora* and Salavon's amalgamations.[71] Their holism is one of continuous aggregation and entanglement instead of smoothing through the process of averaging. The question is whether averaging is more invested in calculating sameness than amalgamating is in generating relationality, and in turn if a digital aesthetic sensibility would be governed by sameness (after all, it is predicated upon interchangeability of elements) or difference. I would argue that averaging leads to an entropic state that deviates from the energy present in aggregative pieces such as *MicroImage*. Furthermore, pace Gilles Deleuze, I would contend that not necessarily difference but relationality and indeed nuance can be located in repetition, of units, for example. Works such as *MicroImage* are inspired by Reas's interest in artificial life but should not merely be seen as "demonstrations" of computational evolutionary algorithms insofar as they are a very particular aesthetic manifestation of an analogico-digital system predicated upon the relational movement of digital units and the entanglement of their linear paths. These overall patterns of delicate lines, circles, or shapes reminiscent of underwater plants reveal what occurs when the disjunct digital "vehicles" are let loose, leaving behind their imprints as layers of color and etched-in afterimages of their generative, relational elements.

■ Processes as "Painting": Painting and Digital Media

In several recent Processes, Reas puts into play the various slips, gaps, and incommensurabilities that occur between the various instantiations of the underlying "idea." In fact, it is after his *{Software} Structures* project that Reas begins to allow the digital literally to parallel the analog aesthetic exhibited in *Tissue*. Reas's works after 2004, which he calls "Processes," exhibit a tripartite structure, in which natural language "instructions," in homage to LeWitt, are accompanied by a divided screen. The divided screen of Reas's Processes display

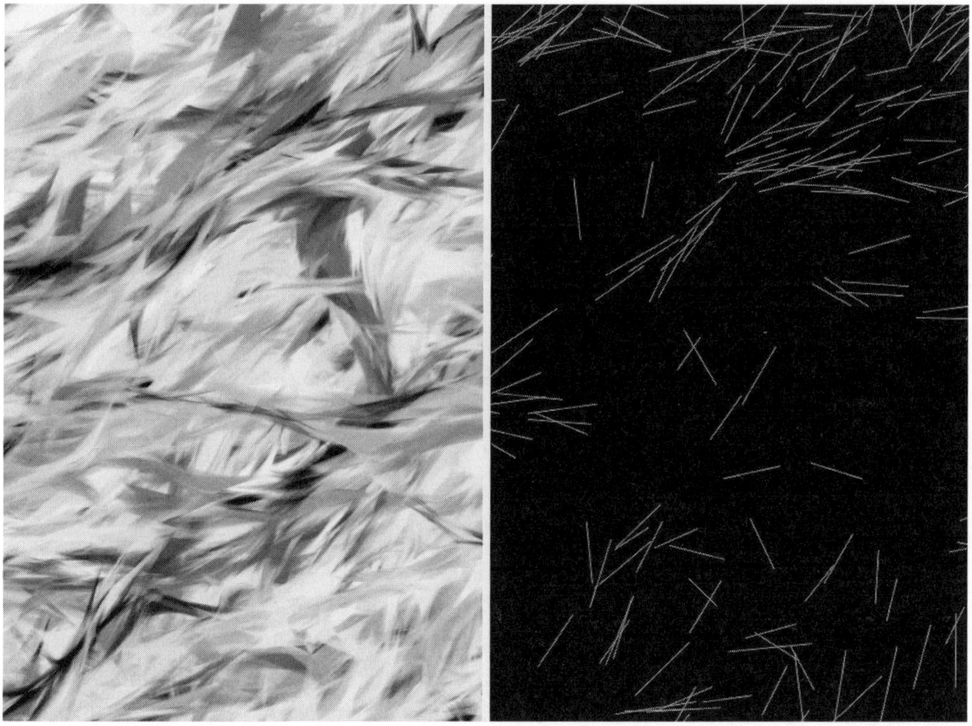

FIGURE 4.4 ▪ Casey Reas, *Process 18*. Unique custom software. Dimensions variable. 2007. © Casey Reas.

on their right half a simplified notation of the underlying processes, while the left half transfers attention from the skeletal structure of the piece to its surface. The visual component of the piece consists of two screens, side by side, each one showing two possible implementations of the instructions. In *Process 18*, the right screen displays a simplified digital schema of the underlying processes of the generative software. Here, a skeletal array of short white lines against a black screen reveals the "mechanism" determining the behavior of individual parts as they touch, collide, and rebound. Similar to *{Software} Structures*, "Structure 003," in which lines demarcating the intersections of the moving circles are shown in the "intermediate" phase of implementation, in *Process 18* the right screen gives up the "trick," the "game," or the "conceptual undergirding" of the work, precisely by showcasing the schematic, digital structure that underlies the painterly swaths on the left screen.

The notational visuality of the right screen more closely approximates the textual form of language-based instructions in the sense that it provides a concrete illustration of the rules governing the behavior of the elements and the surface qualities of the outermost layer or "skin" of the piece. On the left screen the mechanistic structural elements—the skeletal backbones—are erased, as the orthogonals and transversals disappear from a perspective painting, leaving the surface effects—here, curved, layered lines, of varying degrees of transparency and various degrees of saturation on a grayscale—available to sensory apprehension. In contrast to the austere structuralism of the right-hand screen, then, its neighbor on the left reveals the more "painterly" aspect of Reas's multilayered process compendium, offering up an abstract, gestural surface that, minus the textures, is more reminiscent of Jackson Pollock's action painting than Vasarely's heavily digitized *Alphabet Plastique*. However, these works are more "digital" than the others I have discussed because the digital and analog surfaces are placed in parallel. In *Process 18* the side-by-side placement of the screens does not erect a hierarchy in which the analog is granted final pride of place.

In both the "Conceptual" case of *{Software} Structures* and the "organic" cases of *Tissue* and *MicroImage*, digital mechanisms, such as a line of a specific number of pixels, become drawing "agents," but in the act of drawing, they obscure their digitality, rendering the digital, in Reas's practice, a technological rather than an aesthetic category. In *Tissue*, the computationally simulated bots mimicking Braitenburg's neural motors are digital—they are registered by the system in terms of their position at any given moment. But whereas the bot's position is digital—it can only occupy one encoded position at a time, the visible output of the system is continuous, fluid, and aesthetically analog. Despite Reas's claim that the conceptual strain of his practice is "more formal and explores the nature of software, representation, notation, and process," in the end, computational process is foregrounded in both his so-called Conceptual and organic pieces, whereas the digital occupies a more unstable position at both ends of the spectrum. In the end, Reas's work does not evidence two entirely separate strains, one toward the organic and one toward the conceptual. Instead, these two impulses swirl playfully around one another in a noisy feedback loop. They are each practices built on digital platforms but shot through with the specter of the analog.

In contrast to the austere structuralism of the right-hand screen, then, its neighbor on the left reveals the more "painterly" aspect of Reas's multilayered process compendium. Line, color, depth, and volume are all terms used frequently to describe the formal qualities of a painting. But one word I take to be of utmost importance, and one that is elided by the terms above, is *gesture*. As was well demonstrated in Abstract Expressionism, the brushstroke, the direction, force, and texture of the application of paint to a surface bears an indexical relationship to the hand of the markmaker. Reas writes in 2003, "Gesture is a critical aspect of every continuous medium and software has the ability to convey and interpret gesture."[72] While painting bears the indexical impression of the gesture, and as such effects a sense of "presence," no matter how ghostly or distant, software is a medium that can only simulate gesture. It can "recognize" movement and calculate paths of travel. But in and of itself it can only convey theatrically,[73] and interpret computationally. Looking back to Walter Seitter's explication of digitality derived from the individuated "digits" of the hand, a theory based on Leroi-Gourhan's research on the relationship between evolution, physiology, technology, and meaning, we can observe a split in the relationship we have to "the hand" in its figural sense. The hand is, in one instance, an accounting device, a tool, that first exists not as an extension but as part of the body itself, but that leads nevertheless toward the development of tools for abstract, disembodied calculation. This is one extreme. And in the opposite instance the hand becomes something different—a mark of presence, a signature, and an index of movement whose force (pressure) and propulsion (momentum) had been at some point exerted by a living body and is now captured as a trace in a physical medium.[74] In the first example, the hand activates a bond between the body and its technological extensions, while in the second, it acts as a bridge, providing a metonymical link between the mark and the embodied producer of that mark.

In his brief catalog essay for *Code: The Language of Our Time*, the 2003 Ars Electronica festival in Linz, Austria, Reas appends Roy Ascott's and Myron Kruger's characterizations of the visual, cognitive, and relational affordances of computational media. Ascott proposes that we have transitioned from thinking of media tolls in terms of "content, object, perspective, and representation,"[75] all of which derive from the distantiation of sight and intellection from the "lower" end of the human sensorium, to a system in which media are oriented to "context process, immersion, and negotiation."[76] Kruger maintains that human-computer interactions turn on dialog, amplification, ecosystem, instrument, game, and narrative.[77] But Reas suggests that these terms fail to reveal the basic genotype of software-enabled communication; for him, software-generated expressivity emerges from "dynamic form, gesture, behavior, simulation, self-organization, and adaptation."[78]

In LeWitt's wall drawings, aspects of subjectivity (if not the artist's subjectivity but rather the draughtsperson's) are visible in the draughtsperson's particular imagination, configuration, and execution of LeWitt's instructions. Elements of gesture may be found in small irregularities in lines and contours; however, LeWitt's work is far less focused on gesture than Reas's, which ironically contains no actual index of a marking hand. Artist Penny Feuerstein has used her art practice to open dialogs and pathways between the analog and the digital. Feuerstein identifies the deviations not just in the phenomenology of *viewing* painting versus digital structures but in the process of *making* as well. The practice of painting is, for Feuerstein, a highly physical, embodied experience, in which "the tangible, kinesthetic experience of holding a paintbrush in my hands, feeling the movement between brush, oil paint and canvas traveling up my hand, arm, and into my body is totally different from manipulating images with a mouse, on a screen, then clicking a button that tells a machine to print. Paint is thick and juicy. A print is flat and smooth. There is no getting around the visceral differences."[79]

This is not, however, to dismiss the computer as conceptually or perceptually dimensionless. Instead, the construction of digitally rendered imagery encourages her to consider the shape of life "from a subatomic perspective."[80] This seems to be another way of saying that the composite structure of digital artifacts might press us to think more clearly about the architectonics of the material world rather than about the properties of surfaces. Of course, volume and depth—dimension—can all be explored using techniques of applying paint to canvas. A "digital aesthetic," conceived broadly, extending past the technohistorical horizon of the invention of the computer, presents us with a view not just of the surfaces of the material world but also of its architectonic principles: the bits and pieces that comprise it, the dynamic forces that hold these bits together, and the principles of movement and change that permit forms to grow, decay, or recombine.

The following conclusion will explore in further detail the relationship between digital media (technoscience) and painting. This final section will examine the more recent work of Reas, as well as the work of Jason Salavon, an artist who bridges art and technoscience by using computationally generated or digitized data to create painterly visual surfaces deeply resonant of high modernist abstraction. If the visible elements of painting can be transcribed through the action of digital processing, then it must be asked what is achieved by maintaining the distinction between painting and digital imaging. Digital imaging is more often compared to photography than painting, partly because there seems to exist a much larger intuitive gap between painting and digital image production. Painting requires the gestural application of pigment to surface; it communicates on the level not only of shape, color, depth, and volume but also of texture, viscosity, and the materiality of the paint itself that might be sensed as hardness and reflectivity in the case of lacquer or oil paint and soft, diffuse transparency in the case of watercolor. Hand-paintedness does not necessarily imply imprecision, as we have seen in the work of Roy Lichtenstein. Conversely, the use of automated tools is certainly no guarantor of regularity and digital interchangeability, as we can see in the screenprints of Andy Warhol and that we have examined more carefully in the raster paintings of Sigmar Polke. Painting, then, seems to occupy an insistently analogical position on a continuum between "pure" digitality and "pure" analogicity, both of which are nearly counterfactual extremes due to the rarity of their appearance in a pure and unmuddied state.

Conclusion

Amalgamations

From Digital Painting to Information Visualization

The preceding chapters of this book have not, largely, questioned the boundary between art and nonart. The argument has been presented here that pictorialization, as opposed to other forms of symbolic communication, including writing or timekeeping, is expected to conform to analog aesthetic characteristics. Picture-making, as a mode of "capturing" or encapsulating individual views of what the eye sees, or what the eye might see in an alternate physical universe, engages with—even as it twists, anamorphizes, facets, or pixilates the pictorial field—what might be called "natural vision." And while arguments in vision science suggest that vision might itself be digital, the analog experience of vision (as continuously correlated to the perceived surface and as smoothly resolved, in defective cases tending toward blur rather than dissolution into a field of digital granules) means that despite the possibility that physiologically vision is digital, experientially (or phenomenologically) it is analog. This is not to say that all pictures inherently try to imitate "natural vision" (whatever this would be) or to create perfect continuity between real and pictorial space. As we have seen, and as many more examples extending further back into deep and prehistory show, there is far greater evidence that depiction does something else: it does not try to imitate, but instead, as art, it attempts to make strange, to exaggerate, and to defamiliarize.

Many very different scholarly approaches have arrived at this conclusion, taking, for example, "defamiliarization," a term famously applied from the literary arts in 1917 by Russian critic Viktor Shlovsky. According to Shlovsky, "The technique of art is to make objects 'unfamiliar,' to make forms difficult to increase the difficulty and length of perception because the process of perception is an aesthetic end in itself and must be prolonged."[1] In a divergent but subtly related vein, recent arguments by proponents of "neuroaesthetics"[2] have proposed that art carries not only a signifying function but also what I might call a "singularizing" capacity, to make an artifact (signal) stand out from the background (noise). Ellen Dissanayake has argued that making art, what might be called artificing, has an adaptive function and is thus a biological propensity that has been evolutionarily hardwired into human psychology.[3] In particular, what differentiates the aesthetic experience of art from nonart—a marble sculpture from a stunning view of a natural landscape—is the idea that what Dissanayake calls "artifying" is an act of "making special." The distinction here, according to Dissanayake, is that "'making special' not 'beauty' or 'display,' explains the difference between a collection of decorated yams and a field or wildflowers, or a headdress composed of the colored feathers of thousands of birds and the feathers of the bird itself."[4] Making special directly recalls the term *techne*, the act of making itself, which becomes technological. Materials are transformed beyond their basic properties into new configurative schemas imbued with new capacities for dynamism and generativity. Our experiential frameworks are distinctively marked by these artifacts. Consequently, we can say that this process of "making special" bears a marked resemblance to Shlovsky's defamiliarization, despite the very different origins of the theoretical, philosophical, and scientific armature supporting these two terms.

If the culturally and historically narrow definitions of art inherited from Enlightenment ideals[5] are expanded, it is possible to incorporate alternate forms and practices into an artistic canon. Furthermore, if the delineation of pictures from other symbol systems is discarded in order to adapt the idea that artificing or artifying is about "making special," it is not too far a leap to incorporate a category of graphic production not generally included within the fine arts, namely, information visualization, into the art historical canon on the basis of not only its making special but also its making *visible*, at the outset, of patterns of information. That which seemed in the first instance not to have a perceptible "body" is given shape, but it is a shape whose relationship to high art is on shakier ground than even Pop Art was to skeptics in the 1960s.

Moreover, information visualization gives what is perceptually abstract—fields of numerical values, for instance—a concrete shape in which relations between values are made visible. In its most utilitarian guise, information visualization strives for clarity and works to make the invisible visible, but it also renders the visible relational. It shows the interconnectedness of quantized values, and how those connections can take shape, can be shown to exert mutual patterns of influence by creating a meaningful network of relations that possess architectonic features. Information visualization, in other words, shows how unorganized "data" becomes "information" when it is systematized and ordered. Systems of structuring and patterning meaning can be thought of as immaterial architectures that influence or direct human thought, feeling, and behavior. Information visualization shows how even immaterial quantities have distinct material effects.

Nevertheless, these artifacts do not seem to conform to the Western, post-eighteenth-century-criteria accorded to art objects. Utilitarian pictorializations that are designed to visualize information, as do maps and charts, or that illustrate other forms of knowledge, as does a mathematical diagram, do not fit the aesthetic rubric used to define art objects. Musical scores notate an art form but do not themselves, in their state as relatively mute visual artifacts, constitute the art object. Instead, as in the case of Conceptual Art, it is the "idea" (the performance or manifestation) of the content notated on the score that becomes the art. The typeset in which a poem by Shakespeare is printed contains a significantly lower "art quotient" than the strings of words that comprise the poem. Thus, notationality, the overarching framework within which the digital is a categorical subset might be a medium, a channel, or an instrument for the delivery of an art experience, but it is not itself the sine qua non, that is, the endpoint or the final, objectival token of the type known as "art."

To review, there are many reasons for this rejection of digital and notational systems, or at least for the frequent suspicion of their status with respect to normative definitions of art. As previous chapters have argued, within the history of aesthetics it has been presumed that pictures would be a product of analog processes and would therefore exhibit aesthetic features that include continuity, smoothness, and perceptual ambiguity. The analog picture is irreducible, on the level of both form and content, to a distinct quantitatively assessed set of values. In an analog scheme, one can discern, hypothetically, an infinite gradation of detail. The aesthetic markers of analog processing have appeared in many aesthetic models. For example, it can be found in Heinrich Wölflinn's theorization of "the painterly," which is associated with the dissolution of the line, or an "indeterminate character," of depicted forms; it is a roiling, open-ended sense of movement and an indistinct yet insistent gravitational weight conveyed by the play of light and shadow.[6]

The digital emerges from a very different structural logic; digital composition is inherently discrete, schematic, metric, and modular. In Nelson Goodman's classic example of the morphologically similar but semantically distinct illustrations of an EKG and a painting of Mt. Fuji by Katsushika Hokusai, the Hokusai painting is exemplary of analog values, so that every linear modulation, every increase in pressure or thickness of ink, potentially affords a new layer of meaning.[7] The EKG, by contrast, exemplifies a digital system, in which only the abscissas and ordinates bear meaning but the lines connecting them are insignificant. As a subset of notation, the digital is characterized by "digits" that become discrete units for tallying and counting. Information is, of course, processed digitally in today's electronic computers, but the digital as an analytic and a perceptual category can be disaggregated from the technical specificities of today's hardware and software. Rather, the digital refers to a particular configurative schema—to a state in which materials or signals operate and are operated upon as discrete states, as distinct from the continuous variation of the analog. Digital symbol systems may appear in the form of pixels but may also manifest in a variety of other mark-making practices, such as points on a graph, in which a unit of measure has been assigned and outside of which no indeterminate state can be registered.

Digitality renders what might appear to be dense, infinitely graduated, or irreducible to a discretely legible quantity that can then be placed into relationship with other quantities and, ultimately, can be used in calculating processes. Alan Turing's "machine"—the notional thought experiment proposed by Turing in 1950 that simulates all possible computers and thus becomes the basis for computer science—and subsequent instruments of technoscience all require the "finite, fixed" values of a symbol system such as an alphabet or binary ones and zeros, outside of which no intermediate values are permissible, recognizable, and computable by the machine. In an alternate articulation of what has been named density, repleteness, ambiguity, and irreducibility, Warren Sack writes that "Turing's definitions assume that one will ignore 'inconvenient' or 'unprofitable' details, while it is never *a priori* obvious for the functioning of a 'desiring machine' which details are significant and which are to be ignored."[8] In other words, information machines select which values will be communicatively relevant and suppress all (or most) other values, in contrast to the traditional view that works of art are to be accorded *greater* worth based on their irreducible, constantly proliferative and polymorphous zones of meaning. Based on this estimation, the aims of technoscientific machines are fundamentally at odds with the aims of art to make strange, to exaggerate, or to defamiliarize. It is for this reason that Sack goes on to argue that painting should be viewed "*not* as equivalent, in some sense, to the artifacts and processes of high technology but, rather, as distinctly different than the kinds of work that scientists and engineers currently engage in."[9] Technoscience works toward determinacy, quantization, and repeatability, while art creates a field of semantic possibility that cannot be contained in a single interpretive thread.

What is held in common between the two seemingly separate depictive methodologies practiced within "art" and "technoscience," however, is that both art and technoscience use information and other visual models to make visible what had been previously invisible, whether that invisibility is imposed by the limitations of the human eye—its inability to see areas of brain activity or immaterial data sets—or by the oversights produced by normatively constrained "scopic regimes."[10] Information visualization adds another layer of recursion to the process of "digitizing" the world—of parsing the world into discrete units —by translating a data set that has already been quantized into a sensorially apprehensible, qualitative entity. In most cases, information visualization attempts to deliver information with the greatest clarity and efficiency, while also (and this is where the term "aesthetics" as it is mobilized in infographics circles becomes murky) offering up a visually pleasing visual schema. Its primary objective of translating numerical data into digestible visual form with a minimum of loss and obfuscation correlates to the communicative function of art objects, which convey meaning visually. However, "pictorial" meaning is less definite or deterministic than the visual semantic mode of information visualization.

All the artworks discussed in this book have retained a certain degree of analogic ambiguity and as such have not pushed the boundaries of "art" past the breaking point, into the domain of design or information visualization. Nevertheless, they have circled around the trope of information, either raising it as a specter or pulling it directly into the foreground in order to test its aesthetic limits. This conclusion will briefly examine information more directly through the work of Jason Salavon, an artist whose work hovers at the boundaries of art and information visualization, and some additional works by Casey Reas that diverge quite sharply from those discussed in chapter 4. Although the art discussed here ultimately lands on the side of art by obfuscating its data sources rather than working toward visual clarity, the medium under consideration, with which the artists create alternately painterly and digitized abstractions, is information itself.

Jason Salavon, an artist and professor at the University of Chicago, combines his training in fine arts and computer science to create software-based works that blur the line between photography and information visualization. Salavon's "data sets," selected from the cluttered vaults of culturally communal material, have included, among other examples, every *Playboy* centerfold between the years of 1988 and 1997, and state and county information collected by the U.S. census bureau between the years 1790 and 2000. He designs and implements software processes that generate images whose overall shape and structural patterns derive from relationships, computed by the software, between discrete elements of the data that fall within the described parameters for the "set."

But rather than attempting to deliver pertinent information as straightforwardly as possible, the images rendered by Salavon's data-analysis software depict the collapse of information that occurs when the isometric pressure exerted by layering data onto itself becomes too great for the image to maintain a clear distinction between signal and noise. His images are beautiful, fascinating, and even hypnotic; but they are quite a different beast from charts and graphs one might find in science textbooks or on the pages of the *New York Times*. Salavon's art can be read as a series of experiments that test the idea that one can never have too much information. These experiments inquire into the artistic and semantic possibilities that emerge when information is pushed beyond its capacity to transmit data as a range of related but differentiated values.

Why visualize information? What does information visualization try to "do" with data? Typically, the goal of information visualization is to give a perceptible shape, a way of making conceptual and phenomenological sense of a large or complex data set. Emerging as a formal discipline in the early 1980s, when scientists began to consider how to render abstract data more quickly and easily legible at a glance, information visualization set itself to the task of translating numerical data into graphical patterns that would reveal internal relationships between data elements and would make possible the topographical mapping of the informatic territory in question. Martin Wattenberg, a manager at IBM's Visual Communication Lab and a central figure in information visualization (info-vis) and digital art circles alike, points out that "visualization technologies can represent the 'unrepresentable'; things that could not possibly be seen can be visualized. For instance, the flow of blood in a heart cannot be seen, but a visualization generated from sensor data can create an image that represents the flow or lack of it."[11] There is an implicit equation here between visualization and clarity. To visualize a data set within a particular design schema is to make it knowable, sensible, and digestible.

As I have intimated, information visualization, the mode of image-making that motivates the artistic appropriations by Salavon and Reas does not typically fall within the borders of art. Even in its nonartistic instantiations, however, information visualization is representative of a mode of computational depiction invested in aesthetics, and particularly in issues surrounding the effects of aesthetics on visual communication. Data visualization originated in the statistics and science, domains in which empirical verification and the pursuit of objectivity hold sovereignty over such philosophically muddy notions as "aesthetics," "beauty," and "taste." In a 2005 posting to the IBM website, Wattenberg informed curious "info-vis beginners" that

> some of the biggest scientific discoveries hinged on turning data into pictures. One famous example of visualization is the periodic table of elements:

When Mendeleev published a grid-like arrangement of elements for a textbook in 1869, not only did he create a beautifully simple display of known data, but his diagram highlighted gaps in current knowledge that told scientists where to search for new elements.

Visualization has always involved a partnership between science and art. A wonderful example is the work of Santiago Ramon y Cajal in the late nineteenth century. Ramon y Cajal, a doctor who trained as an artist, used a new staining technique to examine brain tissue. He created a series of drawings that are so clear and precise they are still used today in introductory neuroscience courses.[12]

Wattenberg emphasizes in this statement the simplicity of Dmitri Mendeleev's periodic table and the precision of Santiago Ramón y Cajal's drawings. Wattenberg's text argues for the effectiveness of simplicity and precision in the visual register but, in so doing, reveals a gap between the notions of aesthetic success in mathematics and in art. According to Gian-Carlo Rota, the phenomenological experience of beauty in mathematics tends to be associated with brevity—a theorem, for example, should arrive at proof in the smallest number of steps.[13] For John Maeda, design should give the viewer just enough information but not too much. Both Rota and Maeda assert that aesthetic principles play an instrumental role in ascertaining the validity of mathematical proof (Rota) or clear communication in design (Maeda).

Because it appears more frequently on Wall Street than in blue-chip galleries, information visualization resides in a liminal state, somewhere between art and industry tool. When it appears in festivals and galleries, information visualization might be considered a form of outsider art that is intellectually interesting to a small number of practitioners and theorists but fails to make the leap into an emergent canon of contemporary art. Although the surface of the image might contain a sufficient degree of complexity and harmony to warrant aesthetic analysis, the foundation of information visualization in statistical notation rather than in the fine arts seems to place it outside of an art-historical chain of reference. However, it is precisely in this resistance to canonization that information visualization shows its potential simultaneously to reproduce and to reflect upon the effects of the figure of information on the contemporary worldview as well as on representation itself.

However, the aesthetic variability in specific info-vis examples shows that effective communication (simplicity and accessibility of design) does not necessarily overlap with the achievement of *artistic* success. Wattenberg's *Map of the Stock Market* is a well-known example of an information visualization piece that rests primarily in the "function" category. It was produced for Smartmoney.com, the website for *SmartMoney* magazine, whose subtitle, *Investing, Saving, and Personal Finance*, identifies the magazine as a decidedly business-oriented publication rather than an artistic one. Wattenberg's map is designed to allow viewers to absorb the state of the world economy at a single glance and to track the rise and fall of each major player without sifting through columns of numbers. The map is laid out in a rectilinear grid format and utilizes a red, green, grey, and black color scheme to convey information. There is less of the poesy or playfulness in this piece that we see in other Wattenberg visualizations. But the crucial thing to consider here is that this work is not typically included in the selection of Wattenberg's work that crosses over from industry to the domain of art festivals, exhibitions, galleries, and so on. Granted, the notion that information visualization fits at all into the art world is contentious, and many practitioners grappling with the issues raised by information visualization, such as Salavon, set themselves more firmly within art-historical and art-institutional contexts.

Many words have been written about Salavon, some emphasizing his reframing of photographic practices, others the formal similarities in his work to painters Kenneth Noland or Giorgi Morandi, and still others the latent commentary in his images about the mass distribution of sexual norms. However, none of them position him squarely within the field of information visualization in its most straightforward sense. It is not just the surface appearance of Salavon's "pictures" that differentiate him from the field. Infographics no longer necessarily conform to the rectilinear patterns imposed on data by charts and graphs, and even employ similar palimpsestic compositional strategies that both visually and conceptually echo Salavon's software-generated averaging processes.[14] For example, Christopher Baker's *American Toys* presents a two-part visualization of five hundred patent applications for toy guns submitted since the 1800s. The primary visual artifact of the project combines the totality of the diagrams of the toy guns into a visual average, similar to Salavon's amalgamations. Alongside this picture, evocative of the form of a charcoal sketch, Baker supplies a page of the individual drawings that comprise the average, arranged on the page in a rectilinear grid format and evoking the official visual language of an informational pictorial array. The authors of *Data Flow* describe the project in somewhat utopian language, claiming that the hazy tangle of black lines "becomes a collective *expression* of the prototypical American toy."[15] When we consider this vague shape in conjunction with its accompanying chart-like array of drawings, arranged not by year but somewhat haphazardly (perhaps by morphological characteristics) we realize that the combinatory picture exhibits "expressionistic" traits; in other words, it carries signifiers of handmadeness in its progression from center to periphery and from densely overlaid black to wispy outlying tracelines. It recalls the sketch, that first stage of pictorial brainstorming in which the artist inscribes his or her first experimental musings onto a material substrate.[16] The accompanying compendium of drawings refers in turn to bureaucratic modes of classification and communication; its arrangement in a grid format seems obvious and transparent in the sense that this layout goes largely unquestioned as a form of information collection, organization, and dissemination. However, another voice is faintly audible through the structure of the grid. Once viewers notice that the drawings are not arranged chronologically, they begin to search for a pattern, a modus operandi governing the sequence in which the data is presented. One begins to wonder if Baker is poking fun at a viewer who accepts unquestioningly bureaucratic rationality. In failing immediately to discern a numeric pattern, one questions whether it is the U.S. Patent Office that sequences the toy guns in this manner or if we are observing a sly authorial intervention into a seemingly mechanized presentation of information. Baker's *American Toys* project, in its mobilization of something akin to a computational palimpsest, is similar to some of Salavon's impressionistic visualizations. In employing traditional tropes of information-bearing graphics, however, Baker maintains a more obvious connection to info-vis practices than to the kind of emphatically inexact painterly adaptation of info-vis performed by Salavon. Ultimately, Baker's finished product adheres more strongly to the semantics and syntactics of a digital format; whereas Salavon's prints evoke (whether critically or not) a painterly sensibility, Baker's argument is made via direct reference to digital parsing and compilation.

Wattenberg's *Map of the Stock Market* provides a convenient foil to Salavon's ghostly amalgamations, but it is by no means the case that info-vis specialists have not attempted, with varying "success" (depending on what one deems as successful), to explode the frame of infographics. The authors of *Data Flow*, a recent book charting trends in visualization, relegate examples of "blocky" graphics to a single chapter out of six.[17] The remaining five quite deliberately collect projects that open themselves to a greater rage of experimentation with the ways visual models can prompt an intuitive absorption of statistical information. While these alternative maps seek to reveal the possibilities wrought by new approaches to visualization, they are often unwieldy and difficult to navigate. As such, their goal seems to be to impart a sense of movement or gestalt more than to facilitate an incisive look into the precise cardinal or ordinal shifts that (a) demarcate elements in the data set and (b) consequently avail themselves to comparison and conceptual organization in the viewer's mind.

But inescapably, *because* he works with the vast accumulation of pop cultural records, and the way these records present themselves as a statistical database, Salavon's artwork must be viewed through the lens of data visualization. Moreover, because the particular materiality of his work is situated at the intersection of traditionally analog imaging technologies (photography, film, and television) and software, Salavon's work is clearly *about* the conversion of analog pictures—that are imprinted or burned in their totality onto celluloid or photographic paper by the chemical processing of light—into digital pictures, which are a radically discontinuous array of bits that only resolve into a recognizable image when instructed by the computer to execute a series of commands. Not only does he gather his subjects from the vast bank of pop-cultural detritus, stored and found on the Internet, but Salavon also asks, without anticipating the answer, how the nature of pictures might change when subjected to particular software-based processes. Thus, we experience the work as a meditation not only on the vastness, ubiquity, or mundanity of digital information but also on what happens between the specificity of a single instance (the irreproducible and the particular) and its exponential multiplication (the generic and the popular). Because Salavon subjects analog images to computational processing, there is some expectation that they must look computed. But what, finally, might this mean?

In his 2005 series *Everything, All at Once*, Salavon filters each video frame of a cable television broadcast through a program that transforms the signals into concentric bands of color that radiate outward to the edges of a wall-sized screen. The hypnotic, sensual rhythms of Salavon's pieces might seem to replicate the spectacular seduction of the televisual image. Or they might simply reinscribe modernist theoretical valorizations of abstraction and pure opticality over academic mimesis. But Salavon's work resists such easy categorization by creating an irreducible play between multiple channels of information transmission. First, Salavon identifies his source material by synchronizing the abstract visual output with the unmodified soundtrack of the TV program. In the corner of the installation space, the unaltered broadcast is presented through the familiar channel of the TV monitor. Typically, the verisimilitude of a live-action video obscures the fact that this "copy" of real life is merely the product of a delivery of a stream of informational bits that are meaningless without their reconstitution into a legible signal. By writing a program that places a filter between input and output, Salavon reveals the deeply mediated nature of recorded images and also radically undercuts the implied truth value of information visualization.

The highly constructed documentary quality of reality TV and network news is evidence enough to obliterate the notion that television delivers information with minimal mediation. But Salavon's work performs the impossibility of a

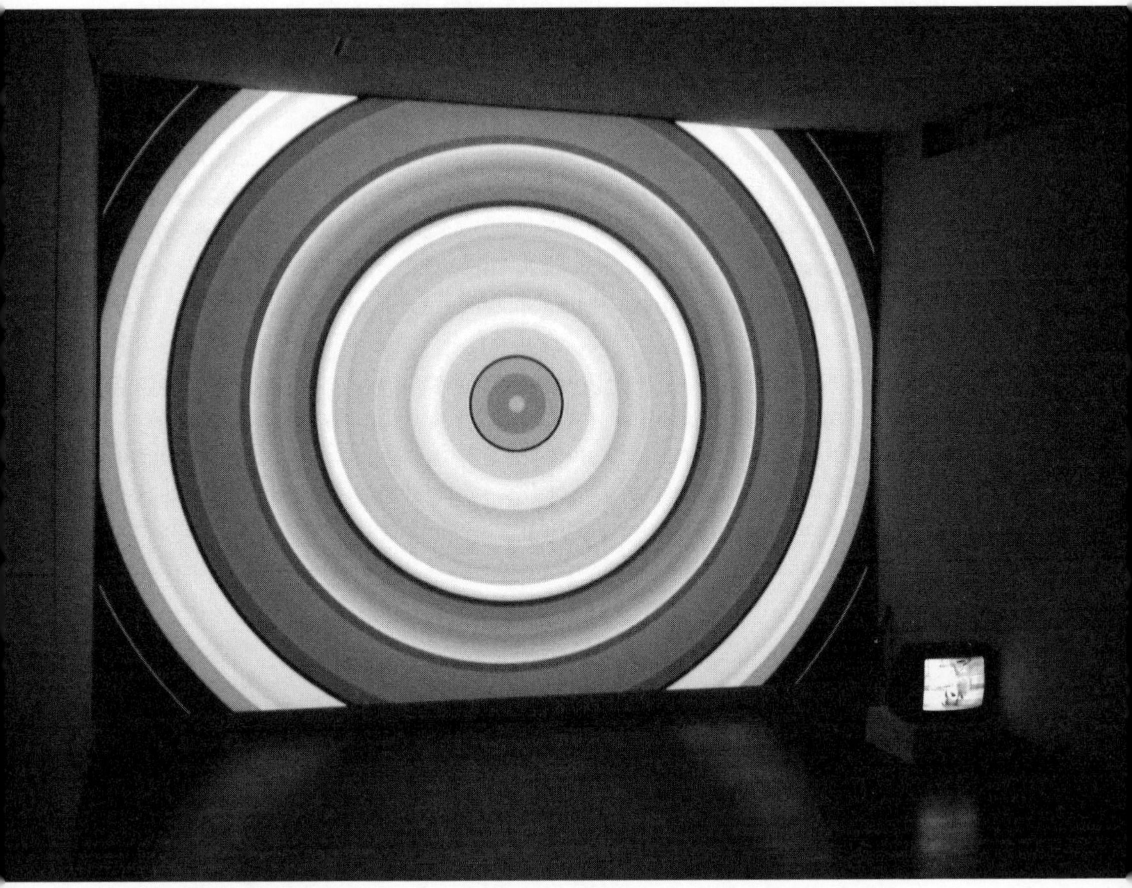

FIGURE 5.1 ▪ Jason Salavon, *Everything, All at Once (Part III)*, 2005. Custom software, workstation, real-time audio/video input, video projector, monitor. Dimensions variable. Ed. 3 + 1 AP. © Jason Salavon.

direct, unmediated link between sender, channel, and receiver. The images filtered through his program are sensually captivating in and of themselves, but Salavon demonstrates that processing the same units of information through different mediating devices can produce a multiplicity of possible results. The magnetic pull of the color bands radiating outward on the wall-sized screen proves the potential for information to be viewed through an aesthetic, rather than a merely utilitarian, lens. At the same time, however, it also resists an uncritical belief in the truth value of information itself and the objectivity of information visualization. What the viewer sees on the screen reveals the capacity of data transmission to exclude or conceal the fundamental mutability of the informatic signal.

In the example of *Everything, All at Once*, Salavon immerses himself deeply in questions about information. What is a unit of information? What happens when an amalgamation of similar informational propositions or data sets reduces precise statistics to an ethereal fog of line and color? Is the resulting image still "informative," and if so does the quality of available information change due to the artist's manipulation? Whereas a straightforward instance of information visualization implicitly assigns aesthetics to a supplemental role by using aesthetics to enhance utility and communicative efficiency, Salavon self-consciously denies the viewer an experience of total mastery over social "data."

Not only does Salavon not give graphical indexes of the type of information he is assessing (announcing that one very blurry, painterly image is an amalgamation of photographs of real estate for sale in a given area of Chicago, for example), but he also refuses to reduce his material to numerical or statistical data. He does not visualize numerical values, such as the cost of a real estate property, nor does he arrange his source material in a relational manner, as a graph or a chart would. Instead, he manipulates and amalgamates *pictures*. Consequently, even if the process of amalgamation or the stripping down of signals to patterns obscures individuating features, leaving only generic outlines, the vestiges of particularity hover within the pictures, provoking a yearning for the familiarity of home in the uncanny muteness of color and mottled texture.

In viewing *Everything, All at Once* it becomes clear that without the successful execution of the encoded instructions described by a program, digitized numerical data can never resolve into a picture. When the program stops running, the image is gone, without a trace. Because the visual manifestation of computational, screen-based images is dependent on electronic execution of code, the ontology of the image is fundamentally unstable and dependent on real-time information processing. In other words, to appear at all, the image must be computed and rendered in real time and will just as quickly disappear as soon as the machine is powered off. Although the computational origin of the mode of pictorialization is often effaced, just as the orthogonals and visual angles are eventually covered over perspective drawing, Salavon's strategy of "anti-visualization"—his actuation of the mutability of code and his methodical decomposition of indexical images—suggests that the aesthetic richness of computational images lies in their fragility and ghostliness. As opposed to the material solidity of painting and sculpture, the computational image is haunted by a strange mortality. In each instance, it is born, dies, and is reborn again, phoenix-like, rising not from its own ashes but from a machine-readable string of ones and zeros.

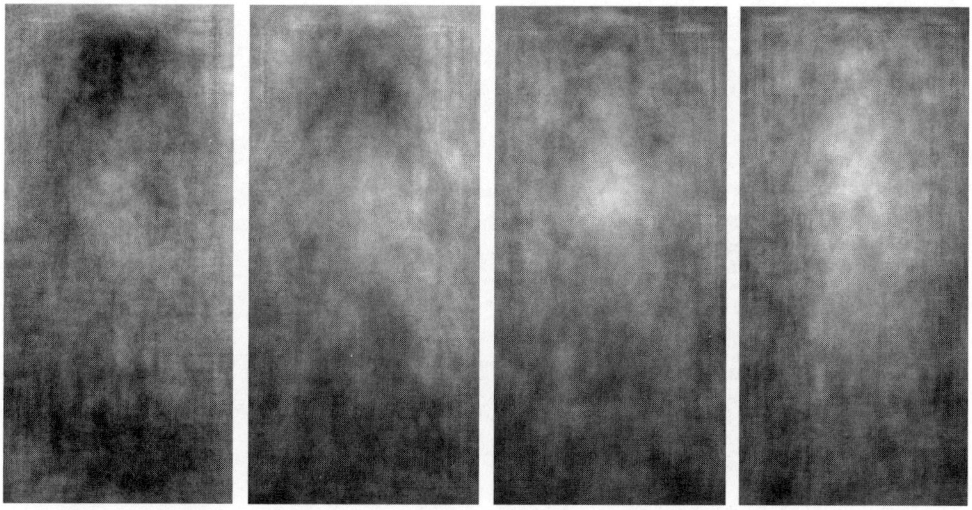

FIGURE 5.2 ▪ Jason Salavon, *Every Playboy Centerfold, The Decades (normalized)*, 2002. Digital C-prints. Ed. 5 + 2 APs. 60 x 29.25 in. © Jason Salavon.

Salavon's exhibited works convey his obsession with what he calls "the relationships between the whole and the part, the individual and the group." Although the thematic content of his works varies widely, each work repeats a seemingly compulsive reenactment of the translation of subjects and substance into statistical data. In *Every Playboy Centerfold*, a program written by Salavon compiles a point-by-point digital average of all *Playboy* centerfold foldouts from January 1988 to December 1997. The seductive poses of these soft-porn icons dissolve into what Salavon calls a "shroudlike," indistinct form. Like a vaguely digitized offspring of Marcel Duchamp's *Nude Descending a Staircase* and Mark Rothko's *Red on Maroon*, the amalgamation of photographs in *Centerfold* allows a few mechanical angles and repeated abstract shapes to surface from a deep, muddy background. In the area where flesh is most concentrated, a reddish, ovoid shape emerges, only to fade away again.

Even at the center of the image this textural quality visually analogizes gestural brushstrokes, which would, if it were a painting, signify gestural style, but here it is a record of digital noise in the averaging process. This noise, however, does not "fail to communicate." It reconfigures the boundaries of information visualization to suggest that digital computation of data can generate poetically resonant, sensuously rich imagery that uses information as its medium but is not dependent on communicating a particular set of statistics for utilitarian ends. The process of averaging would seem to eliminate variation and to depict the informatic world as a flattened, neutral plane of obdurate consistency. But

FIGURE 5.3 ▪ Jason Salavon, *Flayed Figure, Male, 3277½ Square Inches*, 1998. Laminated digital C-print. Ed. 5 + 2 APs. 69 x 47.5 in. © Jason Salavon.

instead, the human figure hovers just outside the limits of perception, and the image acquires a ghostly, pulsating dynamism.

By definition, information visualization as a design practice relies on notational features for its communicative success, but sometimes designers blur either the semantic or the syntactic discreteness for the sake of producing a rather uncritical version of "visual pleasure" dependent on analog aesthetic typology. For example, a graph describing fluctuations in American population and demographics taken from data collected by the census bureau derives its communicative efficacy from the legibility of discrete, distinct values. These values are not inherently digital, insofar as they can appear on an analog scale but nevertheless interrupt the smoothness, fineness, and ambiguity of a classical linear scheme based on *disegno*.

There is a somewhat tragic beauty in Salavon's amalgamations. Salavon writes about his 1998 "self-portrait"—*Flayed Figure, Male, 3277½ Square Inches*—that the photographic deconstruction of the surface of his body into twelve thousand half-inch squares and its subsequent reconstruction into a "complete" image results in a "contradictory self-portrait in which every intimate detail of my body is revealed and yet the clinical detachment of the generic pervades."[18] The pictorial fields in Salavon's amalgamation series hang in suspension between continuous and discrete surface characteristics. Again, "texture" signifies not only artistic intention (the gesture and the deliberate mark) but also the variability and irregularity that is the hallmark of a nonautomated painterly process. In some of Salavon's works, such as *Flayed Figure*, discreteness is not suppressed, as it is in *Every Playboy Centerfold* and his Chicago real estate series, but is made more subtle, more adequate to the brushstroke, than, for example, the pixelated portraits of Chuck Close, whose offering up of a resolved, recognizable portrait is equally compelling to the concomitant invitation to approach each individual pixel in order to examine the (analog, irregular, and clearly handmade) content within. Emphatically in Close's portraits, but more evanescently in Salavon's cutting up and layering of photographic material, the digital comes in and out of focus. Both *Flayed Figure* and *Every Playboy Centerfold* obscure the informational substrate from which the works are configured by producing a gestural, painterly topography. However, they also possess an uncanny quality that derives from the very fact that their underlying materiality—the stacks of photographic images submitted to the compiling and averaging mechanism of the software—has been translated from a continuous whole into discontinuous information. In other words, an analog photograph reads as a fragment of reality, pulled from its situated context, but within the boundaries of its artificial edge it is a single unit, a continuous whole. But once that photograph is subjected to digitization, it disintegrates into a collection of new fragments, each of which is extracted and bounded according to the rule governing the informational content of a single digital unit. The figure, then, is flayed by the digitizing process. The flayed bodily surface is recombined without respect to the laws of biological or organic systems. Instead, the "figure" is further flattened—from the already flattened plane of the photograph—into an abstract field of color values arranged continuously from light to dark.

In an implicit parallel to the rhetorics of genetics and molecular biology, individual bits of data act as the basic code—the DNA—of Salavon's imagery, but the final product does not suggest that the reconstitution of these bits into visual form will reveal the essence of information, just as deciphering human DNA will not reveal the whole truth of what it means to be human. Indeed, Salavon has claimed that at some level his work seeks to "nullify the individual."[19] In *Centerfold*, "as all individual characteristics and overt sexuality are subsumed, abstracted generalization becomes central." Does Salavon's work, then, celebrate likeness over difference, or can it uncover difference within repetition, averaging, and abstraction? In fact, Salavon's apparent nullification of the individual through the processes of averaging and amalgamation ultimately preserves, rather than suppresses, the power of "the part" to mark itself against the grey and brown hues of a data-mined, informatic landscape. While the presence of a central area of color-saturated flesh tone marks the mean or the norm, these less-nuanced regions are less interesting than the wispy traces of outlying color values. Thus, while averaging would seem to crush nuance, deviations haunt this landscape and suffuse it with a much warmer light than we find in the precise, if airbrushed, outlines of *Playboy* centerfolds.

Looking again at Salavon's art through the lens of information visualization, there is at least one statement one can make confidently about how the technological conditions of digitality productively limit the kinds of signification that digital images can produce: the existence of a digital artifact is governed by and predicated upon information processing. Computers are tools that process information at the levels of both input and output. Digital objects of any kind, then, are both composed of information and fundamentally *about* information. Computationally constructed images communicate most successfully about information. But what forms of meaning fall outside the limits of information? Moreover, how do we determine whether information has been communicated successfully or not? The artistic intervention into data visualization practices staged by *Every Playboy Centerfold* activates our capacity to feel aesthetic pleasure and fascination in the *dissolution* of information that occurs, seemingly oxymoronically, at the point of informatic oversaturation. It is in this sense that Salavon's work can be labeled as "anti-visualization."[20] Paradoxically, as the informational content of the data set increases, the putatively information-bearing image blurs into unrecognizability.

Thus, Salavon's images challenge the idea that visualization always aims for clarity or revelation by depicting the deresolution that occurs at the point of informational oversaturation. The field of noise generated by the amalgamation of centerfold photographs reconfigures the boundaries of information visualization to suggest that digital computation of data can create poetically resonant, sensuously rich images that use information as their medium but are not dependent on communicating a particular set of statistics for utilitarian ends. Salavon "hints at profound hidden meaning, but ultimately obscures or ridicules it."[21] As a result, his work follows in the tradition of avant-garde intervention into crystallized and emptied cultural signifiers and practices. We recognize Salavon's work immediately as art because, if it has utility, its function lies partly in its critical appraisal of the effect of digitality on traditional representational models. But to an even greater extent its success can be identified in its resistance to theoretical reduction. The images created by his programs make visible the philosophical and aesthetic complexity of information. Not only does *Every Playboy Centerfold* evoke a continual stream of interpretive possibility, but also its textures, its visual richness, and its mischievous play between high-art formalism and cheap pornographic solicitation make a different kind of information available for sensuous apprehension.

If one of the most powerful attributes of successful art is its capacity to reveal the hidden, unthought, or concealed mechanisms of everyday objects and events (as Martin Heidegger maintains about Vincent van Gogh's shoes in the "Origin of the Work of Art"), Salavon's adoption of information visualization for artistic ends offers the possibility of awakening viewers to unexpected interactions between abstract data and worldly phenomena.[22] Even in moments of failure or breakdown, when visualizations manifest the instability of information or reveal the extent to which accuracy and breadth of communication is dependent on representational codes, Salavon's artworks expose us at an intuitive level to the fluidity of what counts as valid or important information, and ultimately triumph by calling into question the very stuff of which their foundations are built.

The varieties of depiction are, rightly or wrongly, often delineated and compartmentalized into nonintersecting categories such as medium specificity. Here, cases such as Salavon's, in which not only different modes of depiction but also notions such as medium specificity begin to overlap dangerously, are helpful in thinking about how adding the figure of the "digital"—both in its technological and aesthetic sense—to the discursive mix can expand domain of art. Adding the digital to an art-critical vocabulary expands the way art is conceptualized, experienced, and delimited from other forms of cultural production. *Every Playboy Centerfold* calls into question categorical distinctions between abstract painting and information visualization, as well as painting itself and digital artificing.

In September 2015, software artist Casey Reas mounted a solo exhibition entitled *Linear Perspective* at the Charlie James Gallery in Los Angeles, California. The exhibition contained three separate series, consisting of eight real-time video works, all made from "remediated" images—or images that have been appropriated from one media format and "refashioned" into new technical platforms. This reformulation facilitates the construction of unanticipated conceptual frameworks and perceptual experiences.[23] In the *Linear Perspective* series after which the show is titled, images, accompanied (unlike Reas's earlier works) by sound, stream ceaselessly, creating a highly stimulating atmosphere and echoing the attempts of contemporary mass media to immerse the senses. But in this case, the senses are not subject to the suturing effect of social media feeds, Hollywood cinema, or news channels, which more or less efficiently elide gaps in self-identification or smooth out stuttering mishaps in political bombast. But to identify this show *only* with political commentary or statements about locating selfhood within the stream of social media images is to ignore the way in which this particular exhibition performs a discursive *intersection* between a critically self-reflexive approach to software art (software as medium) and a more externally reflective examination of mass and social media.

To contextualize the focus of Reas's practice in terms of its primary art historical, technological, and aesthetic milieu, software art, although it can take many forms, generally deploys computational systems, and particularly code, to explore the generative potential that emerges when a series of instructions is executed in order to produce a work of art. Some theorists of software art, those who are more interested in the procedural and conceptual aspect of the art form than a strictly technological definition of digitally computational software, have argued that "software" does not necessarily involve the use of digital machines; rather, any set of algorithmically executable rules might constitute a piece of software. Florian Cramer uses the example of Tristan Tzara's repeatable directives for creating Dadaist poems by shuffling words cut from a newspaper article. Another instantiation of noncomputational software would be Sol LeWitt's wall drawings, which supply verbal sets of instructions that are then executed visually by draughtspeople. Generally, whether its driving mechanism is derived from digital computation or not, software art is understood as a critically reflexive practice in which the "medium," in this case conceived as software, is used to "expose its instructions and codedness."[24] In this sense, according to Cramer, software art is a logical extension of, or a "subset of" conceptual art.[25] In a different vein, theorists self-identified within a new disciplinary model labeled "software studies" are, to make a generalization, less invested in the legacy of conceptualism to be found in software art and more grounded in technical and materialist explorations of digital software technologies. These scholars and practitioners focus on such issues as the materiality of code and software; connections between biology, information science, and networks; or the history of the graphical user interface.

As we have seen in chapter 4, Reas's earlier work follows directly from the former line of thought. His complex approach to the problematics of software, code, and art would not ignore the principles addressed by the second (more recent) field of enquiry, but both his statements and the distinct aesthetic properties of his early work link his practice to that of both conceptual artists and artists experimenting with the aesthetics of emergence, complexity, and generativity. Within this particular niche, Reas carves out an instantly recognizable aesthetic modality consisting of delicate, intricately entangled arabesques and organic, proliferating, anemone-like forms. This aesthetic sensibility arises from a complex series of translations between text, code, and image. Housed in his encyclopedic "Process Compendium," the textual instructions for Reas's Processes, their expression in code (also documented), and their visual instantiation in a multiplicity of media platforms expose the emergent properties of software-based generative systems. Often, his works are arranged in paired frames to reveal the underlying mechanism of the system. An "element" or "elements" are laid bare in one frame—reflecting upon the basic structure or grammar of the system. In the second frame, the element or elements are then set into motion to produce a complex visualization—the aesthetic potentiality unveiled when the system is allowed to evolve. According to Reas's 2010 description in the Process Compendium, "A Process interpretation in software is a kinetic drawing machine with a beginning but no defined end."[26] Insofar as a Process has no distinct end, it can take on different material forms. Ranging from prints to interactive screens and large-scale projections, Reas's Processes disclose both the basic structures underlying complex systems and the manifold perceptual affordances of software-as-medium. However, these works, unlike Reas's later interrogations of social and news media platforms, reflect more prominently on the internal properties of software as a technical and aesthetic system rather than on the capability of technology to reach outside itself into the socio-political world through the collection and manipulation of data and its visualization.

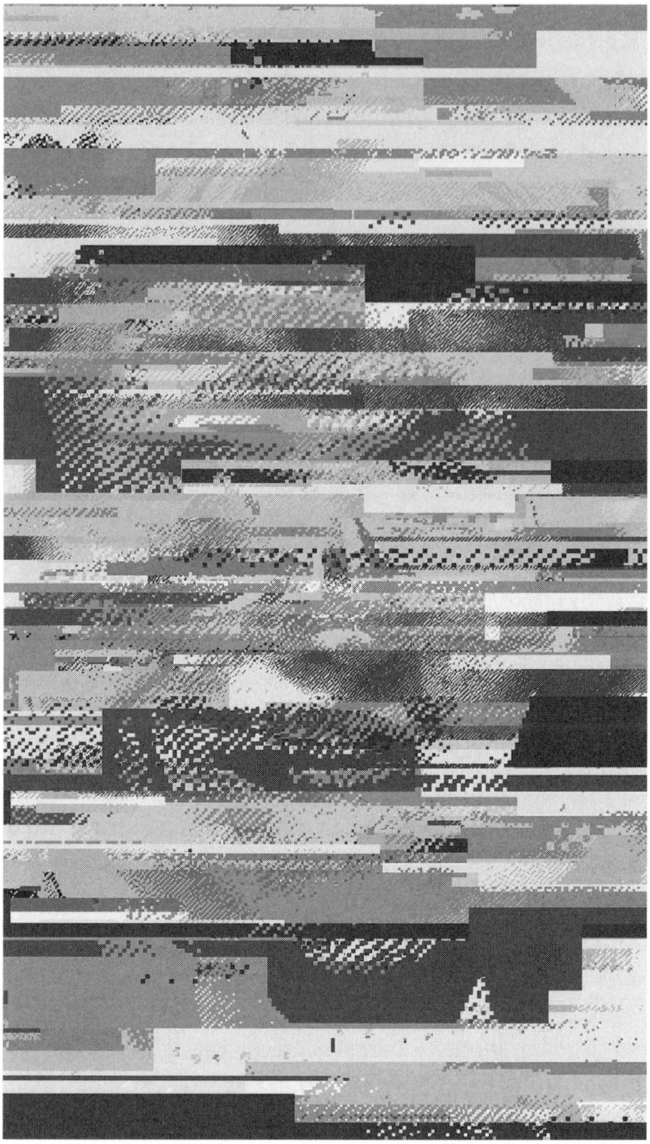

FIGURE 5.4 ▪ Casey Reas, *All Your Face Are Belong to Us (Followers 1K)*. Code, digital images, computer, screen. 1080 x 1920 pixels. 2015. © Casey Reas.

Self-reflexivity and aesthetic sensibility is of course not entirely overturned in Reas's new work. An intermediate stage is introduced in 2013 with his solo exhibition ULTRACONCENTRATED, in which one of the featured series, *Signal to Noise*, scrambles television signals captured live using an antenna from mainstream cable networks such as ABC, NBC, and CBS. Similarly to his 2015 pieces, such as KTTV *(August 2015)*, this series shows how easily legible information can

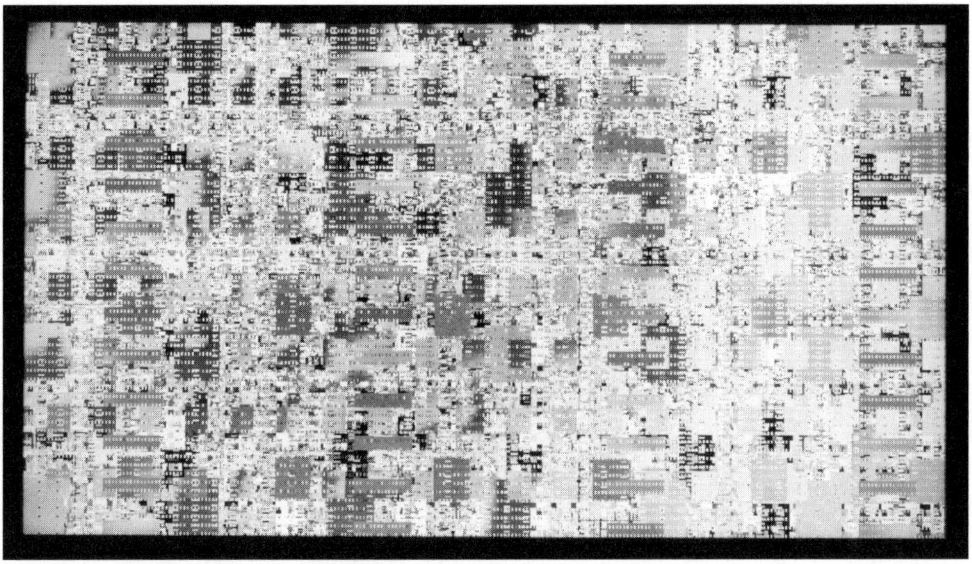

FIGURE 5.5 ▪ Casey Reas, *KTTV (August 2015)*. Code, digital video, computer, screen. 1920 x 1080 pixels. 2015. © Casey Reas.

be divested of its power to signify, transformed into raw, flickering patterns of seemingly meaningless noise. Although invested in the televisual, and in this sense still dealing with mass media, KTTV *(August 2015)*, part of the *Linear Perspective* exhibition, diverges to some degree from the more overtly socially and politically charged series *Linear Perspective* and *All Your Face Are Belong to Us*, working more analogically to his 2013 explorations of information theory. KTTV submits a month of prime-time news to a code-driven dissection, moving into a different aesthetic modality from his earlier organically inspired work, one that is resolutely digital, boasting jagged, aggressively pixilated surfaces fractured into their constitutive graphic units. We have seen how Reas has been conducting visual and conceptual investigations of the transition between digitality, analogity, and hybridity throughout his career but, curiously, has paused until the production of works such as *Signals to Noise* and KTTV *(August 2015)* to so emphatically digitize the surface of his images.

As Reas relates in an interview with Kimberly Nichols, part of his impetus for the 2015 project began with his fascination with not only the large-scale technological transfer of signals from analog to digital but also, "most importantly, how that shift has changed the medium and how we experience it."[27] These televisually based images seem fraught with information—but information legible only to the computational mechanism underlying the graphic output, not to the inquisitive gaze of the viewer. Nichols comments that this dismembering of the image into discrete digital elements effectively renders the sensationalism of the news media null and void, draining content from a communication system that attempts to activate immediate emotional and adrenal responses based on socio-political narratives or pure entertainment. Reas's approach is "extractive," rending pure informational values out of their narrative flow and presenting them instead as apprehensible patterns that speak indirectly to the viewer *about* information. Information is thus a subject under consideration at a meta-level in these works, but in order to achieve this, specific narrative or representational content must be at least partially suppressed.

Reas asks his viewer at what point information begins to "mean." Media theorist Christiane Paul explains that, "in information theory, entropy means the average amount of information contained in each received message. Entropy thereby also becomes a measure of uncertainty: [Claude] Shannon posits that the greater the number of possible messages, the greater the uncertainty."[28] Because the messages contained within these fragmented pieces have been rendered multiple and indeterminate, their level of uncertainty has been increased, which in turn bears a powerful analogy to the overall uncertainty contained within the ostensibly determinate (but of course unstable and contingent) messages of news reporting of all kinds. Moreover, with respect to the model of digital aesthetics discussed throughout these chapters, these projects, again, may not confer meaning in a narrative sense upon the images that render into pixelated abstraction, but they are nevertheless imbued with a different type of content, where type refers to the overall typology of digital symbol systems referring to a digitized world structure.

Quite dissimilar from the phases of production that characterize Reas's work informed chiefly by conceptual art, generative and complexity theory, and information and communication theory, the video works from 2015 comprising the *Linear Perspective* and the *All Your Face Are Belong to Us* series are both technically and personally invested in problems pertaining to mass media, the dissemination of images across technological platforms, and concomitant social issues and formations arising from this distinct image economy. Reas's choice not only to select his sources from contemporary mass and social media but also to reveal traces of the originary pool from which he draws his sound and imagery, marks a radical shift into an exploration of the ways in which information is mobilized in the socio-political sphere. Reas follows the transformations that occur as a massive aggregation of babble, his commentary is taken from sources ranging from news to social media and filtered into feeds and channels that attempt to "make sense" of randomized chatter, which can then be broken back down into

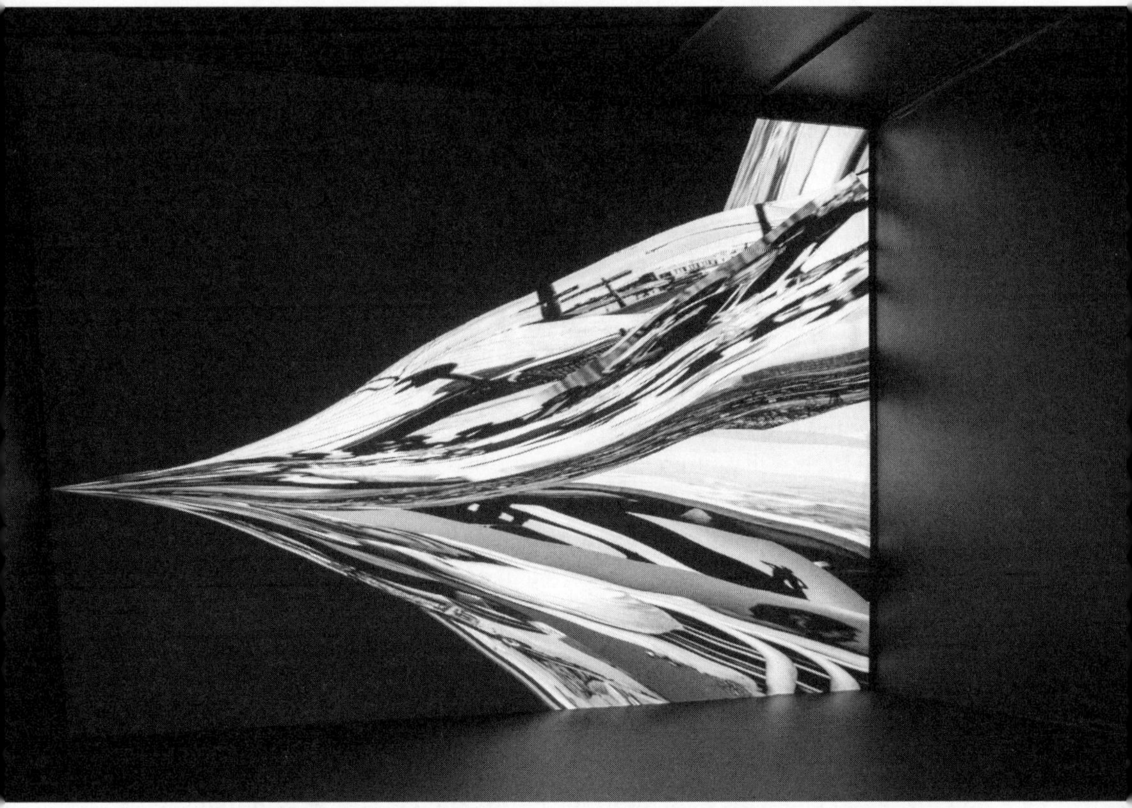

FIGURE 5.6 ▪ Casey Reas, *Linear Perspective*. Code, digital images, computer, projector. Dimensions variable. 1920 x 1200 pixels. 2015. © Casey Reas.

bits and bytes of data and reconstituted into his distorted and pixelated images. Like his TV projects, *Linear Perspective* and *All Your Face Are Belong to Us* projects reveal the underlying datafication of mass media by scattering these channels into visually intriguing but interpretively frustrating patterns of pixels and distorted perspective, but they enact this scattering using systems that leave a trace, or a specter of what we might recognize as nondatafied entities within the pixels or anamorphoses.

In *Linear Perspective*, after which the exhibition is titled, the images bending semi-horizontally along the screen consist of front-page photographs taken from the top half, "above the fold," of *New York Times* newspapers from January 1, 2015, forward, but the contents are warped into near unrecognizability. The images move from left to right, invoking not only the process of reading but also, according to Reas, a progression of the history of image technologies from the camera obscura to the film camera.[29] This is a history of technics representing "an objective and mathematical way of representing space."[30] Christiane Paul writes that "a central element in Reas' project is the uncertainty in the perception and legibility of images."[31] But Reas is, interestingly, utilizing the history of mathematical means of representation in order to reinject a sense of "ambiguity and subjectivity" back into the imagery in these video works.[32]

Paul's assertion about an oscillation between legibility and illegibility holds truer in these social-media- and mass-media-based works than in the pieces more purely concerned information theory. The televisual series that includes KTTV *(August 2015)* and his preceding investigation, the 2013 *Signal into Noise*, perform a more absolute scrambling of informatic signals into noise. But Reas sets loose a cat-and-mouse game between resolution and deresolution in *Linear Perspective* and *All Your Face Are Belong to Us*. In these pieces, there remains a more insistently haunting presence (is that Donald Trump's face oozing across the screen in *Linear Perspective*?) of some residue of social immediacy, of having-been-present, for informational purposes, or perhaps merely for consumption, even as representation is stretched into lugubrious anamorphism or shattered into a field of brightly colored pixelated portraits. Salavon asks his viewer to look closer and then to back away from his images in some effort to achieve the point of fusion at which, for example, a Georges Seurat would cohere into legibility (although of course in Salavon's case this task is Sisyphean, or endlessly frustrated). Similarly, Reas configures these pieces as visual queries for his viewer about the point at which information begins to communicate semantically instead of disaggregating into senseless noise.

The *Linear Perspective* series, as opposed to his social media and televisually driven series, is presented by reviewers Kimberly Nichols and Jody Zellen as projected electronic paintings replete with "digital brushstrokes."[33] Aesthetically, it initiates a painterly sensibility, but it is a painterliness that does not evoke "art for art's sake." These "brushstrokes" actively interrogate the political sphere *as a result of* their references to representational codes and the technologies that produce them—perspective, the camera obscura, and the film camera—unlike Reas's earlier works, which are primarily interested in computational aesthetics and the dynamic possibilities of art generated by code, as was observed in chapter 4. In his more recent engagement with social and news media, the images of highly mediated quotidian contemporary life flicker in and out of view, but more esoteric subjects such as the energetic flow from the intersections of animated Braitenburg bots are abandoned. Certainly, of course, intersections exist; across his work, software, code, data, and the relationships between concept and image, and many other issues persist. The question is what his strategy reveals, or perhaps conceals, about the data he gathers, compresses, and stretches across the screens in painterly swaths of color—whether his subject is organic complexity, the translation of invisible televisual signals into abstract patterns, or the amalgamation of five thousand portraits into a pixelated field of color values.

In the videos belonging to the *Linear Perspective* series, Reas's sources are overtly related to contemporary political situations, but he also incorporates Twitter feeds to target issues of identity in an age when the custody of personhood seems to be governed by the largesse of one's appearance on social media channels. Reas's *All Your Face Are Belong to Us* series consists of three individual "portraits," derived from images collected variously from Kickstarter, Facebook, and Twitter. In *(Followers)*, Reas compresses profile pictures of five thousand of his Twitter followers, creating a sense of instability and change by continuously aggregating new "bits" of different profile pictures into the compressed image. By merging different categories of followers—"some are intimate friends of @REAS, others are acquaintances, and others are complete strangers who share only this online media connection"[34]—Reas creates a contemporary exquisite corpse whose collaboration is activated by code and whose subject is (potentially narcissistic) identity rather than the discovery of unconscious drives. This is an identity based entirely on exteriority, a model of subjectivity that was in some ways prefigured by twentieth-century artists, such as Andy Warhol and Kurt Schwitters, in whom Reas expresses an explicit interest and who operate by "collapsing individual subject and cultural space" through the act of collage.[35] Reas's 2015 works, as well as Salavon's amalgamations, might be regarded as an informatic, often aesthetically digital collage.

As Drucker writes, poetically, in these series, "whether the signals are dithered, scattered, repatterned by stochastic [unpredictable due to influence of random variables] processes or mechanistic [reducible to mechanical principles] ones, the record of lived experience and mediated communication has already become signal—quantized data for which the referent has vanished. Traces remain, and so we focus on them, staring, seeking some meaning in the details and pattern of the whole."[36] In the relationship between quantization, informatics, and statistics and the richness of lived experienced, the fleeting but saturated colors of memory, the images of culture are neither blended nor polarized in these series, nor in any of the projects described in this book. It is an association of struggle, of divergent paths that create their own meaning and then suddenly converge once again as if they had never been apart. Reas's strategy, as with Salavon's, Victor Vasarely's, and Seurat's, is to show not only the deeply, mutually constitutive relationship between different experiential—analog—and digital modalities—all generated by software but also the profound but often unthought necessity to recognize them as theoretically, aesthetically, phenomenologically, and epistemologically distinct *so that* they can build upon one another in a constructive fashion.

Painting the Digital

Now, to come full circle to the beginnings of this exploration of digital practices from early modernity forward, as we have seen throughout this text, the problem of digitality takes a particular shape when reflected not only in computational practices but also in traditionally analog media such as painting. The 2003 exhibition *Painting Pictures* at the Kunstmuseum Wolfsburg, and its accompanying catalog, takes as its central problematic the very *possibility* of painting in the digital age. The catalog essays ask whether "Painting Has Always Been a Digital Affair" or whether it is "A State of Utter Idiocy." It asks how the coming into being of various technologies, from photography forward to digital computers, has fundamentally altered painting practices. But the essay unsurprisingly comes to no stable conclusion other than that painting and technology have always been, and will continue to be, fundamentally linked and mutually influential.

Painting and digital artificing do not seem to render the world in the same way and with the same aims. Metric systems such as perspective mean that the picture is governed by an overarching system that plots the position of any given feature of the painting according to a modular, infinitely extensible grid. Seurat and his fellow pointillists deploy a proto-digital system to produce particular perceptual effects, while Paul Klee incorporates musical notation and digital modules into his painting practices in various ways at various times. Vasarely is the most explicit in his translation of computationalist ideas into plastic forms, due, it must be imagined, at least in part to the fact that his practice, and his process, unfolded around the birth of contemporary computationalist paradigms such as cybernetics. Instances in which painting uncovers its constitutive digitality not only destabilize the conventional association between picturing and analogicity but also reveal how analog and digital modalities rarely remain perfectly distinct from one another. As Turing, John von Neumann, and others have pointed out, even in thought experiments it is only notionally tenable to think that any "discrete state machines" would exist, where, according to Turing, "digital computers . . . may be classified amongst the 'discrete state machines.' These are the machines which move by sudden jumps or clicks from one quite definite state to another. These states are sufficiently different for the possibility of confusion between them to be ignored. Strictly speaking there are no such machines. Everything really moves continuously."[37] Seurat and Klee meshed a traditionally analog medium with a notionally digital procedure, a mixing process that results in artifacts that partially inhabit both states—they are technologically analog but lean toward aesthetic digitality. This book has offered up a series of examples of paintings that are constructed according to a digital logic and has argued that these pictures activate a different set of expectations and perceptual experiences than their analog cousins. When the digital is disaggregated from electronic computational technology, it becomes clear that digital methods have been employed in visualization and depiction for centuries—well beyond the inception of metric perspectival constructions in the Renaissance—though only a very small slice of that history, beginning around the turn of the twentieth century, has been expounded upon here. When the copresence of digital and analog modes in painting and other forms of depiction becomes visible, it prompts a consideration of what kinds of meaning are afforded by each model separately in order to see how they put pressure on one another.

Digital depiction is part of a philosophical worldview that equates knowledge with quantization; digital artificing is eminently concerned with the capacity of representation and symbolic forms to make the world measurable, to create schemas and algorithms that impose regularity and pattern on an otherwise entropic, irreducible, analog universe. According to Félix Guattari, "The paradigms of techno-science place the emphasis on an objectal world of relations and functions."[38] While the conventions of analog pictoriality are, themselves, also about the world of objects, relations between them, and the human perception of them, the paradigm of technoscience, as Guattari describes it, arranges the object-world in terms of functions and coordinates—it makes the world mapable, metric, algebraic, probabilistic, and knowable in terms of all manner of calculations. Art, in contrast, is for Guattari ever more "eccentered"—thrown outward from the confines of "preformed structures and coordinates."[39] Again, we see that while technoscience works toward clarity and disambiguation, art seems to thrive on its irreducible density and ambiguity. And yet, it is in the very impossibility of perfect clarity, articulation, and discretization that the digital becomes an artistic, not merely a technoscientific, communicative form. In seeming to offer the promise of a world that is totally knowable in its utter calculability, the digital ultimately proposes a new set of questions about meaning, a new way of seeing and conceptualizing the world. The digital is thus not merely a technological marvel. If we look closely, through eyes now accustomed to computational formats, the digital makes its presence known, in more and less subtle ways, as a structural principle and structuring force that shapes the architecture of depiction. I have set forth a genealogical model that allows the paradigms and scopic regimes of the contemporary moment both to inflect our investigations of and to revise existing theories of the forms of the past, so that digital strategies become visible in a particular way. Thus, it is contemporaneity that provides the language for the past to speak, but it is the deep historicity of digital modes of inscription that imbues this language with a new vitality and capacity for meaning. By reaching past the contemporary technological milieu, it is possible to connect what seems radically new to a long but often silent history of digital knowledge and digital depiction.

From the outset, this book has presupposed that works of art emerge as such through a series of critical reflections on the part of the viewer. Art is distinguished from nonart based on expectations for how a work of art should look and what effects it should produce in the beholder. An artifact fails as a work of art if it falls outside the sphere of qualities that, tautologically, provide the definition of art by which the work is then judged. I have taken up a series of examples that possess certain characteristics that hover at the margins of aesthetic success, which has added a measure of controversy to their reception or position within the art historical canon. After all, traditionally speaking, fine art should be irreducible, dense, and continuous—in short, it should be analog, not digital. Moreover, fine art should explore and reflect upon an analog world. The examples here, however, to different degrees engage in the construction of a digital world. This world is structured according to different properties than an analog one and thus must be perceived and understood within a different aesthetic and theoretical framework. In essence, then, this book has addressed the aesthetics of structure and the way in which the understanding of the digital, as an alternate structural model from the analog, expands the possibilities for art to be named and reflected upon. This is especially crucial in a time in which everyday objects operate and are structured based on digital principles, whether or not the object dissimulates analogicity, as in the case of naturalistic, immersive video games. Basic inquiries into these artifacts must take into account that analog and the digital models are different structures and provide different ways of structuring knowledge itself.

The foregoing chapters have proffered a typology of digitality: the digital can reveal itself in a range of modes, from the aesthetic to the technological. The aesthetic of digitality does not necessarily rely on electronic computational processing for its realization. In other words, it need not be technologically digital in order to present a digital surface and a digital worldview. It need only present an array of discrete, discontinuous, and interchangeable units that make up the building blocks, and indeed the very materiality, of the world in question. By contrast, a technologically digital system does not by definition reveal its constitutive digitality on its surface. A computational system can create a visual experience that is aesthetically analog and thus fail to challenge the boundaries of art delineated by the expectation of analogicity.

This typological analysis of the analogico-digital distinction and its variants (hybridity, multiplicity, and so forth) seeks to provoke an expansion of the field of art theory and generally to broaden the inquiry into the nature of art. The nature of art cannot be limited by expectations that it conform to an analog worldview, particularly in a digital age. The examples deployed here reveal the development of a digital consciousness that begins long before the invention of the electronic computer. Artists such as Vasarely imagined new systems for constructing objects that, if examined thoroughly, provide a perceptual pathway into understanding digital operations and digital structure. Vasarely creates a specifically digital materiality that can only be enfolded into a definition of art if his philosophical and aesthetic mission is made clear. Other artists, such as Casey Reas, show how there is a continuum between digital and analog. While theoretically the two terms present a polarity, in practice the two modes often commingle, creating an oscillatory movement that can only be experienced to the fullest extent if the theoretical distinction between digital and analog is tacitly understood. Digitally structured art, then, challenges historical ideas about what art is taken to be. If attention is given to this alternate aesthetic paradigm, the notion of what art can be, and what artifacts can be included in the artistic canon becomes radically expanded. While Seurat in his own time could not have been understood as operating within a digital aesthetic paradigm, it is possible to see, retrodictively, the seed of a digital universe developing from a perspective situated in the contemporary moment, in which digitality has come to technological and aesthetic fruition. This book has made a historical claim about how the very idea of a work of art constantly multiplies, creating new phylogenetic trees and seductive offspring from strange couplings of new genetic strands. Without an understanding of the genetics of images—their underlying structure—the encounter with new aesthetic species can only be met with frustration and misapprehension. But if such an encounter is facilitated by the introduction of new interpretive schema, the nature of art evolves into ever-more-complex and intriguing territories.

Notes

Introduction—The Digital: An Aesthetic Ontology

1. Transparency occurs when all signs of artifice and mediation "disappear" from a picture, leaving the viewer instead with an impression of a naturalistic, three-dimensional illusionism or "virtualization." For more on transparency, see Jay David Bolter and Diane Gromala, *Windows and Mirrors: Interaction Design, Digital Art, and the Myth of Transparency* (Cambridge, MA: MIT Press, 2003).

2. In vector graphics, the "digital depiction" becomes, in theory, infinitely expandable and compressible, because the appearance of a line is independent of the arrangement of pixels on a bitmap, instead derived from equations that are transposable to a screen of any size or resolution.

3. Nelson Goodman, *Languages of Art: An Approach to a Theory of Symbols* (Indianapolis: Hackett, 1976). See also Robert Pepperell, "Seeing without Objects: Visual Indeterminacy and Art," *Leonardo* 39, no. 5 (2006): 394–400; and Timothy J. Clark, "Preliminaries to a Possible Treatment of 'Olympia' in 1865," *Screen* 21, no. 1 (1980): 18–41.

4. Clark identifies in the writings on and caricatures of *Olympia* "the figures which indicate the ways in which the hand of Olympia—the one spread over her pubic hair—disobeys, crucially, the conventions of the nude. The hand is *shamelessly flexed*, it is *improper*, it is *in the form of a toad*, it is *dirty*, it is in a state of *contraction*. It comes to stand for the way Olympia's whole body is disobedient: the hand is the sign of the unyielding, the unrelaxed, the too-definite where indefiniteness is the rule" ("Preliminaries," 25).

5. Clark, "Preliminaries," 29.

6. Clark, "Preliminaries," 36.

7. Paul Gordon has argued with respect to aesthetics in the literary and critical tradition that aesthetic discourse becomes distinct from other discursive models by virtue of its emphasis and performance of duality, or the "critical double." Paul Gordon, *The Critical Double: Figurative Meaning in Aesthetic Discourse* (Tuscaloosa: University of Alabama Press, 1994).

8. For more on the extensions and distortions performed by digital spatial modeling and special effects, see Kristen Whissel, "Tales of Upward Mobility: The New Verticality and Digital Special Effects," *Film Quarterly* 59, no. 4 (2006): 23–34. For Jameson's account of the postmodern space of capital, see Frederic Jameson, *Postmodernism; or, the Cultural Logic of Late Capitalism* (Durham, NC: Duke University Press, 1991).

9. D. N. Rodowick has claimed that digital processes do not make images at all, in the sense of making a stable visual object that is "identical to itself." Instead, digital graphics rendered on electronic displays have an elusive presence and a notorious ephemerality. "Having disappeared into information, the image can be reborn or reconstituted only as

an electronic signal." D. N. Rodowick, *The Virtual Life of Film* (Cambridge, MA: Harvard University Press, 2007), 131, 134.

10. See, for example, Sean Cubitt, *Digital Aesthetics* (London: Sage, 1998); Anna Munster, *Materializing New Media: Embodiment in Information Aesthetics* (Hanover, NH: University Press of New England, 2006); and Johanna Drucker, *SpecLab: Digital Aesthetics and Projects in Speculative Computing* (Chicago: University of Chicago Press, 2009).

11. In a slightly different vein than Rodowick, Whitney Davis has also advanced a theory about how a series of marks comes to be recognized as a "picture" in his writings on Paleolithic art. He begins with the following question: "Many things resemble many other things without being images of them. How do we know how to distinguish an image from any chance resemblance?" Davis ultimately argues that images develop through strategies of context-driven and convention-dependent replication that perform the translation of physiological "seeing" into the cognitive symbolic register of "seeing-as." However, Davis not only outlines a set of conditions an inscription must fulfill to become a picture but also adapts Goodman's analog-digital distinction to Paleolithic mark-making. This application of the analytic parameters of analog and digital becomes useful to my discussion of the deep history of digitality in chapter 1. Whitney Davis, "Replication and Depiction in Paleolithic Art," *Representations*, no. 19 (Summer 1987): 117.

12. For a thorough examination of strains of mysticism and transcendentalism that float through techno-utopian narratives, see Richard Coyne's study of technology and romanticism. "For romantic narrative, which privileges the subjective, the one is presented as an issue of the unity, which is the unity of humankind with nature, beyond the individuation and classification considered necessary for objectivity. For romanticism, objectivity divides the world into many parts and is obsessed with individuation." Richard Coyne, *Technoromanticism: Digital Narrative, Holism, and the Romance of the Real* (Cambridge, MA: MIT Press, 1999), 90.

13. Johanna Drucker provides a helpful series of distinctions between calculation, computation, digital processing, classification, and electronic communication. Most applicable here are calculation and computation; while calculation entails the automated representation of numerical content, computation is more generalized in the sense that it can represent any type of information (not just numerical) as long as that information can be processed within the rules of formal logic. Drucker, *SpecLab*, 23.

14. Digitality is often conflated with the figure of information, in part due to the fact that information quantities, as measured by Claude Shannon's information theory, are converted into discrete values. In addition, the information revolution progresses hand in hand with the development of computing devices, which are themselves digital processors.

1. From Analog Pictures to Digital Notations

1. Frank Dietrich, "The Computer: A Tool for Thought Experiments," *Leonardo* 20, no. 4 (1987): 317. Even if in 1987, the year this article was published in *Leonardo* (still among the most prominent journals cataloging the intersections of art, science, and technology), "computer art" was still more often addressed through the lens of formalist art history, in recent years archaeologies of digital media have shown that the threshold between analog

and digital media may prove to be indistinct at best. Examples of recent publications that adopt an archeological approach to "media" include Anne Friedberg, *The Virtual Window: From Alberti to Microsoft* (Cambridge, MA: MIT Press, 2006). See also Siegfried Zielinski, *Deep Time of the Media: Toward an Archaeology of Hearing and Seeing by Technical Means* (Cambridge, MA: MIT Press, 2006).

2. Whitney Davis's essay on this topic, "How to Make Analogies in a Digital Age," poses these questions in order to address the hybridity found in many examples of contemporary art, in which the smoothness of the pictorial surface, which may or may not be combined with a visual emphasis on artificiality, renders the digital or analog ontology of the picture indiscernible. Whitney Davis, "How to Make Analogies in a Digital Age," *October* 117 (2006): 71–98.

3. Sean Cubitt, "Analogue and Digital," *Theory, Culture and Society* 23, no. 2/3 (2006): 250–251.

4. Cubitt, "Analogue and Digital," 250.

5. This claim is clearly indebted both to Foucauldian epistemology and, most directly, to Thomas Kuhn's theory of the changes in worldview led by revolutions in scientific paradigms, in which, "led by a new paradigm, scientists adopt new instruments and look in new places. Even more important, during revolutions scientists see new and different things when looking with familiar instruments in places they have looked before." Thomas Kuhn, *The Structure of Scientific Revolutions* (Chicago: University of Chicago Press, 1962), 111. See also Michel Foucault, *The Order of Things: An Archaeology of the Human Sciences* (New York: Vintage Books, 1994).

6. Henry Jenkins, *Convergence Culture: Where Old Media and New Media Collide* (New York: New York University Press, 2008).

7. According to David Summers, "*to consider an artifact in terms of its facture is to consider it as a record of its own having been made*. . . . Facture is *indexical* in semiotic terms, that is, it implies immediate relation to a prior cause, as a footprint implies the former immediate presence of a foot." David Summers, *Real Spaces: World Art History and the Rise of Western Modernism* (London: Phaidon, 2003), 74.

8. "Analog, n.," *Oxford English Dictionary Online*, 2 April 2010, http://dictionary.oed.com/

9. "Digital, n.," *Oxford English Dictionary Online*, 2 April 2010, http://dictionary.oed.com/.

10. Davis, "How to Make Analogies," 82.

11. Lev Manovich, *The Language of New Media* (Cambridge, MA: MIT Press, 2001), 52.

12. For more on pixels and noise in digital imaging, see William J. Mitchell, *The Reconfigured Eye: Visual Truth in the Post-Photographic Era* (Cambridge, MA: MIT Press, 1992).

13. Manovich reminds his readers that "even pixel-based representation, which appears to be the very essence of digital imaging, cannot be taken for granted." Fixed-resolution image-editing programs convert pixels into a series of mathematical equations. By manipulating these equations, the user can effectively alter the resolution capabilities of the image, so that the threshold of visibility attains a new upper limit. Manovich, *Language of New Media*, 53. Vector graphics offer another possibility for designing non-pixel-based images. I should point out at this juncture that although I have been referring to photographic technology, the same argument can be applied to drawing, painting, and even sculpture,

all of which can be carried out through analog or digital means, for example, using rapid prototyping in the case of sculpture.

14. Bernard Stiegler, "The Discrete Image," in *Echographies of Television*, ed. Jacques Derrida and Bernard Stiegler, 145–163 (Malden, MA: Blackwell, 2002), 154.

15. Manovich, *Language of New Media*, 53.

16. Davis, "How to Make Analogies," 84.

17. Svetlana Alpers's and Michael Baxandall's research on the effects of nonart artifacts and practices provide seminal examples of an approach to art through visual culture. Alpers's appraisal of the "mapping impulse" in seventeenth-century Dutch art, and Baxandall's study of the fifteenth-century "period eye," in which artists seduce their patrons' eyes by engaging their ability to calculate volume, a skill necessary to merchants at that time for quickly and easily assessing the weight and value of goods, show how various models of visual computing factor into the aesthetic experience and interpretation of pictures. Svetlana Alpers, *The Art of Describing: Dutch Art in the Seventeenth Century* (Chicago: University of Chicago Press, 1984); Michael Baxandall, *Painting and Experience in Fifteenth-Century Italy: A Primer in the Social History of Pictorial Style* (Oxford: Oxford University Press, 1972).

18. Martin Heidegger, "The Question concerning Technology," in *The Question concerning Technology and Other Essays*, trans. William Lovitt, 3–35 (New York: Harper Torchbooks, 1977), 23.

19. Heidegger, "Question concerning Technology," 23.

20. Katherine N. Hayles, *How We Became Posthuman: Virtual Bodies in Cybernetics, Literature, and Informatics* (Chicago: University of Chicago Press, 1999).

21. The documentation of these first three conferences, compiled by Warren McCulloch, is held in a private collection. I am using an account given by Claus Pias, a historian of cybernetics and technology, as my primary reference here. Claus Pias, "Analog, Digital and the Cybernetic Illusion," *Kybernetes* 34, nos. 3/4 (2005): 543–550.

22. John von Neumann, "General and Logical Theory of Automata," ed. A. H. Taub, in *Collected Works*, vol. 5: *Design of Computers, Theory of Automata and Numerical Analysis*, 288–328 (New York: Pergamon, 1963).

23. Claus Pias, *Cybernetics/Kybernetik: The Macy Conferences, 1946–1953* (Zurich: Diaphanes, 2003).

24. Von Neumann, "General and Logical Theory," 293.

25. Von Neumann does acknowledge that even digital machines do not produce absolutely accurate results; there is some degree of error in a digital machine. Von Neumann explains, "This error is, or course, not a random variable like the noise in an analogy machine. It is, arithmetically, completely determined in every particular instance. Yet its mode of determination is so complicated, and its variations throughout the number of instances of its occurrence in a problem so irregular, that it usually can be treated to a high degree of approximation as a random variable" ("General and Logical Theory," 295).

26. Pias, *Cybernetics/Kybernetik*, 158.

27. Von Neumann, "General and Logical Theory," 296.

28. Timothy Binkley, "Digital Dilemmas," *Leonardo* 3 (supplemental issue; Digital Image, Digital Cinema: SIGGRAPH '90 Art Show Catalog) (1990): 13–19.

29. Claus Pias, "Analog, Digital and the Cybernetic Illusion," *Kybernetes* 34, nos. 3/4 (2005): 548.

30. Pias, "Analog, Digital," 548. See also man as the empirico-transcendental doublet, the new trope of the eighteenth century, as discussed in Foucault, *Order of Things*.

31. Pias avers that "Shannon's information theory and McCulloch's logical calculus are completely dependent on digital notions, and that means that the whole new universal cybernetic epistemology would not work if it is not based on digital terms." Pias, "Analog, Digital," 546.

32. Pias, "Analog, Digital," 546.

33. Pias, "Analog, Digital," 546.

34. Vincent Müller, "Representations in Digital Systems," Interdisciplines, 25 June 2007, accessed 24 March 2008, http://www.interdisciplines.org/.

35. Goodman, *Languages of Art*, 131.

36. Immanuel Kant, *Critique of Judgment*, trans. Werner S. Pluhar (Indianapolis: Hackett, 1987), 174.

37. In a recent book investigating the "myth of transparency" nearly endemic to interface design, Jay David Bolter and Diane Gromala draw on the legend of Zeuxis, whose flawless painterly technique caused birds to try in vain to pluck grapes from the bunches painted in his murals. Bolter and Gromala use this myth to demonstrate the ways in which interface designers attempt to naturalize their work, to make the surface, the appearance of constructedness and mediation, disappear. "Before there were computers," the myth goes, "people saw things as they really were: there were no pixels, no aliasing, and no need for Web-safe colors. Objects were present to people; the rays of light reflected by objects entered their eyes undistorted by any intervening medium (other than the air itself). Today, a good computer interface gets the user as close to that original experience as possible." According to Bolter and Gromala, this uncritical validation of transparency becomes subject to play and critique in digital art. Bolter and Gromala, *Windows and Mirrors*, 49.

38. Maureen Turim, "Artisanal Prefigurations of the Digital: Animating Realities, Collage Effects, and Theories of Image Manipulation," *Wide Angle* (Ohio University School of Film) 21, no. 1 (January 1999): 49.

39. Goodman, *Languages of Art*, 134.

40. "Nothing is intrinsically a representation; status as representation is relative to symbol system. A picture in one system may be a description in another; and whether a denoting symbol is representational depends not upon whether it resembles what it denotes but upon its own relationships to other symbols in a given system." Goodman, *Languages of Art*, 226.

41. Goodman defines repleteness in opposition to attenuation. Repleteness signifies which features are salient in a given symbol scheme. Here, he deploys his now-classic distinction between the electrocardiogram and a painting of a mountain by Katsushika Hokusai. In the former, only the ordinates and abscissas through which the lines passes are significant, and the thickness or thinness, color, or other visible features of the symbol scheme inflect the information given. In the latter, on the other hand, any fluctuation in the line, any detail down to the darkness of the ink or texture of the paper, is potentially

significant. Thus, while the two cases are morphologically similar, their capacity for meaning and the kind of information they convey is radically different. The aesthetic manifestation of this difference obtains in that the diagrammatic symbol scheme is attenuated while the pictorial scheme is replete. Goodman, *Languages of Art*, 229.

42. Goodman, *Languages of Art*, 136.

43. Davis, "How to Make Analogies," 76.

44. Goodman, *Languages of Art*, 153.

45. David Lewis, "Analog and Digital," *Noûs* 5, no. 3 (September 1971): 321.

46. Davis, "How to Make Analogies," 72.

47. Goodman, *Languages of Art*, 160.

48. Davis, "How to Make Analogies," 73.

49. Goodman, *Languages of Art*, 38.

50. Dominic McIver Lopes, "From *Languages of Art* to Art in Mind," *Journal of Aesthetics and Art Criticism* 58, no. 3 (Summer 2000): 228.

51. Goodman, *Languages of Art*, 38.

52. Lopes, "From *Languages of Art*," 229.

53. The history and aesthetics of letters, alphabets, and typography present another theoretical model and another parallel historical trajectory within which to consider digital media. See, for example, Johanna Drucker's sweeping account of the design of alphabets and letters from the classical age to the twentieth century. A reproduction of Adobe's master font for the letter O and other electronically manipulated letter forms is given in her chapter on the twentieth-century typographic imagination. Johanna Drucker, *The Alphabetic Labyrinth: The Letters in History and Imagination* (London: Thames and Hudson, 1995), 284.

54. Lewis, "Analog and Digital," 322.

55. "The interface is the basic aesthetic form of digital art. Just as literature has predominantly taken place in and around books, and painting has explored the canvas, the interface is now a central aesthetic form conveying digital information of all kinds." Soren Pøld, "Interface Realisms: The Interface as Aesthetic Form," *Postmodern Culture* 15, no. 2 (2005).

56. James Blachowitz, "Analog Representation Beyond Mental Imagery," *Journal of Philosophy* 94, no. 2 (February 1997): 71.

57. Lewis, "Analog and Digital," 322.

58. Citing Nicolas Negroponte's definition of a bit, which "has no color size or weight, It is a state of being: on or off, true or false, up or down, black or white," Müller rejoins, "Which of the black things are bits? What determines whether something is a bit?" Müller, "Representations." See also Nicolas Negroponte, *Being Digital* (New York: Vintage, 1995), 14.

59. Müller, "Representations."

60. Zenon Pylyshyn, *Computation and Cognition* (Cambridge, MA: MIT Press, 1984), cited in Müller, "Representations."

61. Müller, "Representations."

62. Müller, "Representations." Likewise, Goodman differentiates between schemes and systems, so that for a symbol scheme, defined as a label that sorts objects/symbols

into classes (e.g., sorts blue objects from other colors of objects), to be analog it requires only syntactic density, and an analog system is both syntactically and semantically dense. Goodman, *Languages of Art*, 160.

63. Müller emphasizes the role of function in digital modularity. "If someone would fail to recognize that my laptop computer has binary digital states, they would have failed to recognize the proper function of these states for the purpose of the whole system—namely what it was made for. . . . (And the fact that it computes is crucial to its function, but not to that of, say, my shaving brush—so pancomputationalism seems misleading here)." Müller, "Representations."

64. "Just as a fractal has the same structure on different scales, a new media object has the same modular structure throughout." Manovich goes on to write that "structural computer programming, which became standard in the 1970's, involves writing small and self-sufficient modules (called in different computer languages *subroutines, functions, procedures*, scripts), which are then assembled into larger programs." Lev Manovich, *Language of New Media*, 30, 31.

65. Müller, "Representations."

66. The five principles include numerical representation, modularity, automation, variability, and transcoding. See the chapter "Principles of New Media" in Manovich, *Language of New Media*, 27–48.

67. Manovich, *Language of New Media*, 28.

68. Manovich, *Language of New Media*, 28.

69. Manovich, *Language of New Media*, 29.

70. Manovich, *Language of New Media*, 29. See also Michel Foucault, *Discipline and Punish: The Birth of the Prison*, trans. Alan Sheridan (New York: Random House, 1979).

71. Walter Benjamin's essays on modernity, Siegfried Kracauer's *Mass Ornament*, and Martin Heidegger's later writings on science and technology offer some of the most compelling illustrations of modernity, its iconic figures and paradigmatic structures. Walter Benjamin, *The Arcades Project*, trans. Howard Eiland and Kevin McLaughlin (Cambridge, MA: Harvard University Press, 1999); Martin Heidegger, *The Question concerning Technology and Other Essays* (New York: Harper Torchbooks, 1977); Siegfried Kracauer, *The Mass Ornament: Weimar Essays*, trans. Thomas Y. Levin (Cambridge, MA: Harvard University Press, 1995).

72. For example, see Arthur Kroker and Marilouise Kroker, "Code Warriors: Bunkering In and Dumbing Down," in *The Cybercultures Reader*, ed. D. Bell and B. M. Kennedy, 96–106 (New York: Routledge, 2000). See also W. Gibson, *Neuromancer* (New York: Ace, 1984).

73. Mark B. N. Hansen, *Bodies in Code: Interfaces with Digital Media* (New York: Routledge, 2006); Anna Munster, *Materializing New Media: Embodiment in Information Aesthetics* (Hanover, NH: University Press of New England, 2006).

74. André Leroi-Gourhan, *Gesture and Speech*, trans. Anna Bostock Barger (Cambridge, MA: MIT Press, 1993).

75. Jacques Derrida, *Of Grammatology*, trans. Gayatri Chakravorty Spivak (Baltimore: Johns Hopkins University Press, 1998). Bernard Stiegler, *Technics and Time*, vol. 1: *The Fault of Epimetheus*, trans. Richard Beardsworth and George Collins (Stanford, CA: Stanford

University Press, 1998). Bernard Stiegler, *Technics and Time*, vol. 2: *Disorientation*, trans. Stephen Barker (Stanford, CA: Stanford University Press, 2009). For more on the relationship between Stiegler, Leroi-Gourhan, as well as between Jacques Derrida and Georges Bataille, see Charlie Gere, *Art, Time, and Technology* (Oxford, UK: Berg, 2006), 13–34.

76. Whitney Davis, *Replications: Archaeology, Art History, Psychoanalysis* (University Park: Pennsylvania State University Press, 1996).

77. Heidegger, *Question concerning Technology*, 115–141.

78. Henri Bergson, *Creative Evolution*, trans. Arthur Mitchell (Mineola, NY: Dover, 1998).

79. Müller, "Representations."

80. See Whitney Davis's arguments about how, due to the increasing indiscernability of digital and analog systems, it becomes more interesting to consider both digital and analog artworks and artifacts in terms of how they "analogize" or "look like"—bear certain aesthetic characteristics of—digital and analog systems. Davis, *Replications*, 89.

81. In his discussion of analog and digital representations of time, Müller postulates that Pylyshyn would argue that regardless of whether a hand advances one click forward or if a digit changes on the screen, if the "underlying mechanism" of the device is digital, the clock will necessarily be digital. I take issue with this on several levels; at the most general level, if the underlying mechanism is not perceivably digital, the relevance of its digitality may be negligible. This, of course, is the issue at the crux of my entire project. But even at a more particular level, the tendency toward regress manifests when we realize the "underlying mechanism" of timekeeping, or more applicably, time-measuring, instruments is precisely the discretization or *punctuation* (Bergson) of time itself.

82. For an extensive analysis of the disciplinary forms that arose to organize bodies, both individual and in group formations, to subdivide both bodily movements and time itself, see Michel Foucault, "Docile Bodies," in *Discipline and Punish*, 135–169. See also, on the invention of clock time, Lewis Mumford, *Technics and Civilization* (New York: Harcourt, Brace, 1934), 12–18.

2. Points, Divisions, and Pixels: From Modern to Contemporary Digitality

1. See Lewis, "Analog and Digital."

2. Stiegler, "Discrete Image," 149.

3. Leroi-Gourhan, *Gesture and Speech*, 264.

4. Leroi-Gourhan, *Gesture and Speech*, 264.

5. Walter Seitter, "Painting Has Always Been a Digital Affair," in *Painting Pictures: Painting and Media in the Digital Age*, ed. Kunstmuseum Wolfsburg, 30–35 (Bielefeld, Germany: Kerber Verlag, 2003).

6. Seitter, "Painting Has Always," 30.

7. Knut Ebeling, "The Painting of the Men from Mars," in *Painting Pictures: Painting and Media in the Digital Age*, ed. Kunstmuseum Wolfsburg, 36–40 (Bielefeld, Germany: Kerber Verlag, 2003).

8. Laura U. Marks, "Infinity and Accident: Strategies of Enfoldment in Islamic Art and Computer Art," *Leonardo* 39, no. 1 (2006): 40.

9. For Lev Manovich, the modular structure of new media is one of its fundamental

characteristics. His definition of the module analogizes the structure of fractals, in which the form of the constituent parts of the fractal is replicated at every scale, so that if we are confronted with a star-shaped fractal, when we "zoom in" to the figure, we will see that that the macroscopically visible star is composed of many smaller stars. This definition deviates from, for example, David Summers's, which emphasizes not the part-whole relationship but rather the metric function of the module, as the smallest part according to which "the notional surface is infinitely multipliable or divisible, and is reconcilable with any other measure." See Manovich, *Language of New Media*, 30. See also Summers, *Real Spaces*, 411.

10. See Leroi-Gourhan's chapter "The Expanding Memory," in *Gesture and Speech*, 258–266.

11. Seitter, "Painting Has Always," 31.

12. For example, neo-Impressionism can be read as an informed response to the Impressionists' experimental method of immediately capturing and rendering on canvas a direct, unfiltered recording of imperfect, ephemeral human sensory perception. For more on "the impression" of impressionism, see Paul Smith, "Defining Impressionism," in *Impressionism: Beneath the Surface*, 7–32 (New York: Abrams, 1995).

13. William Innes Homer, *Seurat and the Science of Painting* (Cambridge, MA: MIT Press, 1964).

14. Rood's text, originally published in 1879, was familiar to Seurat through its 1881 translation into French, under the title *Théorie scientifique des couleurs*. For the English edition, see Ogden Rood, *Modern Chromatics, with Applications to Art and Industry* (New York: Appleton, 1879).

15. Alan Lee, "Seurat and Science," *Art History* 10, no. 2 (1987): 203–224.

16. Norma Broude, *Seurat in Perspective* (Englewood Cliffs, NJ: Prentice-Hall, 1978), 42.

17. Martin Kemp, *The Science of Art: Optical Themes in Western Art from Brunelleschi to Seurat* (New Haven, CT: Yale University Press, 1990).

18. Martin Kemp, "The Impressionists' Bible," *Nature* 543 (1 May 2008): 37.

19. Seitter, "Painting Has Always," 31.

20. See, for example, Erwin Panofsky, *Perspective as Symbolic Form*, trans. Christopher S. Wood (New York: Zone Books, 1997). See also Hubert Damisch, *The Origin of Perspective*, trans. John Goodman (Cambridge, MA: MIT Press, 1994).

21. John Gage, "The Technique of Seurat: A Reappraisal," *Art Bulletin* 69, no. 3 (1987): 452; Meyer Schapiro, "Seurat," in *Modern Art, 19th and 20th Centuries: Selected Papers*, 101–109 (New York: George Braziller, 1978), 102.

22. For more on Seurat's scientific and theoretical sources, see Homer, *Seurat*, 129–131.

23. Schapiro, "Seurat," 102.

24. Seurat quoted in Gage, "Technique of Seurat," 448n1.

25. Félix Fénéon, "Le Néo-Impressionnisme," *L'art moderne*, 1 May 1877, 139. Cited in Homer, *Seurat*, 170. Italics added.

26. George Sheldon, *Recent Ideals of American Art* (New York, 1890), 160. Cited in Homer, *Seurat*, 294n103.

27. Homer, *Seurat*, 173.

28. Gage, "Technique of Seurat," 452.

29. Gage, "Technique of Seurat," 452n34.

30. Schapiro, "Seurat," 103.

31. Roger Fry, *Seurat* (London: Phaidon, 1965), 14.

32. Lee, "Seurat and Science," 222.

33. See, for example, Norma Broude's essay tracing the possible influences on Seurat's technique and worldview of the invention of photomechanical color printing in the 1880s. Norma Broude, "New Light on Seurat's 'Dot': Its Relation to Photo-Mechanical Color Printing in France in the 1880's," *Art Bulletin* 56, no. 4 (December 1974): 581–589.

34. Lee, "Seurat and Science," 208.

35. Gage, "Technique of Seurat," 452.

36. Stephen F. Eisenman, "Mass Culture and Utopia: Seurat and Neoimpressionism," in *Nineteenth Century Art: A Critical History*, ed. Stephen F. Eisenman and T. Crow (London: Thames and Hudson, 1994), 281.

37. As Schapiro has admonished proponents of scientifically inflected interpretations of Seurat's work, "how to paint brightly is no secret requiring a special knowledge of science." Schapiro, "Seurat," 101.

38. Schapiro, "Seurat," 108.

39. For further consideration of the dominance of allographic arts in traditional aesthetics, and of the challenges posed by the introduction of autographic technologies and movements, see chapter 3 on algorithmic art and the aesthetics of code. See also Kirk Pillow, "Did Goodman's Distinction Survive LeWitt?" *Journal of Aesthetics and Art Criticism* 61, no. 4 (Autumn 2003): 365–380.

40. Schapiro, "Seurat," 103.

41. Schapiro, "Seurat," 102.

42. Schapiro, "Seurat," 102.

43. Seitter, "Painting Has Always," 31.

44. Seitter, "Painting Has Always," 31.

45. Eisenman, "Mass Culture," 278.

46. Eisenman, "Mass Culture," 277.

47. Fry, *Seurat*, 7. See also Eisenman, "Mass Culture," 277.

48. Seurat cited in Gage, "Technique of Seurat," 448n2.

49. Schapiro, "Seurat," 108.

50. Fry, *Seurat*, 9.

51. "And yet, for all this close adherence to observation, how unlike anything natural these pictures are! How utterly fixed and immovable everything is! His pictures are alive, indeed, but not with the life of nature." Fry, *Seurat*, 10.

52. Schapiro, "Seurat," 106.

53. Schapiro, "Seurat," 101.

54. Ileana Marcoulesco, "Unclassifiable Klee," in *A Piece of the Moon World*, by Paul Klee, 13–27 (Houston: Menil Collection, 1995), 16.

55. Richard Wagner, "Outlines of the Artwork of the Future: The Artwork of the Future 1849," in *Multimedia: From Wagner to Virtual Reality*, ed. R. Packer and K. Jordan, 3–9 (New York: Norton, 2001).

56. Wassily Kandinsky, *Concerning the Spiritual in Art*, trans. M. T. H. Sadler (New York: Dover, 1977), 25.

57. Kandinsky, *Concerning the Spiritual*, 20.

58. Goodman, *Languages of Art*, 178.

59. Manovich, *Language of New Media*, 45.

60. All quotations from Paul Klee, "Creative Credo," in *Theories of Modern Art: A Source Book by Artists and Critics*, ed. H. B. Chipp, 182–186 (Berkeley: University of California Press, 1968). Italics added.

61. I am not treating here Klee's engagement with alphabets and writing, not because this aspect of his work is less important or less notational. In fact, I am addressing his engagement with music as one possible notational form among many, and as such it functions as an example rather than the single authoritative case for Klee's deep, career-long explorations of the possible intersections and deviations between pictorial and notational depiction. For more on Klee's incorporation of language and alphabetic notation into his depictive schemas, cf. K. Porter Aichele, *Paul Klee's Pictorial Writing* (Cambridge: Cambridge University Press, 2002). Also see Rainer Crone and Joseph Leo Koerner, *Paul Klee: Legends of the Sign* (New York: Columbia University Press, 1991).

62. Hajo Düchting, *Paul Klee: Painting and Music* (New York: Prestel, 1997), 35–36.

63. Düchting, *Paul Klee*, 45.

64. Klee, cited in Petra Petitpierre, *Aus der Malklasse von Paul Klee* (Berne, Switzerland: Benteli, 1957), 19. Cited in Düchting, *Paul Klee*, 45.

65. Victor Vasarely, *Vasarely*, trans. I. Mark Paris (New York: Alpine Fine Arts Collection, 1979), 8.

66. Paul Klee, *The Thinking Eye: The Notebooks of Paul Klee*, ed. Jürg Spiller, trans. Ralph Mannheim (London: Percy Lund, Humphries, 1961), 8.

67. Klee, *Thinking Eye*, 8.

68. Klee, *Thinking Eye*, 8.

69. Klee, *Thinking Eye*, 8.

70. Klee, *Thinking Eye*, 8, 10.

71. Klee, *Thinking Eye*, 10.

72. Chapter 4 will introduce Casey Reas, an artist whose work involves a strong pedagogical aspect. While Klee used his notebooks, and many of his drawings and paintings, as pedagogical tools for his students at the Bauhaus, Reas also produces a handbook for his own, fully computational programmatic language, *Processing*, in 2008. Similarly, Victor Vasarely, the primary subject of chapter 3, envisioned a fully programmatic visual alphabet that could be taught to and replicated by future generations of artists.

73. Paul Klee, *Notebooks*, vol. 2: *The Nature of Nature*, ed. Jürg Spiller, trans. Heinz Norden (New York: George Wittenborn, 1973), 231.

74. Klee, *Nature of Nature*, 377.

75. Mitchell, *Reconfigured Eye*, 69.

76. Manovich, *Language of New Media*, 30.

77. Manovich, *Language of New Media*, 30, 31.

78. Klee, *Nature of Nature*, 53.

79. Klee, *Nature of Nature*, 53.

80. Klee, *Nature of Nature*, 183.

81. Marcoulesco, "Unclassifiable Klee," 26.

82. Considering Klee's work in terms of a dynamism activated by particles conjures Henri Bergson's profoundly antidigital theory of duration and movement. Bergson calls up Zeno's paradox, in which a flying arrow must be conceived as being motionless if at every moment it occupies a single position. For, in this estimation, the arrow occupies each separate, distinct, disjunct, and therefore digital position successively, leaving no room for movement between positions. Bergson, then, would most likely determine that a fully digital system would result in stultification, where movement and duration become, impossibly, a series of immobilities. Bergson, *Creative Evolution*, 308–309.

83. K. Porter Aichele has argued that a series of early illustrations by Klee to Voltaire's Candide, examined in conjunction with concurrent diary entries, can be viewed as experiments in the visual modeling of the conceptus of kinetic energy and "nervous energy" set forth by Jean Perrin and Wilhelm Ostwald, respectively. This suggests that Klee's concept of nature, which was a primary subject of his artistic writings, teachings, and practice, would have been informed by scientific models and specifically turn-of-the-century energetic and atomic theories. K. Porter Aichele, "Paul Klee and the Energetics-Atomistics Controversy," *Leonardo* 26, no. 4 (1993): 309–315.

84. Klee, *Thinking Eye*, 63–66.

85. Klee, "Creative Credo," 182.

86. Norbert Lynton, *The Story of Modern Art* (London: Phaidon Press Ltd., 1989), 23

87. Frank Reijnders, "Painting? A State of Utter Idiocy," in *Painting Pictures: Painting and Media in the Digital Age*, ed. Kunstmuseum Wolfsburg, 20–29 (Wolfsburg, Germany: Kerber Verlag, 2003), 24.

88. Reijnders, "Painting?" 24.

89. Goodman, *Languages of Art*, 158.

90. Masters of calligraphy claim such acute control of their brushes that even the finest, seemingly microscopic traces of ink spidering off the path of the primary brushstroke and the most subtle variations in tone due to shifts in pressure of brush to paper, speed of application of ink, and amount of ink contained on the brush are the result of intention, not accident.

91. This distrust of the capacity of technology to aid in the production of fine art is observable also in the history of cinema and photography. See, for example, Maxim Gorky, "The Lumière Cinematograph," in *The Film Factory: Russian and Soviet Cinema in Documents 1896–1939*, ed. I. Christie and R. Taylor, 25–26 (New York: Routledge, 1994).

92. "In modernism, the sign of the contemporary was a geometrical simplicity that mirrored mechanical forms, both being manifestations of a Platonic ideal; in the age of simulation, the sign of the contemporary is the completeness of naturalistic illusion." Julian Stallabrass, *Internet Art: The Online Clash of Culture and Commerce* (London: Tate Publishing, 2003), 34.

93. Pøld, "Interface Realisms."

94. Friedrich Kittler, "Gramophone, Film, Typewriter," *October* 41 (Summer 1987): 102.

95. Andreas Gursky has become the exemplar of uncannily and often invisibly manipulated photographs. See also Mitchell, *Reconfigured Eye*.

96. Paul Virilio, *Art and Fear*, trans. Julie Rose (New York: Continuum, 2003), 48.

97. Eisenman, "Mass Culture," 279.

98. Reijnders, "Painting?" 25.

99. Reijnders, "Painting?" 25.

100. Reijnders, "Painting?" 25.

101. Reijnders, "Painting?" 24.

102. Reijnders, "Painting?" 27.

3. Vasarely, Watz, and the New Abstraction: From Op Art to Generative Art

1. See, for example, Larry Cuba's *3/78 (Objects and Transformations)* (1978), John Whitney's *Arabesque* (1975), and Stan Van Der Beek's *Poem Field 2* (1978).

2. Vasarely, *Vasarely*, 11.

3. Each element, discrete unit, or "pixel" on his raster grid is delimited by its uniform coloration. In other words, there is no color gradation within the unit; instead, form and color, usually held to be distinct, are collapsed together so that the unity of color and form defines the discrete alphabetic particle.

4. Robert Morgan, *Vasarely* (New York: George Braziller, 2004), 18.

5. For the seminal account of Op Art in America, see the exhibition catalog for *The Responsive Eye*. William C. Seitz, *The Responsive Eye* (New York: Museum of Modern Art, 1965), 5.

6. Jonathan Crary has traced the history of artistic transpositions of scientific discoveries in optics and physiological basis of vision in the communication between eye and brain. See Jonathan Crary, *Techniques of the Observer: On Vision and Modernity in the Nineteenth Century* (Cambridge, MA: MIT Press, 1990).

7. Seitz, *Responsive Eye*, 3.

8. "Stripped of conceptual association, habits, and references to previous experience, perceptual responses would appear to follow innate laws, limited though our understanding of them might be." Seitz, *Responsive Eye*, 7.

9. Seitz, *Responsive Eye*, 8.

10. Johanna Drucker makes a distinction between the closed loop of the digital humanities, which employ digital tools to the data mining of humanistic—primarily textual—artifacts, and her open-ended experiments in speculative computing, which thrives on rather than disavowing irregularities, indeterminacies, and inconsistencies in a text. Drucker then lists the principles that generally define the expectations for and constraints of electronic computing technology: (1) calculation, (2) computation, (3) digital processing, (4) classification, and (5) electronic communication. Drucker, *SpecLab*, 23–24.

11. Vasarely, *Vasarely*, 15.

12. While Vasarely's supporters have pointed out with great frequency the fact that he seems to mimic the technics of computer graphics long before the invention of the graphical user interface (GUI), he does not take his interest in physics and the physical construction of matter as a fascination with "newness" or novel scientific theorizations of world and nature. In fact, in 1947 he wrote that "the overvaluation of the bizarre, the

extraordinary and the novel ultimately sinks into boredom. . . . The wondrous discoveries of the accidental, like the excessive love of technology, are leading towards superficiality." Gaston Diehl, *Vasarely*, trans. Eileen Hennessey (New York: Crown, 1972), 15.

13. Vasarely, *Vasarely*, 15.

14. Simulation produces a copy of an existing system, but there is an associated implication that the copy, while it perhaps ultimately replaces and obscures any memory of an original, per Baudrillard, produces a weak version, an insufficient or distorted replica that lacks certain elements of the real while overamplifying others. For the classic humanistic text outlining simulation and hyperreality, see Jean Baudrillard, *Simulations*, trans. Paul Foss, Paul Patton, and Philip Beitherman (New York: Semiotext[e], 1983). Extreme proponents of complexity theory and producers of Artificial Life (A-Life) systems would claim not simply that the behaviors of A-Life programs *imitate* biological and physical patterns and behavior in nature but also that the complexity visible in computer programs is coextensive with nature—that A-Life is not merely a metaphor but rather puts into action natural laws. See Stepfan Helmreich, *Silicon Second Nature: Culturing Artificial Life in a Digital World* (Berkeley: University of California Press, 1998).

15. For a more in-depth discussion of the term "wetware," see Richard Doyle, *Wetwares: Experiments in Postvital Living* (Cambridge, MA: MIT Press, 2003).

16. I use this example in the broadest illustrative sense, leaving aside the myriad and complex distinctions that arise with respect to questions about intellection and consciousness, the degree to which other sentient creatures experience consciousness, and of course the role of intuition, emotion, and other prepropositional forms of knowledge that might be considered inextricable from intellectual activity, and thus the reasons that computers cannot, ultimately, *think*. See Hubert Dreyfus, *What Computers Still Can't Do: A Critique of Artificial Reason* (Minneapolis: University of Minnesota Press, 1992).

17. Jean-François Lyotard, *The Inhuman: Reflections on Time*, trans. Geoffrey Bennington (Stanford, CA: Stanford University Press, 1992), 2.

18. This equivalence of map and territory is the famous illustration of the simulacrum presented by Jean Baudrillard, which is itself a citation of Borges. See Baudrillard, *Simulations*, 1.

19. In his "Notes for a Manifesto," Vasarely wrote of his "plastic unit," comprised of an inextricable bond of form and color, that "through it material structure is comprehended; the mathematics of the universe, everything in its intellectual superstructure. The unit is the abstract essence of the beautiful, the basic form of sensibility. Conceived with art, it makes a work, a poetic equivalent of the world it signifies." Victor Vasarely, "Notes for a Manifesto," in *Data: Directions in Art, Theory and Aesthetics*, ed. A. Hill, 101–103 (Greenwich: New York Graphic Society, 1968), 101.

20. See Jasia Reichardt, *Cybernetic Serendipity* (New York: Praeger, 1969).

21. Jasia Reichardt, "Cybernetics, Art and Ideas," in *Cybernetics, Art and Ideas*, 11–17 (London: Studio Vista, 1971), 14.

22. Reichardt wrote that "intellect has its own pleasures but these are not a substitute for direct emotional response. The central core of a work of art, which is the transformation of the material which makes up the sum of its parts, has so far defeated all analytical

attempts." Presciently to the problems that persist in Generative Art today, she goes on to write, "Both Max Bense and Abraham Moles approach such an analysis from the peripheries of the structure of the work, but to this day there isn't a single masterpiece that has been made according to the principles of generative aesthetics." In an odd conclusion to her statement she adds, "This essential core of a work of art remains still to be fragmented, rationalized and reconstructed." This last sentence is particularly odd in its prescription for discovering art in the very action it is claiming that has not been yet reconciled with the aims of art: the digitization or transformation of matter into an endlessly reconfigurable, replicable, and additive series of ones and zeros. She suggests here that the intellectual act of rationalization will solve the problem of an approach to art practice that fails to catalyze the emotional response necessary to classify a work as art. Reichardt, "Cybernetics," 14.

23. In the acknowledgments section of the catalog, Seitz says that the roots of "optical" or "opthalmic" painting stretch "beyond what we call 'art' into graphic design, technology, psychology, and other sciences," and then later in the text concedes that of the works selected for the exhibition, certain of them bear "a stronger family resemblance to mechanical patterns, scientific diagrams, and even to screens and textured surfaces than to relational abstract art." Seitz, *Responsive Eye*, 3, 8.

24. For further discussion of this topic in philosophy, see Alva Noë, *Out of Our Heads: Why You Are Not Your Brain, and Other Lessons from the Biology of Consciousness* (New York: Hill and Wang, 2009). In vision science ("visual studies"), see David Marr, *Vision: A Computational Investigation into the Human Representation and Processing of Visual Information* (San Francisco: W. H. Freeman, 1982). For a neuroscientific approach to art history, see John Onians, *Neuroarthistory: From Aristotle and Pliny to Baxandall and Zeki* (New Haven, CT: Yale University Press, 2008).

25. C. P. Snow, "The Two Cultures," in *The Two Cultures*, 1–41 (New York: Cambridge University Press, 1998).

26. Regardless of its use value for the humanities, digital technology is grounded in formal logic and as such is subject both to the advantages and to the constraints of working within the strict parameters of a formal-logical system. See Drucker, *SpecLab*.

27. This is a reference to Eco's *Opera Aperta* (*The Open Work*), which is a model that applies not only to Vasarely's multimedia practice but also to the generative software systems authored by Casey Reas, the subject of the following chapter. Umberto Eco, *The Open Work*, trans. Anna Cancogni (Cambridge, MA: Harvard University Press, 1989).

28. "If humans are born human, as cats are born cats (within a few hours), it would not be . . . I don't even say desirable, which is another question, but simply possible, to educate them. That children have to be educated is a circumstance which only proceeds from the fact that they are not completely led by nature, not programmed. The institutions which constitute culture supplement this native lack." Lyotard, *Inhuman*, 3.

29. For an engaging interpretation of the spatial and technological dynamics of *Tron*, see Scott Bukatman, *Terminal Identity: The Virtual Subject in Post-Modern Science Fiction* (Durham, NC: Duke University Press, 1993), 215–227.

30. Michèle Vasarely, *L'affaire Vasarely: Art, pouvoir et corruption* (Aix-en-Provence, France: Vents contraires, 2002).

31. Michèle Vasarely, "Victor Vasarely: Chronology; The Father of Op Art," Galeria Renes, accessed 6 May 2010, http://renes.com.pl/.

32. M. Vasarely, "Victor Vasarely."

33. V. Vasarely, *Vasarely*, 11.

34. Diehl, *Vasarely*, 64.

35. This last term I borrow directly from Vasarely: "The format of every abstract composition is expandable-compressible." V. Vasarely, *Vasarely*, 14.

36. Diehl, *Vasarely*, 55.

37. Diehl, *Vasarely*, 55.

38. Lyotard, *Inhuman*, 3.

39. V. Vasarely, *Vasarely*, 15.

40. John Maeda is most famously the champion of simplicity in the field of computer art and design. See also Edward Tufte for further reflections on the value of simplicity in information visualization. John Maeda, *The Laws of Simplicity* (Cambridge, MA: MIT Press, 2006); Edward R. Tufte, *The Visual Display of Quantitative Information* (Cheshire, CT: Graphics Press, 2001).

41. Summers, *Real Spaces*, 18.

42. Summers, *Real Spaces*, 36.

43. Summers, *Real Spaces*, 21.

44. Summers, *Real Spaces*, 21.

45. For more about the distinctions between space and place, see Edward S. Casey, *The Fate of Place: A Philosophical History* (Berkeley: University of California Press, 1997).

46. Sabine Eckmann and Lutz Koepnick, *Grid/Matrix* (St. Louis: Mildred Lane Kemper Museum, 2006).

47. Casey, *Fate of Place*, 24.

48. Eckmann and Koepnick, *Grid/Matrix*, 16.

49. Eckmann and Koepnick, *Grid/Matrix*, 16.

50. "Insofar as its order is that of pure relationship, the grid is a way of abrogating the claims of natural objects to have an order particular to themselves; the relationships in the aesthetic field are shown by the grid to be in a world apart and, with respect to natural objects, to be both prior and final. The grid declares the space of art to be at once autonomous and autotelic." Rosalind Krauss, "Grids," *October* 9 (Summer 1979): 50, 52.

51. I am here referring to the etymological and philosophical roots of the term matrix, specifically the account of it given by Plato in the *Timaeus*, as explicated Edward Casey in his remarkable study of space and place, *The Fate of Place*. In his chapter on the *Enuma Elish* and the *Timaeus*, Casey discusses the philosophical valences of the matrix as the generative source of matter, energy, and the ordering force, which precipitates the architectural formation of world and universe. Casey, *Fate of Place*, 23–49.

52. David Summers calls this the metaoptical cube, in which a modular division of space along x, y, and z axes creates an infinitely extended cube, measured in the regular intervals provided by the module. Any point might be feasibly mapped in relation to any other point within this cube, which "might in fact be extended in thought (if not in imagination) to be coextensive with the universe itself. This would be the universe conceived as

an infinite, isometric matrix preceding any object that might appear in it." Summers, *Real Spaces*, 560.

53. Summers, *Real Spaces*, 550.

54. Moreover, indices of a fully rationalized or a rudimentary perspectival configuration are often visible in the inclusion of painted floor tiles in the image, which conform to the diegetic world of the picture but also reveal the modular construction of space, the structural framework the conditions that possibility for that world to appear.

55. Vasarely, *Vasarely*, 13.

56. L. Lippard, "Constellation in Harsh Daylight: The Whitney Annual," *Hudson Review* 21, no. 1 (Spring 1968): 180.

57. Vasarely, *Vasarely*, 13.

58. This tendency also begins to gain momentum outside the realm of visual art, as we see in structuralism and semiotic theory and, I would argue, is a symptom of the informatic worldview that comes to fruition in the mid-twentieth century with the advent of cybernetics.

59. Vasarely, *Vasarely*, 14.

60. Vasarely, *Vasarely*, 14.

61. Vasarely, *Vasarely*, 14.

62. Vasarely, *Vasarely*, 14.

63. Siegfried Kracauer, "Photography," in *Mass Ornament*, 47–63.

64. Morgan, *Vasarely*, 30.

65. James Elkins has referred to a subtle and all-too-often unremarked "anti-naturalism" in his discussions of digital modeling of the human body. Particularly germane here is the "stickiness," the slightly-too-dense rubberlike solidity that marks an image of a cross-sectioned mummy's head as a digital rather than a photographic artifact. James Elkins, "Art History and the Criticism of Computer-Generated Images," *Leonardo* 27, no. 4 (1994): 338.

66. Götz, cited in Christine Mehring, "Television's Abstract Starts: Europe circa 1944–1969," *October* 125 (Summer 2008): 37.

67. Vasarely, *Vasarely*, 7.

68. Vasarely, *Vasarely*, 14.

69. For discussion of the relation of art and *techne*, see Martin Heidegger, "The Origin of the Work of Art," in *Poetry, Language, Thought*, 15–86 (New York: Perennial); and Heidegger, "The Question concerning Technology." Both are also available in Martin Heidegger, *Basic Writings*, ed. David Krell (New York: Harper and Row, 1977).

70. Tom Gunning, "The Cinema of Attractions: Early Film, Its Spectator, and the Avant-Garde," in *Early Cinema: Space, Frame, Narrative*, ed. T. Elsaesser and A. Barker, 56–86 (London: British Film Institute, 1990).

71. Marius Watz, "*ElectroPlastique #1* (2005)," accessed 6 April 2010, http://www.unlekker.net/.

72. Marius Watz, "Theory: Vague Terrain," Generator.x, 6 June 2006, accessed 6 April 2010, http://www.generatorx.no/.

73. Diehl, *Vasarely*, 44.

74. Benjamin H. D. Buchloh, "Conceptual Art 1962–1969: From the Aesthetics of Administration to the Critique of Institutions," *October*, no. 55 (Winter 1990): 105–143.

75. Diehl, *Vasarely*, 44.

76. "Perceptual and kinetic art have an intertwined development that cannot be totally disentangled; nevertheless perceptual, optical, or 'virtual' movement—which always exists in tension with factual immobility—is an experience of a different order. Carefully controlled static images have the power to elicit subjective responses that range from a quiet demand make on the eyes to distinguish almost invisible color and shape difference to arresting combinations that cause vision to react with spasmodic afterimages." Seitz, *Responsive Eye*, 9.

4. Spectral Analogies: From Wall Drawing to the Art of Programming

1. Casey Reas, "*{Software} Structures*: A Text About Software and Art," Artport, 2004, accessed 16 April 2010, http://artport.whitney.org/.

2. Casey Reas and Ben Fry, *Processing: A Programming Handbook for Visual Designers and Artists* (Cambridge, MA: MIT Press, 2007), xxiii.

3. I am once again referencing Whitney Davis's term here. Reas's "programmed paintings," as I am calling them, analogize the analog by "looking like" analog painting. Thus, "the looking-like—the noetic resemblance—can be secured and relayed in analog *or* digital modes or in analog *and* digital modes or in what *seem* to be analog and/or digital modes." Davis, "How to Make Analogies," 88.

4. Casey Reas, "Process/Drawing," ed. Mike Silver, *Architectural Design* 76, no. 4 (July/August 2006): 29.

5. Warren Sack, "Aesthetics of Information Visualization," in *Context Providers: Conditions of Meaning in Media Art*, ed. Victoria Vesna, Margot Lovejoy, and Christiane Paul, 123–150 (Bristol, UK: Intellect, 2011), accessed 24 June 2009, http://hybrid.ucsc.edu/; Eve Meltzer, "The Dream of the Information World," *Oxford Art Journal* 29, no. 1 (2006): 115–135; Edward Shanken, "Art in the Information Age: Technology and Conceptual Art," *Leonardo* 35, no. 4 (2002): 433–438.

6. Donald B. Kuspit, "Sol LeWitt: The Look of Thought," *Art in America* (September/October 1975): 48.

7. Katherine Hayles has defined informatics as "the material, technological, economic, and social structures that makes the information age possible. Informatics includes the late capitalist mode of flexible accumulation; the hardware and software that have merged telecommunications with computer technology; the patterns of living that emerge from and depend upon access to large data banks and instantaneous transmission of messages; and changing habits of posture, eye focus, hand motions, and neural connections that are reconfiguring the human body in conjunction with information technologies." Hayles attributes the initial use of the term to Donna Haraway, who employs the term to differentiate traditional (modern) systems of information and control to the (postmodern) informatics of domination. Katherine N. Hayles, "The Materiality of Informatics," *Configurations* 1, no. 1 (1993): 149.

8. Meltzer, "Dream of the Information World."

9. Meltzer, "Dream of the Information World," 132.

10. Reas, "Process/Drawing," 33.

11. These artists include A. Michael Noll, Manfred Mohr, Georg Nees, and Vera Molnar.

12. Kuspit, "Sol LeWitt."

13. Reas, "Process/Drawing" 33.

14. Johanna Drucker, "Digital Ontologies: The Ideality of Form in/and Code Storage —or—Can Graphesis Challenge Mathesis?" *Leonardo* 34, no. 2 (2001): 141.

15. Drucker, "Digital Ontologies," 141.

16. Shanken, "Art in the Information Age."

17. Gene Youngblood, "Calculated Movements: An Interview with Larry Cuba," *Video and the Arts Magazine*, Winter 1986; Gene Youngblood and Larry Cuba, "Calculated Movements: An Interview with Larry Cuba," Larry Cuba, accessed 16 April 2010, http://www.well.com/.

18. Buchloh, "Conceptual Art."

19. Buchloh, "Conceptual Art," 130.

20. Wendy Chun, "On Software: Or the Persistence of Visual Knowledge," *Grey Room*, no. 18 (Winter 2004): 26–51.

21. Sack, "Aesthetics of Information Visualization," 8.

22. Sack, "Aesthetics of Information Visualization," 11.

23. Sack, "Aesthetics of Information Visualization,"6.

24. In "Serial Project #1," LeWitt describes the ethos of the serial artist as follows: "The aim of the artist would be to give viewers information. . . . He would follow his predetermined premise to its conclusion voiding subjectivity. . . . The serial artist does not attempt to produce a beautiful or mysterious object but functions merely as a clerk cataloguing the results of his premise." Sol LeWitt, "Serial Project #1," ed. B. O'Doherty, *Aspen Magazine* 5–6 (17 September 1967).

25. See, for example, Douglas Engelbart's "Augmenting Human Intelligence: A Conceptual Framework," in which his vision of augmented intelligence is tantamount to the development through technological means of a hyperproductive office worker bee: "The objective of this study is to develop a conceptual framework within which could grow coordinated research an development program whose goals would be the following: (1) to find the factors that limit the effectiveness of the individual's basic information-handling capabilities in meeting the various needs of society for problem solving in its most general sense; and (2) to develop new techniques, procedures, and systems that will better match these basic capabilities to the needs, problems, and progress of society." Douglas Engelbart, "Augmenting Human Intellect: A Conceptual Framework," in *Multimedia: From Wagner to Virtual Reality*, ed. R. Packer and K. Jordan, 64–90 (New York: Norton, 2001), 69. See also Jean-François Lyotard on the topic of performativity and pedagogy applied to operational logic. Jean-François Lyotard, *The Postmodern Condition: A Report on Knowledge*, trans. Brian Massumi (Minneapolis: University of Minnesota Press, 1984), 51–52.

26. Victor Burgin clarifies the interlocking mechanisms of art and ideology. First asserting the deep investment in socialist ideals endemic in the conceptualist ethos, he goes on to claim that "the first requirement of a socialist art practice is that it should engage

those codes and contents which are in the public domain. These present themselves, and thus ideology, as natural and whole; a socialist art practice aims to deconstruct these codes, to unpick the apparent seamless ideological surface they present. Victor Burgin, "Socialist Formalism," *Studio International* 191, no. 980 (March/April 1976): 148–152.

27. In order to do so, of course, he first must take the step of defining software *as* a medium. "I like to think of software as a medium and my work is not possible without it. I didn't create any form of art before I began creating software. I've drawn my whole life and I didn't approach drawing with the rigor I now produce software. The essence of my work is dynamic systems and software is the medium in which I'm able to construct my vision." Casey Reas, "Organic and Conceptual Systems: Casey Reas Answers Bert Balcaen's questions for Sonic Acts X, Amsterdam 2004," Reas, 2004, accessed 18 April 2010, http://reas.com/.

28. Inke Arns, "Read_Me, Run_Me, Execute_Me: Software and Its Discontents, or: It's the Performativity of Code, Stupid!" in *Read_Me: Software Art and Cultures Conference*, ed. O. Goriunova and A. Shulgin, 176–193 (Åarhus, Denmark: University of Åarhus Press, 2004).

29. Arns, "Read_Me," 178.

30. Linguistic articulation already imposes a layer of filtration on the Idea and therefore cannot be considered pure or unmediated.

31. Donald Kuspit in 1975 discussed cogently the counterfactual stability of the "idea." While LeWitt proposes, tongue in cheek or not, that the idea should resist the discrepancies in communicative facility that inevitably occur between different media, it is clear that media are not, and cannot be, equivalent; they cannot transmit the same aspects of the same idea in the same manner. At the very least, then, they expose the idea as open to variable interpretation by shifting focus from one facet of the idea to another. Kuspit argues that LeWitt does not attempt to hide the incommensurability of media but rather "exploits the insoluble paradox" of medial nonequivalence. Kuspit, "Sol LeWitt," 44–45. See also Sol LeWitt, "Paragraphs on Conceptual Art," *Artforum* 5, no. 10 (Summer 1967): 79–84. Reprinted in Alexander Alberro and Blake Stimson, *Conceptual Art: A Critical Anthology* (Cambridge, MA: MIT Press, 1999), 12–16.

32. The instructions for this piece read, "All two part combinations of blue arcs from corners and sides and blue straight, not straight, and broken lines." This was written in blue crayon and included site-specific dimensions.

33. The opening three statements in LeWitt's "Sentences on Conceptual Art," which Reas includes in his documentation of *{Software} Structures* read, "1. Conceptual Artists are mystics rather than rationalists. They leap to conclusions that logic cannot reach. 2. Rational judgments repeat rational judgments. 3. Irrational judgments lead to new experience." Benjamin Buchloh has claimed, with respect to LeWitt's address of mysticism, that these statements throw into high relief "the radical difference between the logic of scientific production and that of aesthetic experience." Where positivism, a product of modernist self-reflexiveness, ends in a *reductio ad absurdum* of empiricism—that is, the "condition of tautology" performed programmatically by Kosuth, mystical experience would be associated with the model of aesthetics that is now most often ignored, if not outright

denigrated, a model characterized in terms of a cult of beauty and outmoded universalist theories of shared subjective response. Buchloh, "Conceptual Art," 141.

34. Reas, "Process/Drawing," 27.

35. "85. Same as 63, but with four colors. 63. A Wall is divided into four horizontal parts. In the top row are four equal divisions, each with lines in a different direction. In the second row, six double combinations; in the third row, four triple combinations; in the bottom row, all four combinations superimposed." Reas, "*{Software} Structures*."

36. Reas, "*{Software} Structures*."

37. Reas, "*{Software} Structures*."

38. In his 1986 interview with Gene Youngblood, Cuba describes his iterative process and the effects of using new tools to generate depictions that are irreproducible across platforms. "There was an evolution of the tool simultaneously with the evolution of the pictures—to the extent that I'd get way down the line and look back at the early pictures and realize I couldn't generate those pictures anymore because the software had evolved. I'd opened up new dimensions and closed off others." Youngblood, "Calculated Movements."

39. Meltzer, "Dream of the Information World," 126.

40. One particularly relevant passage from his "Paragraphs on Conceptual Art" compares his visual/spatial module to a biorhythmic pulse or a musical beat. "The intervals and measurements can be important to a work of art. If certain distances are important they will be made obvious in the piece. If space is relatively unimportant it can be regularized and made equal (things placed equal distances apart) to mitigate any interest in interval. Regular space might also become a metric time element, a kind of regular beat or pulse. When the interval is kept regular whatever is irregular gains more importance." By invoking these alternate sensorial modalities LeWitt successfully disrupts the one-to-one feedback loop between intellection and visuality—the notion that seeing is the sense most closely related to reason and propositional knowledge. See Martin Jay, *Downcast Eyes: The Denigration of Vision in Twentieth-Century French Thought* (Berkeley: University of California Press, 1993). In this brief passage LeWitt also activates the figure of difference through repetition, theorized famously by Gilles Deleuze. Here metrics do not serve a totalizing or totalitarian regime; instead, a regularized structure can act as a support for subtle shifts and nuances to appear, as a slight irregularity in an otherwise smoothly woven fabric. Gilles Deleuze, *Difference and Repetition*, trans. Paul Patton (New York: Columbia University Press, 1994).

41. Reas, "Organic and Conceptual Systems."

42. Max Bense, the German mathematician and physicist made famous in media studies for coining the term "information aesthetics," defined "generative aesthetics" in a brief essay published for a companion volume to the exhibition *Cybernetic Serendipity*. "The aim of generative aesthetics is the artificial production of probabilities, differing from the norm using theorems and programs." Max Bense, "The Project of Generative Aesthetics," in *Cybernetics, Art and Ideas*, ed. J. Reichardt, 57–60 (London: Studio Vista, 1971), 58.

43. In a foreshadowing moment in 1975, Donald Kuspit remarked on Sol LeWitt's own elaborate, inconcise use of natural language to articulate his instructions for his *Variations of Incomplete Open Cubes*. Kuspit dismisses LeWitt's foregrounding of process as simultane-

ously unwieldy and ascetic. With respect to the diagrams and handwritten descriptions of each item's location within the floorplan of the John Weber Gallery, Kuspit declares that "written in archaic (from today's point of view, belletristic) mathematical language, they described positions that could equally well have been expressed succinctly in algebraic form, as a function of coordinates." The issue here is not the threat of algebra's obsolescence, but it is demonstrative of the tension that appears between language systems when art begins to take on the look of technology. Kuspit, "Sol LeWitt," 43.

44. Umberto Eco, *The Open Work*, trans. Anna Cancogni (Cambridge, MA: Harvard University Press, 1989).

45. Casey Reas, "Beyond Code," in *Network Practices: New Strategies in Architecture and Design*, ed. A. Burke and T. Tierney, 166–177 (Princeton, NJ: Princeton Architectural Press, 2007), 166.

46. Reas, "Organic and Conceptual Systems."

47. Philip Galanter, "What Is Emergence? Generative Murals as Experiments in the Philosophy of Complexity," Philip Galanter, 2004, accessed 18 April 2010, http://philipgalanter.com/research.

48. Reas, "Organic and Conceptual Systems."

49. Reas, "Process/Drawing," 29.

50. Reas, "Process/Drawing," 29.

51. Reas, "Organic and Conceptual Systems."

52. Bernice Rose, "Sol LeWitt and Drawing," in *Sol LeWitt*, ed. A. Legg, 31–42 (New York: Museum of Modern Art, 1978), 31.

53. "The aim of the artist would not be to instruct the viewer but to give him information. Whether the viewer understands this information is incidental to the artist; he cannot foresee the understanding of all his viewers. He would follow his predetermined premise to its conclusion avoiding subjectivity. Chance, taste, or unconsciously remembered forms would play no part in the outcome. The serial artist does not attempt to produce a beautiful or mysterious object but functions merely as a clerk cataloging the results of his premise." LeWitt, "Serial Project #1." Reprinted in Gary Garrels, ed., *Sol LeWitt: A Retrospective* (New Haven, CT: Yale University Press, 2000), 373.

54. The only given about the status of visuality in LeWitt is that it is stubbornly paradoxical. Whereas Lucy Lippard in 1971 attempts to recuperate his "idea art" to a standard of beauty and visual pleasure, Kuspit insists on the outmodedness of beauty as an evaluative criterion for art criticism. To Lippard's avowal of the beauty of LeWitt's structures, and her claim that he embraces the paradox in making visual art while proclaiming the utter lack of consequence in the look of art, Kuspit rejoins, "The paradox is that LeWitt's objects barely generate any sensuous intensity, and instead seem to generate an intellectual response." Kuspit, "Sol LeWitt," 43.

55. Reas, "Beyond Code," 4.

56. Mitchell Whitelaw, "More Is More: Multiplicity and Generative Art," *The Teeming Void* (blog), 29 October 2007, accessed 28 November 2009, http://teemingvoid.blogspot.com/.

57. Douglas Edric Stanley, "Complexity and Gestalt," *Abstractmachine* (blog), 6 October 2007, accessed 28 November 2009, http://abstractmachine.net/.

58. To illustrate, the first chapter contains painstaking and minute descriptions of the plants in Mr. Palomar's garden, which introduce questions of identification, classification, perception, and the organization of perceptions that repeat on a larger and larger scale until, at the end of the book, Mr. Palomar's thoughts have replicated and expanded upon the themes elicited by his garden meditation to a contemplation of the nature of the universe.

59. Lev Manovich, "Abstraction and Complexity," in *Abstraction Now*, 80–85 (Vienna: Edition Camera Austria, 2004), accessed 28 November 2009, http://www.abstraction-now.at/.

60. Manovich, "Abstraction and Complexity," 85.

61. Maeda, *Laws of Simplicity*, i.

62. Stanley, "Complexity and Gestalt."

63. Manovich, "Abstraction and Complexity," 81.

64. Whitelaw, "More Is More."

65. Whitelaw, "More Is More."

66. Matthew Mirapaul, "In John Simon's Art, Everything Is Possible," *New York Times* on the Web, 17 April 1997, accessed 30 November 2009, http://www.nytimes.com/.

67. Mirapaul, "In John Simon's Art."

68. John F. Simon, "Artist's Statement," Numeral, accessed 24 June 2009, http://numeral.com/.

69. Reas, "Organic and Conceptual Systems."

70. Sebastian Campion, "Code: In Conversation With Casey Reas," Artificial.dk, 10 October 2003, accessed 1 May 2009, http://www.artificial.dk/.

71. Reas, "Organic and Conceptual Systems."

72. Casey Reas, "Programming Media," in *Code: The Language of Our Time*, 174–179 (Ostfildern-Ruit, Germany: Hatje Cantz Verlag, 2003), 177.

73. I use the term "theatrically" in its pejoratively loaded sense—in the sense of an attenuated or inauthentic performance of sincerity, as J. L. Austin would use it, or with inflections of another kind of inauthenticity: the aggressive, hulking anthropomorphism of "theatrical" sculpture derided by Michael Fried. J. L. Austin, *How to Do Things with Words* (Oxford: Oxford University Press, 1976); Michael Fried, "Art and Objecthood (1967)," in *Art and Objecthood: Essays and Reviews*, 148–172 (Chicago: University of Chicago Press, 1998).

74. For more on the relationship between hand and inscription, and technological mediations between the markmaker and the mark as trace, see Jacques Derrida, "The Word Processor," in *Paper Machine*, trans. Rachel Bowlby, 19–32 (Stanford, CA: Stanford University Press, 2005). See also Jacques Derrida, "Signature Event Context," in *Limited Inc.*, 1–23 (Evanston, IL: University of Chicago Press, 1988).

75. Roy Ascott, "Moist Ontology," in *The Art of Programming* (Amsterdam: Sonic Acts Press, 2002). Cited in Reas, "Programming Media," 175.

76. Reas, "Programming Media," 175.

77. Myron Kruger, "Responsive Environments," in *Multimedia: From Wagner to Virtual Reality*, ed. R. Packer and K. Jordan, 104–120 (New York: Norton, 2001).

78. Reas, "Programming Media," 175.

79. Penny L. Feuerstein, "How Does the Analog Talk to the Digital? The Art of Penny Feuerstein," Generative Art, 12–14 December 2007, accessed 18 April 2010, http://generativeart.com/.

80. Feuerstein, "How Does the Analog Talk?"

Conclusion—Amalgamations: From Digital Painting to Information Visualization

1. Viktor Shlovsky, "Art as Technique," in *The Critical Tradition: Classic Texts and Contemporary Trends*, ed. D. H. Richter, 716–726 (Boston: Bedford Books, 1998), 720.

2. The field of neuroaesthetics advances the notion that there are underlying neural, evolutionarily developed, adaptive, biological structures of the brain that can explain not only why humans make art but also how biologically hardwired aspects of "human nature" validate the occurrence of cross-culturally and transhistorically common aesthetic responses.

3. See Ellen Dissanayake, "The Arts after Darwin: Does Art Have an Origin or an Adaptive Function?" in *World Art Studies: Exploring Concepts and Approaches*, ed. K. Zijlmans & W. van Damme, 241–261 (Amsterdam: Valiz, 2008), 252.

4. Ibid., 252.

5. Enlightenment ideals might be said to be based on ideas of the autonomous art object, the cult of artistic genius, the nonutility (or purposiveness without purpose of art), the valorization of art's stimulation of contemplation, and its ability to remove the viewer from, instead of reasserting his or her embeddedness in, everyday life.

6. Heinrich Wölflinn, *Renaissance and Baroque* (Ithaca, NY: Cornell University Press, 1964), 29.

7. Goodman, *Languages of Art*, 229. See also, for a more detailed account of this distinction, Davis, "How to Make Analogies," 75.

8. Warren Sack, "Painting Theory Machines," *Art and Design* (May 1996): 83.

9. Sack, "Painting Theory Machines," 82.

10. Martin Jay, "Scopic Regimes of Modernity," in *Vision and Visuality*, ed. H. Foster, 3–23 (New York: New Press, 1988).

11. Martin Wattenberg, "Introduction to Visualization: From Data to Pictures to Insight," IBM, 16 May 2005, accessed 18 April 2010, http://www.alphaworks.ibm.com/.

12. Wattenberg, "Introduction to Visualization."

13. Gian-Carlo Rota, "The Phenomenology of Mathematical Beauty," in *The Visual Mind II*, ed. M. Emmer, 3–14 (Cambridge, MA: MIT Press, 2005), 3.

14. A question that arises here is how, or whether, Salavon's visual model establishes itself as in any way unique, or if his blurry, impressionistic surfaces lose something by simply reflecting an automated process. In other words, painting, even in its most "automated" instantiations (Andy Warhol), always invokes the gesture, with all its connotations of flawedness and subjectivity. Also recall the oscillations between mechanical and gestural occurring in Sigmar Polke and Gerhard Richter. Does Salavon's "painterly" aesthetic thus contain an element of disingenuousness? Might it be a "gimmick" used to mask the coldness of the work's basis in digital processing?

15. Robert Klanten et al., *Data Flow* (Berlin: Gestalten, 2008), 209, emphasis added.

16. The word "sketch" is problematized when we consider the notion of a computational sketch made, for example, in Processing, as was demonstrated in the previous chapter.

17. Klanten et al., *Data Flow*.

18. Jason Salavon, "Celebrating/Nullifying the Individual," *CIRCA: Irish and International Contemporary Visual Culture* 90 (Winter 1999–2000), http://www.recirca.com/.

19. Salavon, "Celebrating/Nullifying."

20. Marius Watz, "Salavon's Golem," Generator.x, 2 December 2005, accessed 18 April 2010, http://www.generatorx.no/.

21. Watz, "Salavon's Golem."

22. Martin Heidegger, "The Origin of the Work of Art," in *Basic Writings*, ed. David Ferrill Krell, rev. ed. (San Francisco: HarperCollins, 1993), 139–212.

23. Johanna Drucker, "Nostalgia for the Lost Subject of Technology in the Work of Casey Reas," *Los Angeles Review of Books*, 29 January 2016, accessed 7 May 2016, https://lareviewofbooks.org/.

24. Florian Cramer, "Concepts, Notations, Software, Art," Netzliteratur.net, 23 March 2002, accessed 7 May 2016, http://www.netzliteratur.net/.

25. Ibid.

26. Casey Reas, "Process Compendium," 2004–present, updated 20 August 2010, accessed 7 May 2016, http://reas.com/compendium_text.

27. Kimberly Nichols, "Casey Reas' Linear Perspective," *Artdependence Magazine*, 20 May 2016, accessed 7 May 2016, http://artdependence.com/.

28. Christiane Paul, "Essay by Christiane Paul," accessed 7 May 2016, http://landmarks.utexas.edu/.

29. Nichols, "Casey Reas' Linear Perspective."

30. Ibid.

31. Paul, "Essay by Christiane Paul."

32. Nichols, "Casey Reas' Linear Perspective."

33. Nichols, "Casey Reas' Linear Perspective." Jody Zellen, "Exhibition Review: Casey Reas; Linear Perspective," *AfterImage: The Journal of Media Arts and Cultural Criticism* 43, no. 4 (January 2016): 36.

34. Casey Reas, "AYFABTU (Followers)," Reas.com, accessed 7 May 2016, http://reas.com/ayfabtu/.

35. Drucker, "Nostalgia for the Lost Subject."

36. Ibid.

37. Alan Turing, "Computing Machinery and Intelligence," in *The New Media Reader*, ed. N. Montfort and N. Wardrip-Fruin, 49–64 (Cambridge, MA: MIT Press, 2003), 53.

38. Félix Guattari, *Chaosmosis: An Ethico-Aesthetic Paradigm*, trans. Paul Bains and Julian Pefanis (Bloomington: Indiana University Press, 1995), 100.

39. Guattari, *Chaosmosis*, 101.

Bibliography

Aichele, K. P. (1993). "Paul Klee and the Energetics-Atomistics Controversy." *Leonardo, 26* (4), 309–315.

———. (2002). *Paul Klee's Pictorial Writing*. Cambridge: Cambridge University Press.

Alberro, A., & Stimson, B. (1999). *Conceptual Art: A Critical Anthology*. Cambridge, MA: MIT Press.

Alpers, S. (1984). *The Art of Describing: Dutch Art in the Seventeenth Century*. Chicago: University of Chicago Press.

Arns, I. (2004). "Read_Me, Run_Me, Execute_Me: Software and Its Discontents, or: It's the Performativity of Code, Stupid!" In O. Goriunova & A. Shulgin (Eds.), *Read_Me: Software Art and Cultures Conference* (pp. 176–193). Åarhus, Denmark: University of Åarhus Press.

Ascott, R. (2002). "Moist Ontology." In *The Art of Programming*. Amsterdam: Sonic Acts Press.

Austin, J. L. (1976). *How to Do Things with Words*. Oxford: Oxford University Press.

Baudrillard, J. (1983). *Simulations*. (P. Foss, P. Patton, & P. Beitherman, Trans.). New York: Semiotext[e].

Baxandall, M. (1972). *Painting and Experience in Fifteenth-Century Italy: A Primer in the Social History of Pictorial Style*. Oxford: Oxford University Press.

Benjamin, W. (1999). *The Arcades Project*. (H. Eiland & K. McLaughlin, Trans.). Cambridge, MA: Harvard University Press.

Bense, M. (1971). "The Project of Generative Aesthetics." In J. Reichardt (Ed.), *Cybernetics, Art and Ideas* (pp. 57–60). London: Studio Vista.

Bergson, H. (1998). *Creative Evolution*. (A. Mitchell, Trans.). Mineola, NY: Dover.

Binkley, T. (1990). "Digital Dilemmas." *Leonardo, 3* (supplemental issue; Digital Image, Digital Cinema: SIGGRAPH '90 Art Show Catalog), 13–19.

———. (1995). "Transparent Technology: The Swan Song of Electronics." *Leonardo, 28* (5), 427–432.

Blachowitz, J. (1997, February). "Analog Representation Beyond Mental Imagery." *Journal of Philosophy, 94* (2), 55–84.

Bolter, J. D., & Gromala, D. (2003). *Windows and Mirrors: Interaction Design, Digital Art, and the Myth of Transparency*. Cambridge, MA: MIT Press.

Broude, N. (1974, December). "New Light on Seurat's 'Dot': Its Relation to Photo-Mechanical Color Printing in France in the 1880's." *Art Bulletin, 56* (4), 581–589.

———. (1978). *Seurat in Perspective*. Englewood Cliffs, NJ: Prentice-Hall.

Buchloh, B. H. D. (1990, Winter). "Conceptual Art 1962–1969: From the Aesthetics of Administration to the Critique of Institutions." *October* (55), 105–143.

Bukatman, S. (1993). *Terminal Identity: The Virtual Subject in Post-Modern Science Fiction.* Durham, NC: Duke University Press.
Burgin, V. (1976, March/April). "Socialist Formalism." *Studio International*, 191 (980), 148–152.
Campion, S. (2003, 10 October). "Code: In Conversation with Casey Reas." Retrieved 1 May 2009 from Artificial.dk: http://www.artificial.dk/.
Casey, E. S. (1997). *The Fate of Place: A Philosophical History*. Berkeley: University of California Press.
Cave, D. (2008). "'Born Digital'—Raised an Orphan? Acquiring Digital Media through an Analog Paradigm." *Moving Image*, 8 (1), 2–13.
Chun, W. (2004, Winter). "On Software: Or the Persistence of Visual Knowledge." *Grey Room* (18), 26–51.
Clark, T. J. (1980). "Preliminaries to a Possible Treatment of 'Olympia' in 1865." *Screen*, 21 (1), 18–41.
Clauser, H. R. (1988). "Towards a Dynamic, Generative Computer Art." *Leonardo*, 21 (2), 115–122.
Coyne, R. (1999). *Technoromanticism: Digital Narrative, Holism, and the Romance of the Real.* Cambridge, MA: MIT Press.
Cramer, F. (2002, 23 March). "Concepts, Notations, Software, Art." Retrieved 7 May 2016 from Netzliteratur.net: http://www.netzliteratur.net/.
Crary, J. (1990). *Techniques of the Observer: On Vision and Modernity in the Nineteenth Century.* Cambridge, MA: MIT Press.
———. (1999). *Suspensions of Perception: Attention, Spectacle, and Modern Culture*. Cambridge, MA: MIT Press.
Crone, R., & Koerner, J. L. (1991). *Paul Klee: Legends of the Sign*. New York: Columbia University Press.
Cubitt, S. (1998). *Digital Aesthetics*. London: Sage.
———. (2006). "Analogue and Digital." *Theory, Culture and Society*, 23 (2/3), 250–251.
Damisch, H. (1994). *The Origin of Perspective*. (J. Goodman, Trans.). Cambridge, MA: MIT Press.
Davis, W. (1987, Summer). "Replication and Depiction in Paleolithic Art." *Representations* (19), 111–147.
———. (1996). *Replications: Archaeology, Art History, Psychoanalysis*. University Park: Pennsylvania State University Press.
———. (2006). "How to Make Analogies in a Digital Age." *October*, 117, 71–98.
Deleuze, G. (1994). *Difference and Repetition*. (P. Patton, Trans.). New York: Columbia University Press.
Derrida, J. (1988). "Signature Event Context." In *Limited Inc.* (pp. 1–23). Evanston, IL: University of Chicago Press.
———. (1998). *Of Grammatology*. (G. C. Spivak, Trans.). Baltimore: Johns Hopkins University Press.
———. (2005). "The Word Processor." In *Paper Machine* (R. Bowlby, Trans., pp. 19–32). Stanford, CA: Stanford University Press.

Diehl, G. (1972). *Vasarely*. (E. Hennessey, Trans.). New York: Crown.
Dietrich, F. (1987). "The Computer: A Tool for Thought Experiments." *Leonardo*, 20 (4), 315–325.
Dissanayake, E. (2008). "The Arts after Darwin: Does Art Have an Origin or an Adaptive Function?" In K. Zijlmans & W. van Damme (Eds.), *World Art Studies: Exploring Concepts and Approaches* (pp. 241–261). Amsterdam: Valiz.
Doyle, R. (2003). *Wetwares: Experiments in Postvital Living*. Cambridge, MA: MIT Press.
Dreyfus, H. (1992). *What Computers Still Can't Do: A Critique of Artificial Reason*. Minneapolis: University of Minnesota Press.
Drucker, J. (1995). *The Alphabetic Labyrinth: The Letters in History and Imagination*. London: Thames and Hudson.
———. (2001). "Digital Ontologies: The Ideality of Form in/and Code Storage—or—Can Graphesis Challenge Mathesis?" *Leonardo*, 34 (2), 141–145.
———. (2016, January 29). "Nostalgia for the Lost Subject of Technology in the Work of Casey Reas." *Los Angeles Review of Books*. Retrieved 7 May 2016 from https://lareviewofbooks.org/.
———. (2009). *SpecLab: Digital Aesthetics and Projects in Speculative Computing*. Chicago: University of Chicago Press.
Düchting, H. (1997). *Paul Klee: Painting and Music*. New York: Prestel.
Ebeling, K. (2003). "The Painting of the Men from Mars." In Kunstmuseum Wolfsburg (Ed.), *Painting Pictures: Painting and Media in the Digital Age* (pp. 36–40). Bielefeld, Germany: Kerber Verlag.
Eckmann, S., & Koepnick, L. (2006). *Grid/Matrix*. St. Louis: Mildred Lane Kemper Museum.
Eco, U. (1989). *The Open Work*. (A. Cancogni, Trans.). Cambridge, MA: Harvard University Press.
Eisenman, S. F. (1994). "Mass Culture and Utopia: Seurat and Neoimpressionism." In S. F. Eisenman & T. Crow (Eds.), *Nineteenth Century Art: A Critical History* (pp. 274–287). London: Thames and Hudson.
Eisenman, S. F., & Crow, T. (Eds.) (1994). *Nineteenth Century Art: A Critical History*. London: Thames and Hudson.
Elkins, J. (1994). "Art History and the Criticism of Computer-Generated Images." *Leonardo*, 27 (4), 335–342.
———. (1995). "Art History and Images That Are Not Art." *Art Bulletin*, 77 (4), 553–571.
Engelbart, D. (2001). "Augmenting Human Intellect: A Conceptual Framework." In R. Packer & K. Jordan (Eds.), *Multimedia: From Wagner to Virtual Reality* (pp. 64–90). New York: Norton.
Fénéon, F. (1877, 1 May). "Le Néo-Impressionnisme." *L'art moderne*, 139.
Feuerstein, P. L. (2007, 12–14 December). "How Does the Analog Talk to the Digital? The Art of Penny Feuerstein." Retrieved 18 April 2010 from Generative Art: http://generativeart.com/.
Foucault, M. (1979). *Discipline and Punish: The Birth of the Prison*. (A. Sheridan, Trans.). New York: Random House.

———. (1994). *The Order of Things: An Archaeology of the Human Sciences*. New York: Vintage.
Fried, M. (1998). "Art and Objecthood (1967)." In *Art and Objecthood: Essays and Reviews*, 148–172. Chicago: University of Chicago Press.
Friedberg, A. (2006). *The Virtual Window: From Alberti to Microsoft*. Cambridge, MA: MIT Press.
Fry, R. (1965). *Seurat*. London: Phaidon.
Gage, J. (1987). "The Technique of Seurat: A Reappraisal." *Art Bulletin*, 69 (3), 448–454.
Galanter, P. (2004). "What Is Emergence? Generative Murals as Experiments in the Philosophy of Complexity." Retrieved 18 April 2010 from Philip Galanter: http://philipgalanter.com/research.
Galloway, A. (2006). *Gaming: Essays on Algorithmic Culture*. Minneapolis: University of Minnesota Press.
Garrels, G. (Ed.) (2000). *Sol LeWitt: A Retrospective*. New Haven, CT: Yale University Press.
Gere, C. (2006). *Art, Time, and Technology*. Oxford, UK: Berg.
Gibson, W. (1984). *Neuromancer*. New York: Ace.
Goodman, N. (1976). *Languages of Art: An Approach to a Theory of Symbols*. Indianapolis: Hackett.
Gordon, P. (1994). *The Critical Double: Figurative Meaning in Aesthetic Discourse*. Tuscaloosa: University of Alabama Press.
Gorky, M. (1994). "The Lumière Cinematograph." In I. Christie & R. Taylor (Eds.), *The Film Factory: Russian and Soviet Cinema in Documents 1896–1939* (pp. 25–26). New York: Routledge.
Guattari, F. (1995). *Chaosmosis: An Ethico-Aesthetic Paradigm*. (P. Bains & J. Pefanis, Trans.). Bloomington: Indiana University Press.
Gunning, T. (1990). "The Cinema of Attractions: Early Film, Its Spectator, and the Avant-Garde." In T. Elsaesser & A. Barker (Eds.), *Early Cinema: Space, Frame, Narrative* (pp. 56–86). London: British Film Institute.
Hansen, M. B. N. (2004). *New Philosophy for New Media*. Cambridge: MIT Press.
———. (2006). *Bodies in Code: Interfaces with Digital Media*. New York: Routledge.
Hayles, K. N. (1993). "The Materiality of Informatics." *Configurations*, 1 (1), 147–170.
———. (1999). *How We Became Posthuman: Virtual Bodies in Cybernetics, Literature, and Informatics*. Chicago: University of Chicago Press.
Heidegger, M. (1971). "The Origin of the Work of Art." In *Poetry, Language, Thought* (pp. 15–86). New York: Perennial.
———. (1977). *Basic Writings*. (D. Krell, Ed.). New York: Harper and Row.
———. (1977). *The Question concerning Technology and Other Essays*. (W. Lovitt, Trans.). New York: Harper Torchbooks.
———. (1993). "The Origin of the Work of Art." In D. F. Krell (Ed.), *Basic Writings*, rev. ed. San Francisco: HarperCollins.
Helmreich, S. (1998). *Silicon Second Nature: Culturing Artificial Life in a Digital World*. Berkeley: University of California Press.
Homer, W. I. (1964). *Seurat and the Science of Painting*. Cambridge, MA: MIT Press.

Humphries, H. (2003). "A Philosophical Inquiry into the Nature of Computer Art." *Journal of Aesthetic Education*, 37 (1), 14–31.

Jameson, F. (1991). *Postmodernism; or, the Cultural Logic of Late Capitalism*. Durham, NC: Duke University Press.

Jay, M. (1988). "Scopic Regimes of Modernity." In H. Foster (Ed.), *Vision and Visuality* (pp. 3–23). New York: New Press.

———. (1993). *Downcast Eyes: The Denigration of Vision in Twentieth-Century French Thought*. Berkeley: University of California Press.

Jenkins, H. (2008). *Convergence Culture: Where Old Media and New Media Collide*. New York: New York University Press.

Kandinsky, W. (1977). *Concerning the Spiritual in Art*. (M. T. H. Sadler, Trans.). New York: Dover.

Kant, I. (1987). *Critique of Judgment*. (W. S. Pluhar, Trans.). Indianapolis: Hackett.

Kemp, M. (1990). *The Science of Art: Optical Themes in Western Art from Brunelleschi to Seurat*. New Haven, CT: Yale University Press.

———. (2008, 1 May). "The Impressionists' Bible." *Nature*, 543, 37.

Kittler, F. (1987, Summer). "Gramophone, Film, Typewriter." *October*, 41, 101–118.

Klanten, R., et al. (2008). *Data Flow*. Berlin: Gestalten.

Klee, P. (1961). *The Thinking Eye: The Notebooks of Paul Klee*. (J. Spiller, Ed., & R. Mannheim, Trans.). London: Percy Lund, Humphries.

———. (1968). "Creative Credo." In H. B. Chipp (Ed.), *Theories of Modern Art: A Source Book by Artists and Critics* (pp. 182–186). Berkeley: University of California Press.

———. (1973). *Notebooks, vol. 2: The Nature of Nature*. (J. Spiller, Ed., & H. Norden, Trans.). New York: George Wittenborn.

Klutsch, C. (2007). "Computer Graphic-Aesthetic Experiments between Two Cultures." *Leonardo*, 40 (5), 421–425.

Kracauer, S. (1995). *The Mass Ornament: Weimar Essays*. (T. Y. Levin, Trans.). Cambridge, MA: Harvard University Press.

Krauss, R. (1979, Summer). "Grids." *October*, 9, 50–64.

———. (1979). "Sculpture in the Expanded Field." *October*, 8, 30–44.

———. (1985). *The Originality of the Avante-Garde and Other Modernist Myths*. Cambridge, MA: MIT Press.

Krauss, R., Michelson, A., Bois, Y.-A., Buchloh, B. H., Foster, H., Hollier, D., et al. (1997). *October: The Second Decade, 1986–1996*. Cambridge, MA: MIT Press.

Krauss, R. E. (1985). *The Originality of the Avant-Garde and Other Modernist Myths*. Cambridge, MA: MIT Press.

Kroker, A., & Kroker, M. (2000). "Code Warriors: Bunkering In and Dumbing Down." In D. Bell & B. M. Kennedy (Eds.), *The Cybercultures Reader* (pp. 96–106). New York: Routledge.

Kruger, M. (2001). "Responsive Environments." In R. Packer & K. Jordan (Eds.), *Multimedia: From Wagner to Virtual Reality* (pp. 104–120). New York: Norton.

Kuhn, T. (1962). *The Structure of Scientific Revolutions*. Chicago: University of Chicago Press.

Kunstmuseum Wolfsburg (Ed.) (2003). *Painting Pictures: Painting and Media in the Digital Age*. Wolfsburg, Germany: Kerber Verlag.
Kuspit, D. B. (1975, September/October). "Sol LeWitt: The Look of Thought." *Art in America*, pp. 43–49.
Lee, A. (1987). "Seurat and Science." *Art History*, 10 (2), 203–224.
Leroi-Gourhan, A. (1993). *Gesture and Speech*. (A. B. Barger, Trans.). Cambridge, MA: MIT Press.
Lewis, D. (1971, September). "Analog and Digital." *Noûs*, 5 (3), 321–327.
LeWitt, S. (1967, Summer). "Paragraphs on Conceptual Art." *Artforum*, 5 (10), pp. 79–84.
———. (1967, 17 September). "Serial Project #1." (B. O'Doherty, Ed.). *Aspen Magazine* (5–6).
———. (2000). "Serial Project #1." In G. Garrels (Ed.), *Sol LeWitt: A Retrospective* (p. 373). New Haven, CT: Yale University Press.
Lippard, L. (1968, Spring). "Constellation in Harsh Daylight: The Whitney Annual." *Hudson Review*, 21 (1), 180.
Lippard, L., & Chandler, J. (1999). "The Dematerialization of Art." In A. A. Stimson (Ed.), *Conceptual Art: A Critical Anthology* (pp. 46–51). Cambridge, MA: MIT Press.
Lopes, D. M. (2000, Summer). "From *Languages of Art* to Art in Mind." *Journal of Aesthetics and Art Criticism*, 58 (3), 227–231.
Lunenfeld, P. (2000). *Snap to Grid: A User's Guide to Digital Arts, Media, and Cultures*. Cambridge, MA: MIT Press.
Lynton, N. (1989). *The Story of Modern Art*. London: Phaidon.
Lyotard, J.-F. (1984). *The Postmodern Condition: A Report on Knowledge*. (B. Massumi, Trans.). Minneapolis: University of Minnesota Press.
———. (1992). *The Inhuman: Reflections on Time*. (G. Bennington, Trans.). Stanford, CA: Stanford University Press.
———. (1995). "Fait Pictural." (A. Benjamin, Ed.). *Journal of Philosophy and the Visual Arts*, 5, 8–15.
Maeda, J. (2006). *The Laws of Simplicity*. Cambridge, MA: MIT Press.
Manovich, L. (2001). *The Language of New Media*. Cambridge, MA: MIT Press.
———. (2004). "Abstraction and Complexity." In *Abstraction Now* (pp. 80–85). Vienna: Edition Camera Austria. Retrieved 28 November 2009 from http://www.abstraction-now.at/.
Marcoulesco, I. (1995). "Unclassifiable Klee." In P. Klee, *A Piece of the Moon World* (pp. 13–27). Houston: Menil Collection.
Marks, L. U. (2006). "Infinity and Accident: Strategies of Enfoldment in Islamic Art and Computer Art." *Leonardo*, 39 (1), 37–42.
Marr, D. (1982). *Vision: A Computational Investigation into the Human Representation and Processing of Visual Information*. San Francisco: W. H. Freeman.
Mayo, S. (2008). "The Prelude to the Millennium: The Backstory of Digital Aesthetics." *Journal of Aesthetic Education*, 42 (1), 100–115.
McWhinnie, H. J. (1989). "The Use of Computers in the Arts: Simulation versus Abstraction." *Leonardo*, 22 (2), 167–170.

Mehring, C. (2008, Summer). "Television's Abstract Starts: Europe Circa 1944–1969." *October*, 125, 29–64.
Meltzer, E. (2006). "The Dream of the Information World." *Oxford Art Journal*, 29 (1), 115–135.
Mirapaul, M. (1997, 17 April). "In John Simon's Art, Everything Is Possible." Retrieved 30 November 2009 from *New York Times* on the Web: http://www.nytimes.com/.
Mitchell, W. J. (1992). *The Reconfigured Eye: Visual Truth in the Post-Photographic Era*. Cambridge, MA: MIT Press.
Morgan, R. (2004). *Vasarely*. New York: George Braziller.
Müller, V. (2007, 25 June). "Representations in Digital Systems." Retrieved 24 March 2008 from Interdisciplines: http://www.interdisciplines.org/.
Mumford, L. (1934). *Technics and Civilization*. New York: Harcourt, Brace.
Munster, A. (2006). *Materializing New Media: Embodiment in Information Aesthetics*. Hanover, NH: University Press of New England.
Negroponte, N. (1995). *Being Digital*. New York: Vintage.
Nichols, Kimberly. (2016, 20 May). "Casey Reas' Linear Perspective." *Artdependence Magazine*. Retrieved 7 May 2016 from http://artdependence.com/.
Noë, A. (2009). *Out of Our Heads: Why You Are Not Your Brain, and Other Lessons from the Biology of Consciousness*. New York: Hill and Wang.
Onians, J. (2008). *Neuroarthistory: From Aristotle and Pliny to Baxandall and Zeki*. New Haven, CT: Yale University Press.
Panofsky, E. (1997). *Perspective as Symbolic Form*. (C. S. Wood, Trans.). New York: Zone Books.
Paul, C. (2002). "Renderings of Digital Art." *Leonardo*, 35 (5), 471–484.
———. (2016). "Essay by Christiane Paul." Retrieved 7 May 2016 from http://landmarks.utexas.edu/.
Pepperell, R. (2006). "Seeing without Objects: Visual Indeterminacy and Art." *Leonardo*, 39 (5), 394–400.
Petitpierre, P. (1957). *Aus der Malklasse von Paul Klee*. Bern, Switzerland: Benteli.
Pias, C. (2003). *Cybernetics/Kybernetik: The Macy Conferences, 1946–1953*. Zurich: Diaphanes.
———. (2005). "Analog, Digital and the Cybernetic Illusion." *Kybernetes*, 34 (3/4), 543–550.
Pillow, K. (2003, Autumn). "Did Goodman's Distinction Survive LeWitt?" *Journal of Aesthetics and Art Criticism*, 61 (4), 365–380.
Pøld, S. (2005). "Interface Realisms: The Interface as Aesthetic Form." *Postmodern Culture*, 15 (2).
Pylyshyn, Z. (1984). *Computation and Cognition*. Cambridge, MA: MIT Press.
Rajchman, J. (1995). "Another View of Abstraction." (A. Benjamin, Ed.). *Journal of Philosophy and the Visual Arts*, 5, 16–24.
Reas, C. (2003). "Programming Media." In *Code: The Language of Our Time* (pp. 174–179). Ostfildern-Ruit, Germany: Hatje Cantz Verlag.
———. (2004). "Organic and Conceptual Systems: Casey Reas Answers Bert Balcaen's questions for Sonic Acts X, Amsterdam 2004." Retrieved 18 April 2010 from Reas: http://reas.com/.

———. (2004). "{*Software*} *Structures*: A Text About Software and Art." Retrieved 16 April 2010 from Artport: http://artport.whitney.org/.
———. (2004–present). "Process Compendium." Updated 20 August 2010. Retrieved 7 May 2016 from http://reas.com/compendium_text.
———. (2006, July/August). "Process/Drawing." (M. Silver, Ed.). *Architectural Design*, 76 (4), 26–33.
———. (2007). "Beyond Code." In A. Burke & T. Tierney (Eds.), *Network Practices: New Strategies in Architecture and Design* (pp. 166–177). Princeton, NJ: Princeton Architectural Press.
———. (2016). "AYFABTU (Followers)." Retrieved 7 May 2016 from Reas.com: http://reas.com/ayfabtu/.
Reas, C., & Fry, B. (2007). *Processing: A Programming Handbook for Visual Designers and Artists*. Cambridge, MA: MIT Press.
Reichardt, J. (1969). *Cybernetic Serendipity*. New York: Praeger.
———. (1971). "Cybernetics, Art and Ideas." In *Cybernetics, Art and Ideas* (pp. 11–17). London: Studio Vista.
Reijnders, F. (2003). "Painting? A State of Utter Idiocy." In K. Wolfsburg (Ed.), *Painting Pictures: Painting and Media in the Digital Age* (pp. 20–29). Wolfsburg, Germany: Kerber Verlag.
Riddell, A. (2001). "Data Culture Generation: After Content, Process as Aesthetic." *Leonardo*, 34 (4), 337–343.
Rodowick, D. N. (2007). *The Virtual Life of Film*. Cambridge, MA: Harvard University Press.
Rood, O. (1879). *Modern Chromatics, with Applications to Art and Industry*. New York: Appleton.
Rose, B. (1978). "Sol LeWitt and Drawing." In A. Legg (Ed.), *Sol LeWitt* (pp. 31–42). New York: Museum of Modern Art.
Rota, G.-C. (2005). "The Phenomenology of Mathematical Beauty." In M. Emmer (Ed.), *The Visual Mind II* (pp. 3–14). Cambridge, MA: MIT Press.
Sack, W. (1996 May). "Painting Theory Machines." *Art and Design*, 80–92.
———. (2011). "Aesthetics of Information Visualization." In V. Vesna, M. Lovejoy & C. Paul (Eds.), *Context Providers: Conditions of Meaning in Media Art* (pp. 123–150). Bristol, UK: Intellect. Retrieved 24 June 2009 from: http://hybrid.ucsc.edu/.
Salavon, J. (1999–2000, Winter). "Celebrating/Nullifying the Individual." *CIRCA: Irish and International Contemporary Visual Culture*, 90. http://www.recirca.com/.
Schapiro, M. (1978). "Seurat." In *Modern Art, 19th and 20th Centuries: Selected Papers* (pp. 101–109). New York: George Braziller.
Seitter, W. (2003). "Painting Has Always Been a Digital Affair." In Kunstmuseum Wolfsburg (Ed.), *Painting Pictures: Painting and Media in the Digital Age* (pp. 30–35). Bielefeld, Germany: Kerber Verlag.
Seitz, W. C. (1965). *The Responsive Eye*. New York: Museum of Modern Art. Exhibition catalog.
Shanken, E. (2002). "Art in the Information Age: Technology and Conceptual Art." *Leonardo*, 35 (4), 433–438.

Sheldon, G. (1890). *Recent Ideals of American Art*. New York.
Shlovsky, V. (1998). "Art as Technique." In D. H. Richter (Ed.), *The Critical Tradition: Classic Texts and Contemporary Trends* (pp. 716–726). Boston: Bedford Books.
Simon, J. F. (2009). "Artist's Statement." Retrieved 24 June 2009 from Numeral: http://numeral.com/.
Smith, P. (1995). "Defining Impressionism." In *Impressionism: Beneath the Surface* (pp. 7–32). New York: Abrams.
Smithson, R. (1996). "A Museum of Language in the Vicinity of Thought." In *Robert Smithson: The Collected Writings* (pp. 78–94). Berkeley: University of California Press.
Snow, C. P. (1998). "The Two Cultures." In *The Two Cultures* (pp. 1–41). New York: Cambridge University Press.
Stallabrass, J. (2003). *Internet Art: The Online Clash of Culture and Commerce*. London: Tate Publishing.
Stanley, D. E. (2007, 6 October). "Complexity and Gestalt." Retrieved 28 November 2009 from *Abstractmachine* (blog): http://abstractmachine.net/.
Stiegler, B. (1998). *Technics and Time, vol. 1: The Fault of Epimetheus*. (R. Beardsworth & G. Collins, Trans.). Stanford, CA: Stanford University Press.
———. (2002). "The Discrete Image." In J. Derrida & B. Stiegler, *Echographies of Television* (pp. 145–163). Malden, MA: Blackwell.
———. (2009). *Technics and Time, vol. 2: Disorientation*. (S. Barker, Trans.). Stanford, CA: Stanford University Press.
Summers, D. (2003). *Real Spaces: World Art History and the Rise of Western Modernism*. London: Phaidon.
Tomasula, S. (1996). "Bytes and Zeitgeist: Digitizing the Cultural Landscape." *Leonardo*, *31* (5), 337–344.
Tufte, E. R. (2001). *The Visual Display of Quantitative Information*. Cheshire, CT: Graphics Press.
Turim, M. (1999, January). "Artisanal Prefigurations of the Digital: Animating Realities, Collage Effects, and Theories of Image Manipulation." *Wide Angle* (Ohio University School of Film), 21 (1), 48–62.
Turing, A. (2003). "Computing Machinery and Intelligence." In N. Montfort & N. Wardrip-Fruin (Eds.), *The New Media Reader* (pp. 49–64). Cambridge, MA: MIT Press.
Vasarely, M. (2002). *L'affaire Vasarely: Art, pouvoir et corruption*. Aix-en-Provence, France: Vents contraires.
———. (2010). "Victor Vasarely: Chronology; The Father of Op Art." Retrieved 6 May 2010 from Galeria Renes: http://renes.com.pl/.
Vasarely, V. (1968). "Notes for a Manifesto." In A. Hill (Ed.), *Data: Directions in Art, Theory and Aesthetics* (pp. 101–103). Greenwich: New York Graphic Society.
———. (1977). *Vasarely inconnu*. Neuchâtel, Switzerland: Editions du Griffon.
———. (1979). *Vasarely*. (I. M. Paris, Trans.). New York: Alpine Fine Arts Collection.
Virilio, P. (2003). *Art and Fear*. (J. Rose, Trans.). New York: Continuum.
von Neumann, J. (1963). "General and Logical Theory of Automata." (A. H. Taub, Ed.).

In *Collected Works*, vol. 5: *Design of Computers, Theory of Automata and Numerical Analysis* (pp. 288–328). New York: Pergamon.
Wagner, R. (2001). "Outlines of the Artwork of the Future: The Artwork of the Future 1849." In R. Packer & K. Jordan (Eds.), *Multimedia: From Wagner to Virtual Reality* (pp. 3–9). New York: Norton.
Wattenberg, M. (2005, 16 May). "Introduction to Visualization: From Data to Pictures to Insight." Retrieved 18 April 2010 from IBM: http://www.alphaworks.ibm.com/.
Watz, M. (2005). "*ElectroPlastique #1*." Retrieved 6 April 2010 from http://www.unlekker.net/.
———. (2005, 2 December). "Salavon's Golem." Retrieved 18 April 2010 from Generator.x: http://www.generatorx.no/.
———. (2006, 6 June). "Theory: Vague Terrain." Retrieved 6 April 2010 from Generator.x: http://www.generatorx.no/.
Whissel, K. (2006). "Tales of Upward Mobility: The New Verticality and Digital Special Effects." *Film Quarterly*, 59 (4), 23–34.
Whitelaw, M. (2007, 29 October). "More Is More: Multiplicity and Generative Art." Retrieved 28 November 2009 from *The Teeming Void* (blog): http://teemingvoid.blogspot.com/.
Wölflinn, H. (1964). *Renaissance and Baroque*. Ithaca, NY: Cornell University Press.
Youngblood, G. (1986, Winter). "Calculated Movements: An Interview with Larry Cuba." *Video and the Arts Magazine*.
———. (1989). "Cinema and the Code." *Leonardo: Supplemental Issue; Computer Art in Context: SIGGRAPH '89 Art Show Catalog*, 2, 27–30.
Youngblood, G., & Cuba, L. (2010). "Calculated Movements: An Interview with Larry Cuba." Retrieved 16 April 2010 from Larry Cuba: http://www.well.com/.
Zellen, Jody. (2016, January). "Exhibition Review: Casey Reas; Linear Perspective." *AfterImage: The Journal of Media Arts and Cultural Criticism*, 43 (4), 36.
Zielinski, S. (2006). *Deep Time of the Media: Toward an Archaeology of Hearing and Seeing by Technical Means*. Cambridge, MA: MIT Press.

Index

Note: page numbers in *italics* refer to figures; those followed by n refer to notes, with note number.